W9-APF-969
EUROPE
ATLANTIC OCEAN
Black Sea
Caspian Sea
ASIA
Mediterranean Sea
MOROCCO
ATLAS MOUNTAINS
TUNISIA
ALGERIA
LIBYA
EGYPT
Nile
ARABIAN PENINSULA
Western Sahara
Red Sea
MAURITANIA
S A H A R A D E S E R T
MALI
Timbuktu
Niger
NIGER
CHAD
SENEGAL
Khartoum
Blue Nile
ERITREA
SUDAN
Lake Chad
BURKINA FASO
GUINEA
DJIBOUTI
Gulf of Aden
A F R I C A
White Nile
BENIN
NIGERIA
SIERRA LEONE
Freetown
Addis Ababa
IVORY COAST
TOGO
Abeokuta
GHANA
ETHIOPIA
LIBERIA
Abidjan
Lagos
CENTRAL AFRICAN REPUBLIC
SOMALIA
CAMEROON
EQUATORIAL GUINEA
L. Turkana
(L. Rudolf)
Congo
Lake Albert
UGANDA
Gulf of Guinea
Kampala
KENYA
Equator
SAO TOME AND PRINCIPE
GABON
RWANDA
CONGO
Nairobi
DEMOCRATIC REPUBLIC OF THE CONGO
Lake Victoria
INDIAN OCEAN
Mt. Kilimanjaro
BURUNDI
Kinshasa
Cabinda (ANGOLA)
TANZANIA
Zanzibar
Dar es Salaam
ATLANTIC OCEAN
Lake Tanganyika
Luanda
SEYCHELLES
Lake Malawi
(Lake Nyasa)
ANGOLA
COMOROS
MALAWI
ZAMBIA
Zambezi
MOZAMBIQUE
Harare
ZIMBABWE
MADAGASCAR
N
NAMIBIA
BOTSWANA
Windhoek
KALAHARI DESERT
Limpopo
Johannesburg
Maputo
SWAZILAND
LESOTHO
Orange
DRAKENSBERG
0
500
1,000 mi
0
800
1,600 km
SOUTH AFRICA
Cape Town

african BIOGRAPHY

african BIOGRAPHY

Volume 3

Mut-Z

Virginia Curtin Knight, Editor

African Biography

Virginia Curtin Knight, Editor

Staff

Sonia Benson, *U•X•L Senior Editor*
Carol DeKane Nagel, *U•X•L Managing Editor*
Thomas L. Romig, *U•X•L Publisher*

Mary Beth Trimper, *Production Director*
Evi Seoud, *Assistant Production Manager*
Deborah Milliken, *Production Assistant*

Cynthia Baldwin, *Product Design Manager*
Barbara Yarrow, *Graphic Services Director*
Pamela A. E. Galbreath, *Senior Art Director*
Shalice Shah-Caldwell, *Permissions Associate*
LM Design, *Typesetter*

Library of Congress Cataloging-in-Publication Data

African Biography / Virginia Curtin Knight, editor

p. cm.
Includes bibliographic references and index.

Summary: Presents biographical entries on seventy-five noteworthy Africans, historical and contemporary, in a variety of fields, from a wide range of sub-Saharan countries.

ISBN 0-7876-2823-9 (set : alk. paper)
ISBN 0-7876-2824-7 (volume 1)
ISBN 0-7876-2825-5 (volume 2)
ISBN 0-7876-2826-3 (volume 3)

1. Africa, Sub-Saharan—Biography—Juvenile literature. [1. Africa, Sub-Saharan—Biography. 2. Blacks—Africa, Sub-Saharan—Biography.]. I. Knight, Virginia Curtin.

CT1920.A39 1998
920.067—dc21

98-14069
CIP

10 9 8 7 6 5 4 3 2

Contents

Nelson Mandela

Volume 1

Volume 2

Volume 3

Entries by Nationality

Bold numerals indicate volume numbers.

Moshoeshoe

Ethiopia *(Abyssinia; Shoa)*

Ghana *(Gold Coast)*

Guinea

Kenya *(British East Africa)*

Lesotho *(Basutoland)*

Liberia

Madagascar

Malawi *(Nyasaland)*

Mali

Mozambique

Namibia *(South West Africa)*

Nigeria *(Yorubaland, Sokoto Empire)*

Senegal

Sierra Leone

South Africa

Sudan *(The Mahdia)*

Swaziland

Tanzania *(Tanganyika; Zanzibar)*

Uganda *(British East Africa; Buganda)*

Zambia *(Northern Rhodesia)*

Zanzibar *(Tanzania)*

Zimbabwe *(Southern Rhodesia)*

Zululand *(now part of KwaZulu-Natal province, South Africa)*

Entries by Field of Endeavor

Bold numerals indicate volume numbers.

Fela Kuti

Anthropologists

Educators

Environmentalists

Explorers

Heads of Government: prime ministers, presidents, dictators

Heads of International Organization

Labor Leaders

Medicine

Military Leaders

Musicians

Nobel Prize Winners (peace)

Nobel Prize Winners (literature)

Political Activists

Publishers (book)

Publishers (newspaper)

Religious Leaders

Rulers: kings, queens, chiefs, and emperors

Slave Traders

Translators

Writers

Reader's Guide

Miriam Makeba

For students and interested browsers who want to learn more about the world, *African Biography* presents biographical entries on some of its most remarkable people. Spanning most of the recorded history of Africa, this three-volume reference resource includes people living from the year 1182 to modern times from areas that now comprise 23 nations of sub-Saharan Africa. Through reading about the lives of its noteworthy people, the reader will confront many of Africa's important historical and social issues, such as the ancient kingdoms, the early Muslim and Christian influences, Europeans and the devastating slave trade, the colonial governments, African nationalism, and the triumphs and struggles of the newly formed independent nations. The people profiled are the kings, presidents, and dictators, religious and military leaders, musicians, activists, traders, environmentalists, and writers who have helped to shape the continent's history.

In *African Biography* readers will find:

- 75 alphabetically arranged biographical entries, each focusing on the childhood and formative experiences of the subject as well as his or her career; the background and traditions held by the subject; and the overall historical or political situation in the nation or area upon which the subject made an impact.

- Sidebars that provide information on people, events, historical background, and other fascinating facts related to the entry.
- Sources for further reading and a full bibliography that inform students where to delve even deeper.
- More than 150 portraits, illustrations, and maps.
- Locator maps in most entries that identify the nations within the continent.

Each volume of *African Biography* begins with a listing of biographical entries by nationality and by field of endeavor; an introduction to, and timeline of, important events in African history; and a glossary of terms used in the text. Volumes conclude with a subject index so students can easily find the people, places, movements, and events discussed throughout the set.

Acknowledgments

The editor would like to thank the U•X•L staff, particularly the photo research department, for all their hard work behind the scenes. Special thanks to U•X•L senior editor Sonia Benson for her enthusiastic support for this project. Thanks are due also to Remer Tyson who worked on the biographies and enjoyed the research as much as I did.

Special thanks are due for the valuable comments and suggestions of U•X•L adviser Ann Marie Laprise, Detroit Public Library, Elmwood Park Branch, Detroit, Michigan.

Comments and Suggestions

We welcome your comments on *African Biography* as well as your suggestions for topics to be featured in future editions. Please write: Editors, *African Biography,* U•X•L, 27500 Drake Rd., Farmington Hills, Michigan 48331-3535; call toll-free: 1-800-877-4253; or fax (248) 699-8066.

Preface: An Overview of Africa's History

Félix Houphouët-Boigny

The inscription welcoming researchers to the building housing Zimbabwe's historical records says: "There is a history in all men's lives." Just as each person's life holds a history, each life also reveals part of the history of a specific time and place. In these biographies of 75 African men and women, the history of the continent emerges.

The Africans included in these volumes are people living south of the Sahara Desert. For centuries the desert has divided the peoples of the continent. Those living along the Mediterranean and north Atlantic Ocean coasts have a history different from those living to the south. The people in the North were part of the history of Egypt and the early Roman empire while the South remained largely untouched by the experiences of the North.

Historians such as Herodotus (c. 425-484 B.C.) made occasional isolated tours into Africa as early as the fifth century B.C. But historians began to collect comprehensive knowledge of Africans living in the vast regions south of the Sahara with the beginning of Portuguese exploration in the 1400s. From the records and diaries kept by the sailors, priests, and representatives of the kings, the lives of prominent African men and women come alive. Their history and those of future generations reveal a pattern of resistance, perhaps because of the nature of their relationship with the Europeans. In the earlier period, Africans clashed with outsiders who were seeking to exploit the continent's mineral wealth and later to expand the horrendous trade in slaves. Later, resistance took the form of nationalism and demands for independence from European rule. Today, Africans are demanding an end to the corrupt and tyrannical African governments that have cheated them of their share of their countries' resources.

Majesty and wealth

For the early historical period of the great empires in West Africa the documented history is scant. Along the reaches of the Niger and Senegal rivers in West Africa, Africans developed large powerful kingdoms based on trade and warfare. These early empires of the 400s to 1500s—Ghana, Mali, and Songhai—stretched from the Atlantic Ocean as far as the northwest of modern Nigeria. So fabulously wealthy were these kingdoms that Arab traders from the north crossed the Sahara Desert with their huge camel caravans to trading centers like Timbuktu and Gao along the Niger River. There they traded their salt and textiles for the gold of the western African kingdoms. In southern Africa, from the Zambezi River to the Indian Ocean, the rulers of Great Zimbabwe (1000-1400s) controlled the trade in gold and ivory. African traders brought their goods to the Indian Ocean Coast where they traded with Arab merchants from Kilwa and Mombasa along the Kenyan coast.

Along the Red Sea, the Christian kingdom of Aksum reached its height in the 1100s. **Lalibela** (1182-1255), the Emperor of Aksum (Ethiopia), is the first person about whom we have enough information to form a biography. Lalibela was responsible for the construction of 11 Christian churches, still standing today, built into the sides of stone cliffs in northern Ethiopia. In this earlier period **Mansa Musa** (1312-1337), the enormously wealthy ruler of the kingdom of Mali, gained a place in history when he made a pilgrimage, or *haj,* from his capital at Timbuktu to the Muslim holy city of Mecca, in today's Saudi Arabia. The trip took him two years. On his return, he established in Timbuktu one of the leading Islamic intellectual centers in the world.

European interests

In the 1400s the Portuguese sailed around the West African Coast and in their wake European slave traders followed. This trade distorted the normal development of African communities for nearly 500 years. Faced with expanding penetration by Portuguese traders in the East and Arab traders along the Indian Ocean coasts, African communities reacted in several different ways. Some adapted themselves to the trade and grew wealthy from the capture of slaves and the trade in guns. Others resisted.

Sent out by Portuguese Prince Henry the Navigator to make their way around the continent, the Portuguese set up trading posts along the coast. Stimulating the early explorers was the myth of the fabulously wealthy realm of an African Christian king named Prester John. Islam, the faith founded by the prophet Muhammad, had rapidly spread from Saudi Arabia into Africa and Asia from the 600s onward. The Christian church in Europe wanted to believe that Christian kingdoms existed beyond the reach of Islam, and the myth of Prester John suited their purpose. To avoid the Muslim-controlled Sahara Desert, Prince Henry planned to sail along the Atlantic Coast, and then follow the large rivers inland until he found Prester John.

As they explored along the coast, the Portuguese established settlements. Following their discovery of Brazil in the 1500s and the development of plantations there, they began taking slaves from Africa to work these plantations. They sailed around the Cape of Good Hope and along the Indian Ocean Coast. There they explored the inland river systems and wrote descriptions of **Mwene Mutapa Negomo Mupunzagutu,** the ruler of the Mutapa dynasty along the Zambezi River in the 1550s. As in other earlier African kingdoms, the Portuguese were welcomed and provided with accommodation. Often, their Christian priests converted the African rulers and their courts to Christianity. In many instances this caused dissent within the ruler's court between the traditional authorities and priests and those who adopted the new ways. Struggles for power within the kingdom were fueled by the outsiders who supported one side against the another.

Later, other European explorers kept diaries of their contact with African rulers and their societies: among these were the Dutch in the 1600s and the French, British, and Germans in the 1700s and 1800s. On the heels of the explorers came the missionaries, adventurers, and traders. Confronted by European expansion, African societies were forced to turn outward to respond to the pressures. There were some fascinating exceptions, like **Afonso I** of the Kongo in the 1480s, but most ultimately resisted the European presence. Sometimes resistance followed accommodation. The West African kings of Dahomey, for instance, initially profited from the slave trade with the Europeans and strengthened their kingdom. Later, however, French colonial forces defeated the Dahomeans and exiled their king. From the East Coast of Africa, the Arabs and later the Portuguese followed the rivers inland to open up the continent to Europeans from the Indian Ocean Coast.

Anna Nzinga, the queen of the Ndongo in the 1600s in present-day Angola, was a good strategist and formed alliances with the Dutch to try to keep the Portuguese from destroying her kingdom. Ultimately, however, the wealth derived from the trade in slaves won the day. The slavers destroyed African societies, corrupted their leaders, and sent thousands of people into slavery in the Americas. Some men, such as **Olaudah Equiano** and **Samuel Ajayi Crowther,** who were taken as slaves, gained their freedom and wrote descriptions of their experiences. Crowther returned to his native Nigeria and became the first black bishop in the Anglican Church of England. Others became wealthy from trading in slaves. **Tippu Tib** from Zanzibar was one of the greatest African slavers in the interior.

In southern Africa resistance took other forms. Internal conflicts in the region had much more impact on the societies than slavery did. In the early 1800s, **Shaka,** the Zulu king, displaced tens of thousands of people as he sought to increase his powerful kingdom. Later, as the whites from the Cape Colony began moving northward, the conflicts centered on white encroachment and African resistance. The intensity of resistance escalated toward the end of the 1800s as the governments of Europe vied with one another for control of Africa. The British faced armed resistance in southern Africa from the Afrikaners under **Paul Kruger,** from the Zulus under **Cetshwayo**, and from the Matabele under **Lobengula.** In South West Africa (Namibia), **Samuel Maherero,** leader of the Herero, put up stiff resistance to German occupation. Elsewhere in Africa, in the Belgian Congo **Simon Kimbangu** began a religious movement that opposed the repressive, cruel treatment meted out to Africans by the agents of Belgian King Leopold II. In Madagascar, Queen **Ranavalona I** used her authority to keep all

Christian missionaries out of her country for nearly 40 years, thus allowing the traditional culture to flourish unimpeded by European culture. In Ethiopia, **Menelik II** took up arms to defend his country against the Italian invasion. His troops defeated the Italians at the battle of Adowa in 1896, one of the greatest defeats of a European power in Africa.

Demands for independence

During the Second World War, Africans fought in the armies of the colonial powers. When they returned home from the war, they began demanding the same rights for themselves that they had fought for in Europe and Asia. They formed political parties and nationalist movements to rid their countries of European rule. Over a period of 30 years, some by arms and others through negotiation, the African leaders achieved independence for their countries. **Kwame Nkrumah** was the first president of Ghana, the first sub-Saharan African country to win its independence. Nkrumah was a formidable intellectual presence who promoted the idea of Pan-Africanism, a united Africa. During the 1960s, the flood gates opened and in 10 years' time nearly 30 African countries won their independence from their colonial rulers. Some countries under leaders such as **Félix Houphouët-Boigny** in Côte d'Ivoire and **Léopold Sédar Senghor** in Senegal experienced a smooth transition to independence and kept close ties with the French, their former colonial power. Other countries under nationalist leaders like **Patrice Lumumba** in the former Belgian Congo (Zaire and now the Democratic Republic of the Congo) experienced turmoil and bloodshed at independence.

Nationalists and independence leaders

Once African countries had become independent, many leaders experienced difficulties administering their nations and reconciling the conflicting interests of regional and cultural groups. Some leaders like Nigeria's **Abubakar Tafawa Balewa** fell under the gun of military rule. Other rulers ignored constitutional limits and declared themselves presidents for life. Men such as **Hastings Banda** of Malawi, **Kenneth Kaunda** of Zambia, and **Julius Nyerere** of Tanzania all ruled over governments that recognized only one political party—theirs.

In the aftermath of World War II, rivalry grew up between China, the Soviet Union and the Communist bloc countries, and the West. The period of Great Power rivalry is known as the Cold War. It lasted until 1989 when the Communist governments of Eastern Europe fell. During this time, the East and West provided their supporters with arms and ammunition. Africans fought major wars in Angola, Mozambique, Somalia, Ethiopia, and Eritrea. To prevent the East from influencing other governments, the West supported friendly dictators such as **Mobutu Sese Seko** of Zaire to keep them in power. The West wanted to prevent Communist countries from coming in and exploiting the continent's mineral resources and from gaining strategic bases in Africa.

African writers used their powers to criticize and interpret the changes taking place in their societies. Among the most prominent of the writers in the post-World War II period were Nigerians, **Chinua Achebe** and **Wole Soyinka. Alan Paton** used the power of his novel *Cry the Beloved Country* to personalize the plight of Africans in his home country of South Africa. Resistance to the racist policies of the South African government of **Hendrik Verwoerd** continued under such people as Chief **Albert Lutuli, Miriam Makeba, Steve Biko, Winnie Madikizela-Mandela, Nelson Mandela**, and former Archbishop **Desmond Tutu.**

With the collapse of Communism in eastern European and the Soviet Union, the African nations were left alone and some were able to bring stability to their countries. The major benefactors of the end of the Cold War were black South Africans and South Africa's neighbors, Namibia, Mozambique, and Angola. In the absence of the Communist threat, South African National Party leader **Frederick Willem de Klerk** could justify to his followers the advantages of releasing **Nelson Mandela** from nearly 30 years in prison. Mandela's release opened the way to a multiparty system in South Africa and the normalizing of relations with African countries in the southern region.

Today, the leaders of African countries are being evaluated for their competence rather than their loyalties. In many cases they do not stand the test of providing a leadership for the benefit of their people. Many have performed miserably; some have stayed in power for many years and enriched themselves and their families while impoverishing their countries. With the broader vision of democracy and sound economic policies, African societies are beginning to demand a fairer deal from their leaders. In Uganda,

Yoweri Museveni has ended the terrible ethnic fighting and brought stability to his country, although he too refuses to allow competing political parties. In South Africa, **Nelson Mandela** turned over the presidency of his political party to a younger generation, and he has promised to leave office by 1999—setting a precedent that an African leader can serve his or her people by leaving office at the peak of power.

A note about this collection

In these volumes the numbers of prominent political South African activists are greater than in any other single country. Various circumstances account for this. The struggle for freedom and majority rule lasted longer in South Africa than in other countries, and the struggle gave rise to activists, black and white. Of the sub-Saharan African countries, South Africa also has the most developed economy and infrastructure, giving greater opportunities and outlets for activism.

African women are noticeably underrepresented in these biographies. Many African cultures are dominated by men, and they have assigned women to inferior positions. That some women have emerged as powerful leaders is all the more tribute to their strengths and perseverance. In modern Africa, women such as Kenyan environmentalist **Wangari Maathai** are in the forefront of women who have succeeded despite the prejudices of their families, husbands, peers, and governments. Women in many contemporary cultures are challenging the traditional ways that have kept them in subservient positions.

Finally, one of the most difficult aspects of compiling this collection of biographies was to limit the number of entries to 75. Many interesting and noteworthy people were necessarily omitted in an effort to achieve a wide representation of people by region, race, sex, and field of endeavor.

Virginia Curtin Knight
Harare, Zimbabwe
January 1998

Words to Know

Desmond Tutu

A

Abolitionist: someone who is in favor of, or works for, the elimination of slavery.

Advocate: to support or speak in favor of; or someone who speaks in favor of.

African nationalism: a strong loyalty to the traditions and political and economic interests of Africa and its people. The term generally refers to Africans who tried to free Africa from colonial governments and worked for self-rule.

Afrikaans: a language derived from the Dutch language of the seventeenth century, spoken by the Afrikaners or Boers and one of the official languages of the Republic of South Africa.

Afrikaner: an Afrikaans-speaking South African native of European descent, usually Dutch, German, or French. Afrikaners started arriving in South Africa in the middle of the seventeenth century, where the majority became farmers.

African National Congress (ANC): the oldest black political organization in South Africa, founded in 1912 by a group of black lawyers for the purpose of promoting the interests of blacks in the newly created Union of South Africa. After 1948 the organization led the opposition to apartheid, and it was outlawed in the 1960s. In the 1990s the ban on the ANC ended; in 1994 the party won in the first elections open to all races in South Africa.

Afro-Beat: a modern musical style that fuses jazz with the sounds of traditional African music with lyrics in both a native African language and in pidgin English.

Agnostic: someone who believes that human beings cannot know if God or any supreme being exists, or understand what the nature of the supreme being is.

Amnesty: the granting of pardon—forgiveness without punishment—to a group of people by the authorities involved (as a government).

Anarchy: lawlessness or disorder due to the absence of government or authority.

Ancestral lands: lands passed down within a group or family from one generation to the next.

Anthropology: the study of the way humans have lived and developed over the ages.

Apartheid: the policy of segregating and practicing economic and political discrimination against non-European groups; *apartheid* policies were in effect in South Africa from 1948 until the early 1990s.

Archaeology: the study of past human life by digging up and examining the material remains, such as fossils and artifacts.

Asceticism: the practice of strict self-denial for the purpose of gaining spiritual discipline.

Assimilation: the absorbing of an individual or a group into the cultural mainstream.

Atrocities: appalling and brutal acts.

Authoritarianism: placing a nation's power in a leader or group of leaders who are not accountable to the people for their actions.

Autocracy: a government in which one ruler has unlimited power.

Autonomy: self-governing.

Axiom: an established principle or rule.

B

Banning order: legal restrictions imposed by the National party government of South Africa upon an individual that prohibited travel from a set area, speaking in public, appearing in certain public places, and restricted who, or how many people, could visit at one's home, and placed other limitations on the individual's freedoms of movement and speech.

Baptism: a Christian ritual in which a person is purified by means of water and then accepted into the Christian community.

Boer: a South African of the Afrikaans-speaking community.

Boycott: a united effort of refusing to deal with an organization, such as a company, or its products, in order to express disapproval.

Bureaucracy: a system of administration, generally known for its inefficiency, in which decisions and tasks must be filtered through many different specialized officials and conform to many rules in order for an action to be taken.

C

Cabinet: a body of advisers to a ruler.

Caliph: a ruler in an Islamic state who is considered a successor of Muhammad and rules politically as well as spiritually.

Calvinism: a Christian sect developed by John Calvin (1509-1564) that emphasizes the idea of predestination, the belief that some people are fated for salvation and are guided by God.

Capitalism: an economic system in which property and businesses are owned by individuals and corporations (rather than being owned by the government or by the society as a whole). Profits in a capitalistic system are based on competition and enrich the individual owner or the investors in a corporation.

Caravan: a group of people who travel together through deserts or hostile territories.

Censorship: the system of examining public statements or the arts, written or spoken, for ideas or material that is objectionable to the interests of a governing body, and not allowing these statements to be expressed in a public forum.

Centralization: the placement of the majority of power in one concentrated office, as in a strong central government as opposed to a federation of individually governed states.

Civil rights: the nonpolitical rights of a citizen, as in the rights of personal liberty guaranteed to U.S. citizens: equal treatment and equal access to housing, free speech, employment, and education.

Civil disobedience: the refusal to go along with government orders, as in purposely disobeying a discriminatory law or ordinance. Usually *civil disobedience* is carried out by a group in order to protest something or to get concessions from the government.

Civilian government: a government that is not led by the military or police forces.

Coalition government: a temporary joining together of two parties or interest groups within the government for a common goal.

Cold War: a term used to describe the tensions between the West and the Communist bloc countries of Eastern Europe and the former Soviet Union that arose after World War II (1939-45) and ended when the Berlin Wall fell and the Soviet Union dissolved at the end of the 1980s.

Collaboration: cooperation between two individuals or groups that are not normally connected.

Collective farm: a farm formed from many small farms, run jointly by the group of owners and usually supervised by the government.

Colony: a territory in which settlers from another country come to live while maintaining their ties to their home country, often setting up a government that may rule over the original inhabitants of the territory as well.

Colonialism: control by one nation or state over a dependent territory and its people and resources.

Communism: an economic theory in which there is no private property—all goods are owned in common; also the doctrine of the former Soviet Union, in which a single authoritarian governing body controls all means of production.

Confederation: to be united in a league or alliance for mutual support or common goals, as in the union of the 11 states that seceded from the United States in 1860 as the Confederate States of America.

Consensus: an agreement by most or all concerned with an issue.

Conservation: protection and preservation of something (often the environment); a carefully planned management system to prevent exploitation, destruction, or overuse.

Conservative: wishing to preserve what is already established, such as traditions or political or economic structures.

Consolidate: to join different elements or groups together to form one solid unit.

Constitution: a written document that sets forth the basic principles and laws of a nation, establishing the powers and duties of a government and the basic rights of its citizens.

Consul: an official appointed by one nation to live in a foreign country and to represent the business interests of his or her home nation in the foreign country.

Convoy: a protective escort.

Coptic church: a Christian sect that differed from the Western church in the belief that Jesus had only one nature, a divine one; orthodox creed holds that Jesus had both a divine and a human nature.

Corruption: the state of being outside of moral, legal, and proper behavior; acting in ways that benefit oneself or one's connections but hurt the society, such as offering or accepting bribery.

Coup: (from the French *coup d'etat,* "stroke of state") the violent overthrow of a government by a small group.

Cultural integration: to bring many cultures together into a whole as equals within a society, but not necessarily as distinct entities with separate beliefs and traditions.

Culture: the set of beliefs, social habits, and ways of surviving in the environment that are held by a particular social group. *Culture* is also a word for a group that shares these traits.

D

Delegation: a group of people chosen to represent a larger group, such as an organization, a political party, or a nation.

Democracy: a government in which the people hold the power and exercise it either directly or through elected representatives.

Denounce: to publicly criticize, accuse, or pronounce someone or something evil.

Depose: to remove a monarch from the throne or a leader from power.

Dictator: a ruler who has absolute authority and is often oppressive in his use of it.

Diplomacy: the art of handling affairs and conducting negotiations, especially between nations or states, without creating tensions.

Disfranchise: to deprive of the right to vote.

Diviner: someone who practices the arts involved in foreseeing the future or finding hidden knowledge.

Dominate: to exert mastery and control over another.

Dynasty: a powerful family that stays in power over many generations.

E

Elite: a group considered to be socially superior; or a powerful minority group.

Emirate: a state under the control of an *emir,* a ruler in an Islamic country.

Entourage: a group of attendants; the people who surround an important or famous person.

Environmentalist: someone who supports the preservation and improvement of the natural environment.

Ethnic group: a group of people that shares customs, language, beliefs, and a common history and origins.

Evacuate: to leave, or be removed from, a place in an organized way, often for protection from danger.

Évolué: a Western-educated African.

Evolution: in the struggle for survival, the process by which successive generations of a species pass on to their offspring the characteristics that enable the species to survive.

Excavation: to dig up or uncover in order to expose to view, as in digging up ancient fossils.

Exile: removal from one's native country, often forced but sometimes voluntary.

Expatriate: someone who lives in a foreign country.

Expedition: a journey taken for a specific reason.

Expropriate: to take property and put it in one's own name; to take away someone's property rights.

F

Famine: an extreme shortage of food causing starvation within a certain area.

Fascism: a political system headed by a dictator in which the nation is exalted above its individual citizens, all opposition to the government is prohibited, and powerful police and military forces use strong-arm tactics to ensure obedience and conformity to strict government regulation.

Fetish: an object that is believed to have magical powers that will protect its owner.

G

Garrison: a military station.

Genocide: the deliberate killing of everyone belonging to a particular ethnic group.

Grass roots: at the local community level, often referring to rural society away from the political centers.

Guerrilla: someone who fights, generally with a small group of rebels, using nonmilitary methods, such as sabotage and harassment.

H

Harlem Renaissance: a highly creative period among artists and writers in the community of Harlem in New York City that started in the early 1920s and lasted until the Great Depression in 1929.

Hereditary rulers: leaders who inherit the right to rule by reason of being born into a particular station within the ruling family.

Heretic: someone who will not conform to the established beliefs or doctrines of the prevailing religion.

I

Impeach: to accuse a public official or ruler of a crime against his or her office.

Indentured servant: someone who enters into a binding contract to work for someone else for a set period of time and in return usually receives travel and living expenses.

Indigenous: being native to a particular place or having one's origins there.

Inflation: a growing rise in the prices of goods due to an economy in which more money and credit are available than goods.

Infrastructure: the basic structure underlying a system; in a nation, the *infrastructure* includes government and public works, roads and other transportation systems, and communication networks.

Insurrection: rebellion against a government or other authority.

Integration: incorporation of different groups of people into a society as equals.

Isolationism: the chosen condition within a nation or territory of keeping apart from other nations, abstaining from alliances, trade, or intermingling of populations.

J

Judicial system: the system within a state or nation that administers justice, generally through a network of courts and judges.

K

Koran: the holy book of Muslim people, containing sacred writings that are revelations given to the prophet Muhammad by the Muslim god Allah.

L

Labor union: a group of workers organized to bargain together as a strong unit with employers for better wages, benefits, and working conditions.

Legislative body: the group within a government that is in charge of making laws and collecting taxes.

Liberal: broad-minded and open to the reform of established rules, authorities, traditions, and social structures.

Lobby: to attempt to persuade public officials to take action or vote a particular way on an issue.

M

Martial law: the law administered by a country's military forces during a declared emergency situation, when the normal security forces are not sufficient to maintain public safety and order. *Martial law* often involves a temporary suspension of certain individual civil and legal rights.

Mercenary: a soldier who is hired to fight with an army for pay, often coming from a foreign land and serving for profit, without any patriotic motivations.

Migrant worker: a person who moves from place to place to find temporary work.

Migration: the movement of a group of people from a home territory to another region.

Military rule: a government run by the armed forces, as opposed to a civilian government.

Missionary: a person belonging to an organized effort by a religious group to spread its beliefs in other parts of the world.

Monopoly: the exclusive control, ownership, or rights to something, like a product or a particular business.

Mosque: a building where Muslims practice public worship.

Multiparty politics: a political system in which parties representing different interests run against each other in elections, giving individual voters a variety of options and allowing for opposition to be expressed.

Muslim: a follower of the Islam religion, who worships the god Allah as revealed to the prophet Muhammad through the Koran, the holy book of Islam.

Mutiny: resistance to authority; particularly, revolt against a superior officer, as in the crew of a ship against the commander.

Mysticism: the belief that one can obtain a direct knowledge of God or spiritual truth through inner, or subjective, experience.

N

Nationalism: pride and loyalty toward one's nation, usually to the extent of exalting that nation above all others.

Nationalization: investing control and ownership, usually of a business or property, to the national government.

Nation-state: a political unit in which a particular group sharing the same beliefs, customs, history, and political interests comprises its own state and is self-ruled.

Negritude: the state of being pridefully aware of the culture and history of the African people.

Nomad: a member of a group of people who do not live in one set place, but move around as necessary, usually in pursuit of a food supply.

O

Opposition: the position of believing and expressing something contrary to another; in politics, the *opposition* party is one that disagrees with and is ready to replace the party in power.

Organization of African Unity (OAU): An organization founded in 1963, currently with more than 50 member nations, to promote unity among African states, to eliminate colonialism, to develop sound health and economic policies, and to maintain defense of the African nations.

Overlord: a supreme ruler, who rules over other less powerful rulers within his or her realm.

P

Pagan: a word used by Christians and westerners to identify people who believe either in many gods or in no gods.

Pan-Africanism: a movement for greater cooperation and unity among the different regions or nations of the African continent.

Parliament: the highest legislative body of a nation, which meets regularly and is the forum for gathering and discussion among different assemblies.

Pass laws: laws under which blacks in South Africa had to carry documents that identified them and certified that they had authorized jobs in white areas.

Passive resistance: nonviolent defiance of a government or power usually exerted through noncooperation (as in not following commands).

Patronage system: a method of distributing jobs, often used in appointing government jobs, in which jobs are granted as a reward for increasing the political or financial standing of the person or group making the appointments.

Peasant farmers: members of a social class of either small landowners or laborers who work the land, who are generally quite poor and often uneducated and lacking in political influence.

Philanthropist: one who works to promote the welfare of others or the society.

Pidgin English: a simple form of English-based speech used for communication between someone who speaks English and someone who speaks a different language; or, a mixture of English and another language.

Pilgrimage: a journey to a sacred place.

Plantation: a large farming establishment in which the labor is usually provided by workers who live on the premises.

Plateau: a region of high, flat land that is raised sharply above land next to it on at least one side.

Police state: a nation or other political unit under the power of a repressive government that uses a powerful and often secret police force to administer the areas of government usually left to civilians, such as judicial and social matters.

Political prisoner: someone who is jailed because of beliefs or actions that are perceived to be contrary or in opposition to the government.

Polygamy: the practice of having more than one spouse at a time, applicable to either sex.

Polygyny: the practice of a male having more than one wife at a time.

Premier: the prime minister, or the leader who is first in rank as head of the cabinet or ministry of a nation or state.

Prime minister: the leader who heads the cabinet or ministry of a nation or state.

Protectorate: the relationship that occurs when a state assumes the authority position over another state.

Province: a regional division of a nation, like a state, with a regional government of its own, but ruled in federal matters by the national government.

Puppet government: a political body that is controlled by an outside authority, usually referring to a leader who appears to rule but is in fact carrying out the demands of a more powerful and less apparent entity.

Purge: literally, to rid (the nation) of something that is undesirable; *purges* have taken place in many areas in which one ethnic group attempts to destroy another.

R

Recession: a time of decreased economic activity.

Refugee: someone who flees from his or her own country, often to another country, to escape persecution.

Regent: someone who governs a kingdom standing in for the sovereign ruler, generally because the sovereign is under the legal age, absent, or disabled.

Regime: a government in power.

Reparations: payments made after a war by the defeated nation for damages another nation or group of people suffered as a result of the war.

Resistance: the act of opposing the dominant authority; *resistance* can also refer to a political organization that fights an occupying power within its nation, using underground methods such as guerrilla warfare and sabotage.

S

Sabotage: a deliberate act of destruction or obstruction, designed to damage an enemy's ability to carry out its functions.

Sanctuary: a place of protection from persecutors or immunity from the law.

Secession: a formal withdrawal from an organization or a political unit.

Secretary-general: the main administrative officer of an organization.

Socialism: an economic and political system in which the government owns businesses and distributes goods to the people.

Solitary confinement: a punishment used in prisons that involves being placed in a cell by oneself and not allowed to see or speak with others for a set amount of time.

Sovereignty: freedom from controls from outside; self-government.

Statesman: someone who is wise in the arts of leadership and can govern fairly, without becoming involved in factions and partisanship.

Strategic: necessary in the conduct of war and not available in the warring nation's own country; of great importance.

Strike: a stoppage of work by an organized group of workers in order to make an employer respond to demands about wages, job security, or work conditions.

Sub-Saharan Africa: part of Africa south of the Sahara desert (see map, inside front or back cover).

Subsidize: to grant money to a business or another nation in order to provide assistance or to obtain favors.

Subsistence farming: a system of farming in which a family farms a small amount of land to grow just the things they need to live, without significant extra harvest to be sold.

T

Terrorism: using threats and violent acts to inspire extreme fear in an enemy in order to force the enemy to agree to demands.

Textiles: cloth.

Totalitarian: describing a dictatorial state in which one powerful person or group rules with near total control and the state is exalted above the individual.

Tradition: a custom or institution from among the beliefs, social habits, methods, systems, arts, etc., of a people that is handed down from generation to generation, such as a ritual, a story, or a courtship practice.

Treason: the offense of trying to overthrow a government or kill its ruler.

Tribute: a payment made from one nation or group to another, usually when the paying group has been conquerred by the group they are paying. *Tribute* is either payable to the dominant party as a kind of tax, or it is paid in exchange for protection.

Tyranny: excessive and repressive power exerted by the government.

U

Unify: to bring together different elements and make them into a coherent whole.

Unitary state: an undivided state or nation: one with only one political party and a strong central government.

United Nations: an international organization established after World War II for the purpose of maintaining international peace, developing good relations among nations, and finding solutions to economic, social, and humanitarian problems throughout the world.

V

Vanguard: those who lead a movement or action, or the forefront of a movement.

W

West: a term referring to the countries of western Europe and the United States, usually those countries that have not been under Communist regimes in the twentieth century and have some similarities in customs, political and economic philosophy, and ethnicity.

Westernization: the adoption of, or conversion to, traditions and qualities of the West.

White supremacy: a belief in the superiority of the white race over the black race and the consequent need to maintain whites in powerful positions over blacks.

White-minority government: a government led and administered by white people in a population that is comprised of a majority of non-whites who are excluded from the political process.

World Bank: The International Bank for Reconstruction and Development, an agency of the United Nations that loans money to member nations for the purpose of developing economic growth.

Picture Credits

Nadine Gordimer

The photographs and illustrations appearing in *African Biography* were received from the following sources:

On the cover: Haile Selassie I, Miriam Makeba, and Nelson Mandela: **AP/Wide World Photos. Reproduced by permission.**

Photograph by J. P. Laffont. United Nations: xlix; **Photograph by Jerry Bauer. Reproduced by permission:** p. 1; **AP/Wide World Photos. Reproduced by permission:** v, xv, xxiii, lv, lviii, lix, 18, 23, 39, 44, 50, 55, 59, 64, 93, 138,143, 147, 157, 162, 166, 173,175, 177, 181, 183, 229, 232, 235, 261, 269, 283, 306, 309, 315, 328, 346, 359, 379, 396, 400, 418, 433, 437, 441, 448, 454, 466, 471, 498, 502, 504, 510, 525, 530, 534, 543, 554, 562; **Photograph by Reuters/Jeff Christensen. Archive Photos. Reproduced by permission:** p. 28; **Photograph by Rick Wilking. Archive Photos. Reproduced by permission:** 32; **Library of Congress:** 34, 119, 292, 350; **Archive Photos. Reproduced by permission:** lvii, 47, 187, 192, 238, 241, 254, 263, 341, 362, 364, 365, 427, 521, 571, 587, 589, 596; **United Nations:** 62, 578; **Corbis-Bettmann. Reproduced by permission:** lii (top and bottom), 73, 201, 285; **The Granger Collection, New York.**

Reproduced by permission: 79, 220, 388; **Photograph by Howard Burditt. Archive Photos. Reproduced by permission:** 86, 385; **Photograph by Van Lierop. United Nations:** 90; **Illustration by Donna V. Benson, Gale Research:** 95, 195, 294, 459, 478; **Reuters Corbis-Bettman. Reproduced by permission:** lxi, 112, 116, 319; **Photograph by Wyatt Counts. AP/Wide World Photos. Reproduced by permission:** 125; **Photograph by Juda Ngwenya. Archive Photos. Reproduced by permission:** 130, 282; **Reproduced with the kind permission of the Estate of Bessie Head:** 149; **Zimbabwe National Archives. Reproduced by permission:** 246, 248, 249, 515; **Tony Stone Images. Reproduced by permission:** 206; **Photograph by Tom Costello. AP/Wide World Photos. Reproduced by permission:** 212; **Photograph by Robert Caputo. Time Magazine. Reproduced by permission:** 216; **Corbis Images. Reproduced by permission:** 223; **Adrian Arbib/Corbis Images. Reproduced by permission:** 271; **Photograph by Hos Maina. Archive Photos. Reproduced by permission:** 275; **Photograph by Peter Andrews. Archive Photos. Reproduced by permission:** lx, 277; **Photograph by Chester Higgins Jr. Photo Researchers, Inc. Reproduced by permission:** xxi, 304; **Kenya Information Services.** 321; **Corbis Corporation. Reproduced by permission:** 330; **Express Newspapers/L932/Archive Photos. Reproduced by permission:** 353; **Photograph by Reinhard W. Sander. Reproduced by permission:** 443; **The Kobal Collection. Reproduced by permission:** 476; **Mansell Collection/Time Inc/The New York Times Magazine. Reproduced by permission:** li (bottom), 485, 489; **Photograph by Caton Woodville. Mansell Collection/Time Inc/New York Times Magazine. Reproduced by permission:** li (top), 518; **Archive Photos/Trappe. Reproduced by permission:** 536; **Photograph by Y. Nagata. United Nations:** 561; **Photograph by Peter Van Niekerk. Reproduced by permission:** xxxi, 580.

A Timeline of Important Events in African History

Angolan children celebrate their nation's independence.

300 Aksum, the first recorded kingdom of Ethiopia (founded by Arab traders in the first century A.D.), adopts Coptic Christianity.

700 Mombasa (Kenya) develops as a center for Arab trade in slaves and ivory.

1000-1400 Great Zimbabwe, the largest and strongest city of its time in central and southern Africa, controls the gold trade in southern Africa. Lying in the high plateau area of present-day Zimbabwe, the population of Great Zimbabwe reached about 18,000 and its rulers controlled an area of about 60,000 square miles.

1182 Lalibela becomes emperor of Ethiopia.

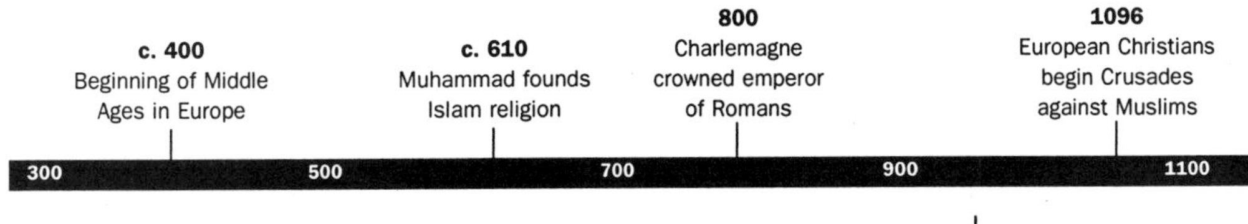
c. 400
Beginning of Middle Ages in Europe
c. 610
Muhammad founds Islam religion
800
Charlemagne crowned emperor of Romans
1096
European Christians begin Crusades against Muslims
300
500
700
900
1100

Slavers moving captives.

1324- 27 Ruler of Mali Kingdom **Mansa Musa** makes pilgrimage to Mecca, the holy city of Islam, and returns to rebuild the capital city of Timbuktu into an urban center of commerce and learning.

1400-96 Sunni Ali, the great leader of the Songhai Empire in Mali, takes Timbuktu; his empire becomes the largest in ancient Western Africa.

1482 Afonso I of the Kongo welcomes Portuguese explorers into his kingdom and establishes relations with Portugal; in addition to bringing Christianity and Western education, the Europeans establish an enormous slave trade in the Kongo kingdom.

1482 The Portuguese establish a trading post at Elmina, Gold Coast.

1505 Portuguese burn Kilwa (in Kenya) and continue penetration along the Indian Ocean Coast and inland.

1550 Mwene Mutapa Negomo Mupunzagutu rules the Mutapa Dynasty in current-day Zimbabwe.

1591 Moroccans invade Songhai, defeat its army, and occupy Timbuktu (in Mali).

1591 The Portuguese invade Angolan kingdoms and increase the slave trade to Brazil.

c. 1600 African trading states develop along the Atlantic Coast as partners of Europeans in slave trade.

1622 Anna Nzinga represents the Ndongo (Angola) in negotiations with the Portuguese.

1652 Dutch East India Company establishes a settlement at the Cape of Good Hope in southern Africa.

1673 Dahomey (Benin) becomes a powerful slave trading kingdom.

1789 Former Nigerian slave **Olaudah Equiano** publishes his memoirs.

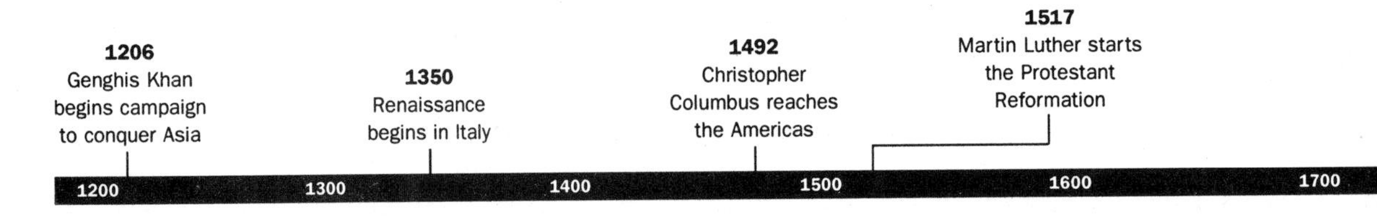
1206
Genghis Khan begins campaign to conquer Asia
1350
Renaissance begins in Italy
1492
Christopher Columbus reaches the Americas
1517
Martin Luther starts the Protestant Reformation
1200
1300
1400
1500
1600
1700

1804 Usuman dan Fodio declares a holy war in northern Nigeria and founds the Islamic Sokoto Empire.

1807 British parliament passes the Slave Trade Abolition Act outlawing maritime (at sea) slave trade.

1815 The British take Cape Colony in southern Africa from the Dutch.

1818 Zulu chief **Shaka** begins 10 years of expansion in southern Africa. His warriors raid villages, causing chaos and forcing millions of people to flee. People displaced by Shaka in turn displace or absorb other peoples, changing forever the mixture of people, language, and culture throughout southern Africa and parts of central Africa. This period in African history is referred to as the *mfecane* or the "crushing."

Shaka meets Lieutenant Farewell.

1818-58 King **Guezo** of a newly strong and independent Dahomey directs his army to move eastward in a relentless pursuit of slaves.

1833 Slavery is outlawed in the British Empire.

1835-43 Afrikaners begin Great Trek northward from Cape Colony in southern Africa to get beyond the influence of the British colonial government.

1835 Queen **Ranavalona I** of Madagascar forbids all religious teaching in the country in an attempt to eliminate foreign influence and preserve the traditional culture of her people.

Ranavalona I.

1843 Gambia and Natal (in southern Africa) become British colonies.

1847 Liberia becomes a republic. American blacks had begun settling there in 1821, and by 1867 approximately 20,000 people had settled in Liberia, mostly on land that had been purchased from local tribes.

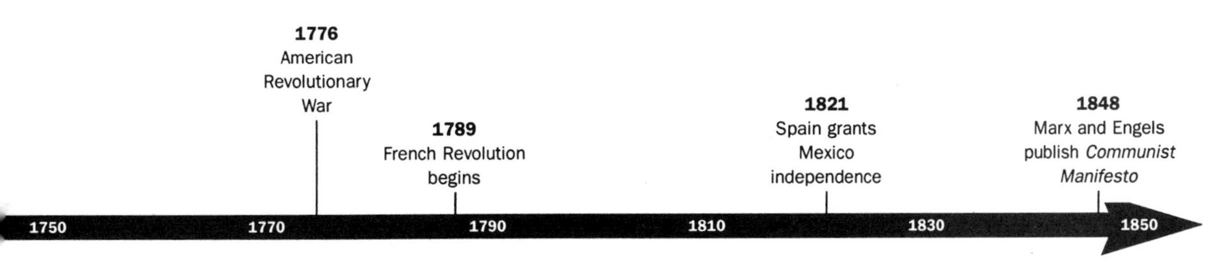
1776
American
Revolutionary
War
1789
French Revolution
begins
1821
Spain grants
Mexico
independence
1848
Marx and Engels
publish *Communist*
Manifesto
1750
1770
1790
1810
1830
1850

Slaves leaving ship.

1860 M'Siri becomes leader of the Katanga Kingdom in Congo. M'Siri expands his territory methodically, taking captives and trading them for more guns and powder, which he uses to take more slaves. At the height of his reign M'Siri controls a territory larger than the state of California.

1861 British establish colonial presence in modern-day Nigeria.

1862 Mutesa I is the first Bugandan king to receive Europeans in his kingdom.

1867 Tippu Tib establishes himself as one of the greatest traders in ivory and slaves in eastern and central Africa. He amasses such a great fortune that he is recognized as the overlord of a vast area.

1868 Moshoeshoe, the chief of a small Sotho clan, arranges for Basutoland to become a British protectorate after Afrikaners move North and settle on land claimed by Moshoeshoe. His diplomacy laid the foundation for the current-day nation-state of Lesotho.

1871 Gold is discovered in the Transvaal (southern Africa).

1873-74 Kumasi (Ghana) is burned in the Ashanti-British War.

1874 The Gold Coast becomes a British colony.

Cetshwayo.

1879 Zulu leader **Cetshwayo**'s army, with weaponry consisting mostly of *assegais* (short stabbing spears) and some firearms, defeats the British army at Isandhlwana (South Africa).

1883 Paul Kruger is elected the first president of the Transvaal Republic (South Africa) after successfully leading his people against the British army in 1880 to restore independence to the Transvaal.

1884-85 At a conference in Berlin, European nations carve out their spheres of influence in Africa.

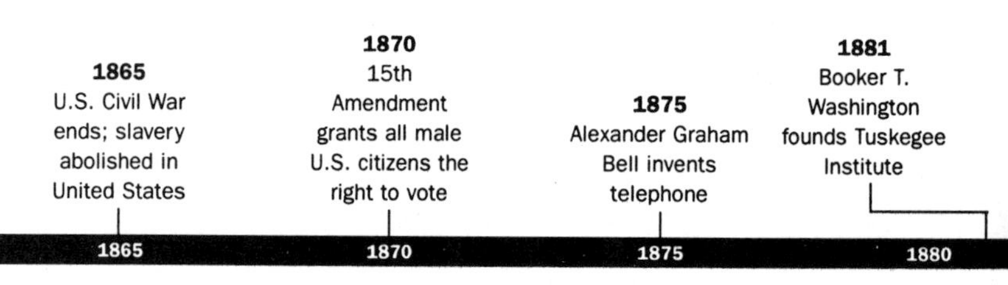

1865
U.S. Civil War ends; slavery abolished in United States
1870
15th Amendment grants all male U.S. citizens the right to vote
1875
Alexander Graham Bell invents telephone
1881
Booker T. Washington founds Tuskegee Institute
1855
1860
1865
1870
1875
1880

1885 The Mahdi, a Muslim visionary who declared himself the successor to the prophet Muhammad, defeats British general Charles Gordon at Khartoum (Sudan) in an uprising against the territory's Egyptian overlords and their British administrators.

1885 King Leopold II of Belgium creates the Belgian Congo as his personal kingdom.

1889 Menelik II becomes emperor of Ethiopia. He is the only African leader to keep control of his country as European powers carve up the continent into colonies.

1889 Great Britain grants the British South Africa Company a royal charter for Rhodesia (Zimbabwe). A large, permanent white settlement is established at Fort Salisbury the next year.

1893-94 Matabele chief **Lobengula** is defeated by British South Africa Company in Rhodesia. With Lobengula's death in 1894, the line of inherited leadership of the Ndebele ends.

1894 Samuel Crowther is consecrated bishop of Nigeria and becomes the first black bishop in the Anglican Church.

1895-96 Ethiopians defeat Italian invaders at the battle of Adowa.

1896 Ashanti king **Prempeh I** negotiates with the British in order to save his 200-year-old kingdom.

1896-97 Ndebele and Shona revolt against the British (in Zimbabwe).

1899-1902 The Boer War is fought between Afrikaners in the Transvaal and Orange Free State against the British. Although the Boers win early victories, the British win the war and the Afrikaners accept British rule.

1900 The first Pan African Congress is held in London. Early Pan-Africanism advocates the merging of smaller African states into one huge African nation.

The Mahdi.

Samuel Crowther.

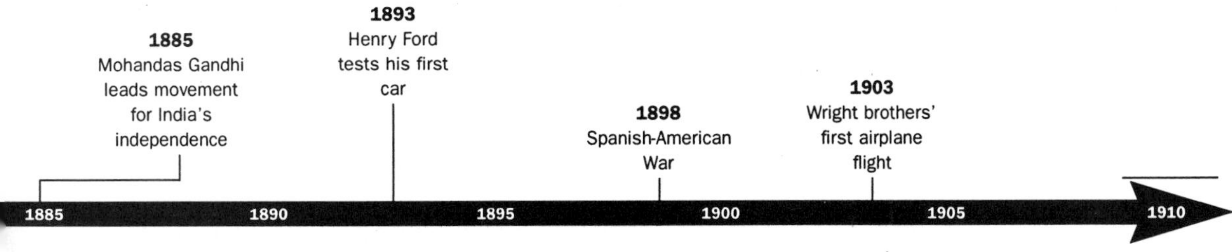
1885
Mohandas Gandhi leads movement for India's independence
1893
Henry Ford tests his first car
1898
Spanish-American War
1903
Wright brothers' first airplane flight
1885
1890
1895
1900
1905
1910

Boer soldiers.

Adelaide Smith Casely Hayford and pupils.

1900 Queen mother of the Ashanti **Yaa Asantewa** leads Ashanti army in war against the British in a heroic but futile battle against the colonizers.

1908 German troops defeat the Herero army at Waterberg (Namibia). **Samuel Maherero,** supreme chief of the Herero nation, makes a brave but ultimately hopeless attempt to get the land back from the Germans. When the Herero revolt begins, the population stands at about 80,000, but within one year more than 65,000 Herero are dead.

1915 Malawi nationalist **John Chilembwe** leads uprising against British colonists. Chilembwe, an African Christian leader in Nyasaland (present-day Malawi) whose "Rising" failed miserably, became a folk hero to the people of Nyasaland, a symbol of resistance to white rule.

1919 Adelaide Smith Casely Hayford establishes her Girls' Vocational and Industrial School in Freetown, Sierra Leone.

1921 Congolese religious leader **Simon Kimbangu** establishes a following after starting one of the most important independent Christian religious movements in central Africa.

1921 Sobhuza II is installed as "Lion" or king of the Swazi. Sobhuza will become the world's longest-reigning monarch, ruling for 60 years.

1930 Haile Selassie I becomes emperor of Ethiopia. During his rule, he abolishes slavery, institutes tax reform, promotes education, creates a constitution, and plays a dominant role in the formation of the Organization of African Unity (OAU).

1935 Italy invades Ethiopia under the orders of Italian dictator Benito Mussolini. **Haile Selassie** appeals to the League of

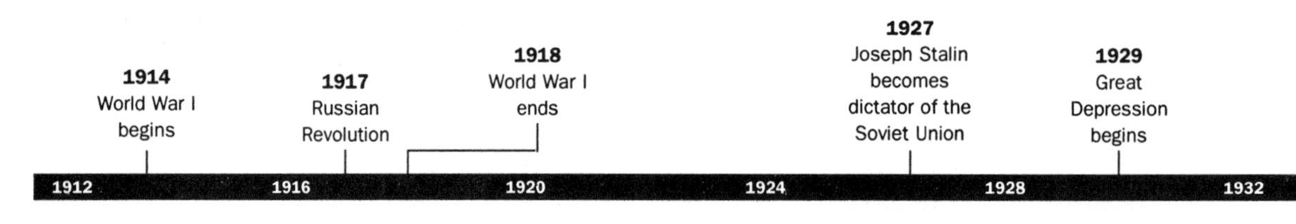
1914
World War I
begins
1917
Russian
Revolution
1918
World War I
ends
1927
Joseph Stalin
becomes
dictator of the
Soviet Union
1929
Great
Depression
begins
1912
1916
1920
1924
1928
1932

Nations for help to stop the Italian invaders, but England and France refused to cooperate. The next year, Italy occupies Ethiopia and Haile Selassie goes into exile.

1941 Italy is evicted from Ethopia; **Haile Selassie** is restored to the throne.

1944 **William V. S. Tubman** is named president of Liberia.

1946 General rise of African nationalism throughout colonial Africa at end of World War II.

1948 Kenyan anthropologist **Mary Leakey** discovers fossilized bones of *Proconsul africanus,* an apelike creature between 25 and 40 million years old. This is the first significant find to suggest that humans may have originated in East Africa

1948 **Olufunmilayo Ransome-Kuti** organizes Nigerian market women. The Abeokuta women's campaign protest abuses of British rule.

1948 The National party, comprised mainly of conservative Afrikaners, wins elections in South Africa and establishes a society based on racial separateness and discrimination, or apartheid.

1948 South African writer **Alan Paton**'s novel *Cry, the Beloved Country* is published, bringing South Africa's racial policies worldwide attention.

1952 The Mau Mau uprising in Kenya begins, a violent rebellion by Kikuyu terrorists who fight against the seizing of Kikuyu land by the British. In the next few years, nearly 3,000 Kikuyu die, many at the hands of the Mau Mau rebels, who terrorize blacks suspected of supporting the white regime. By the end of 1955 the revolt is put down.

Haile Selassie I.

Louis S. B. Leakey.

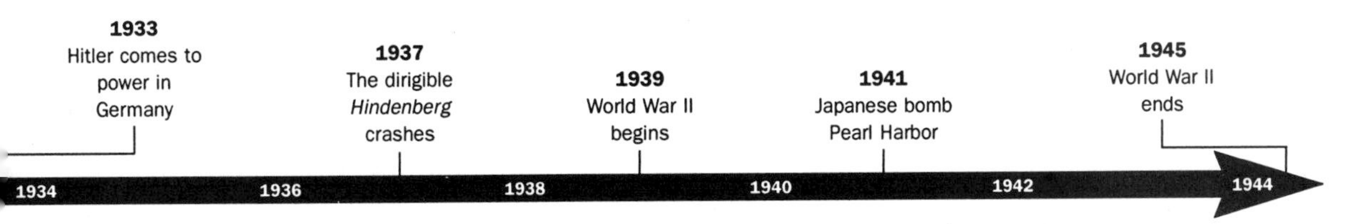
1933
Hitler comes to power in Germany
1937
The dirigible *Hindenberg* crashes
1939
World War II begins
1941
Japanese bomb Pearl Harbor
1945
World War II ends
1934
1936
1938
1940
1942
1944

1953 Federation of Northern and Southern Rhodesia and Nyasaland is formed. Following pressure from the white settler groups in Southern Rhodesia, Northern Rhodesia (now Zambia), and Nyasaland (now Malawi), Great Britain allows the three territories to unite as the self-governing Federation of Rhodesia and Nyasaland. Black Africans strongly oppose the formation of the white-run federation, which lasts until 1963.

1955 Alice Lenshina forms the Lumpa Church, which will become the largest and most powerful peasant movement in Zambian history. The expanding Lumpa Church challenges the state, the established churches, and the traditional leaders.

Sékou Touré, Kwame Nkrumah, and William V. S. Tubman

1957 Kwame Nkrumah becomes prime minister of independent Ghana, the first British colony in Africa to achieve independence after World War II.

1958 Sékou Touré becomes president of Guinea as it achieves independence from France.

1958 Hendrik Verwoerd takes over as prime minister of South Africa and reinforces Bantustan policies that were initiated in South Africa in 1951. Under these policies, citizenship and voting rights for blacks is restricted to nine districts or Bantus. The land reserved for blacks is of poor quality and equals about 14 percent of South Africa's total land, whereas blacks make up about 85 percent of the population.

1958 Nigerian writer **Chinua Achebe**'s *Things Fall Apart* is published.

1960 Joshua Nkomo is elected president of the National Democratic Party, the forerunner to the Zimbabwe African People's Union, one of the main groups that successfully fought for the independence of Rhodesia.

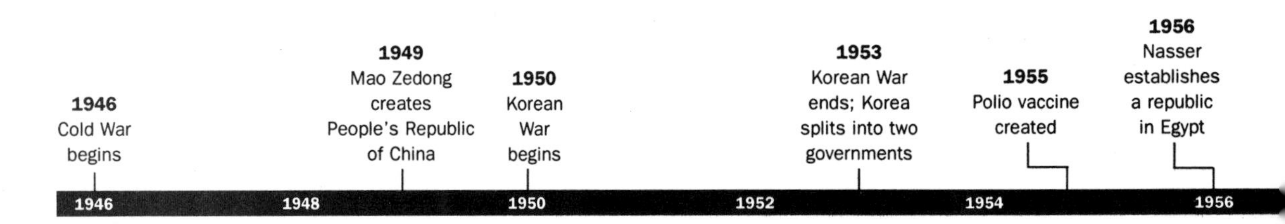
1946 Cold War begins
1949 Mao Zedong creates People's Republic of China
1950 Korean War begins
1953 Korean War ends; Korea splits into two governments
1955 Polio vaccine created
1956 Nasser establishes a republic in Egypt
1946
1948
1950
1952
1954
1956

1960 South African singer and political activist **Miriam Makeba** begins exile from South Africa that will last 30 years. Singing throughout the world, she uses music as her forum in the fight against apartheid and racial discrimination.

1960 At a mass demonstration pushing for an end to pass laws for blacks in Sharpeville, South Africa, policemen fire into a crowd of 5,000 unarmed demonstrators, killing 69 and wounding 300.

1960 **Patrice Lumumba** of the Congo Republic, **Félix Houphouet-Boigny** of Côte d'Ivoire, **Léopold Sédar Senghor** of Senegal, and **Julius Nyerere** of Kenya are sworn in as heads of their newly independent nations.

1960 South African chief and African National Congress (ANC) president **Albert John Lutuli** wins the Nobel Peace Prize.

1960 **Moïse Tshombe** declares Katanga independent from Congo and becomes the president of the secessionist state.

1961 Tanganyika, Rwanda, and Sierra Leone become independent.

1962 Uganda and Burundi achieve independence.

1963 Organization of African Unity is founded to promote unity among African states.

1963 **Nnamdi Azikiwe** becomes president of the Republic of Nigeria.

1964 **Kenneth Kaunda** becomes president of Zambia.

1964 **Jomo Kenyatta** is inaugurated president of Kenya.

1965 Prime Minister **Ian Douglas Smith** declares Rhodesia's independence from Great Britain to avoid an independence granted by the British that would be based on majority rule.

Julius Nyerere

Jomo Kenyatta and Tom Mboya

1959
Castro creates Communist government in Cuba

1961
Berlin Wall divides East and West Germany

1964
First wave of racial riots in large U.S. cities

1965
U.S. troops become involved in Vietnam War

1958 | 1960 | 1962 | 1964 | 1966 | 1968

1966 Nigerian writer **Flora Nwapa** publishes her first novel, *Efuru.*

1966 In a military coup in Nigeria, Prime Minister **Abubakar Tafawa Balewa** is assassinated. Another military coup occurs this year in Ghana.

1966 Hastings Banda becomes president of Malawi.

1966 Sir Seretse Khama becomes president of independent Botswana.

1966 Basutoland becomes independent Lesotho.

Mobutu Sese Seko and troops.

1967-70 Civil war erupts in Nigeria. In the second military coup since independence, military officers from the Muslim North overthrow the existing government. A Muslim-dominated government takes over, and tens of thousands of Ibos who live in the North are killed. The federal government announces plans to split the Eastern Region, the home of the Ibo, into three separate states. In response, the Eastern Region secedes and proclaims itself the independent Republic of Biafra. Nigerian troops go into Biafra to put down the rebellion. A two-and-a-half year bloody conflict follows before Biafra falls to federal forces. An estimated one million Biafrans die of starvation because of the food shortages caused by the war.

Idi Amin being sworn in.

1967-97 Mobutu Sese Seko establishes himself as president of Congo (Zaire).

1968 Swaziland and Mauritius become independent.

1969 Mozambique nationalist **Eduardo Mondlane** is assassinated.

1969 Kenyan trade unionist **Tom Mboya** is assassinated.

1969 Exiled South African writer **Bessie Head** publishes *When Rain Clouds Gather.*

1971 Idi Amin takes power in Uganda.

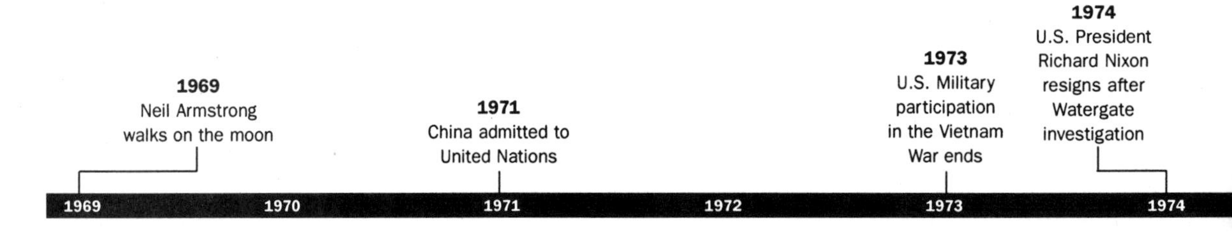
1969
Neil Armstrong walks on the moon
1971
China admitted to United Nations
1973
U.S. Military participation in the Vietnam War ends
1974
U.S. President Richard Nixon resigns after Watergate investigation
1969
1970
1971
1972
1973
1974

1974 A military coup in Portugal ends the fight in Mozambique for independence from Portugal. The Portuguese army—tired of the endless wars they were sent to fight in Africa and desiring a democratic system at home—overthrow the government of Marcello Caetano. The new government in Portugal hold a series of meetings with Mozambique's nationalist leaders and works out a plan for independence.

1974 Ethiopian emperor **Haile Selaisse I** is assassinated.

1975 Mozambique becomes independent.

1976 Soweto, South Africa, erupts in violence as school children demonstrate against the school authorities' decision to use Afrikaans as the language for teaching.

1977 South African authorities banish activist **Winnie Madikizela-Mandela** to Orange Free State for eight years.

1977 South African activist **Steve Biko** dies in police custody.

1977 Kenyan environmentalist **Wangari Maathai** establishes the Green Belt Movement; in years to follow 50,000 people involved in the effort will plant an estimated 10,000,000 trees.

1978 Daniel arap Moi becomes president of Kenya after **Jomo Kenyatta**'s death.

1980 Robert Mugabe becomes prime minister of Zimbabwe, the last of the British colonies in Africa to become independent.

1981 Jerry Rawlings overthrows the elected Ghanaian government in his second coup as Ghana's economy nears collapse.

1984 South African Anglican archbishop **Desmond Tutu** wins Nobel Peace Prize.

1986 Nigerian writer **Wole Soyinka** wins Nobel Prize for literature.

Winnie Madikizela-Mandela.

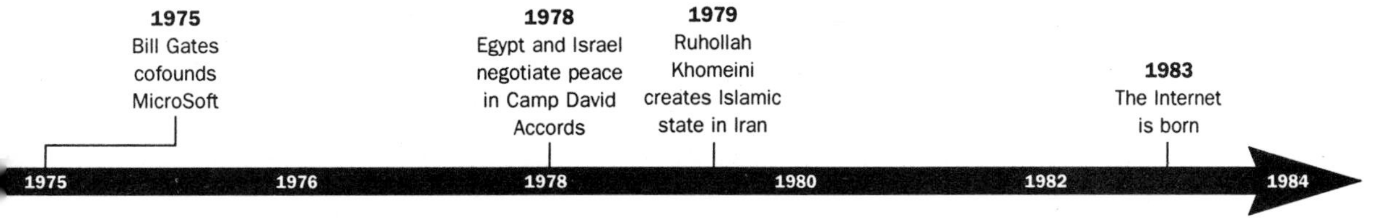

1975
Bill Gates cofounds MicroSoft
1978
Egypt and Israel negotiate peace in Camp David Accords
1979
Ruhollah Khomeini creates Islamic state in Iran
1983
The Internet is born
1975
1976
1978
1980
1982
1984

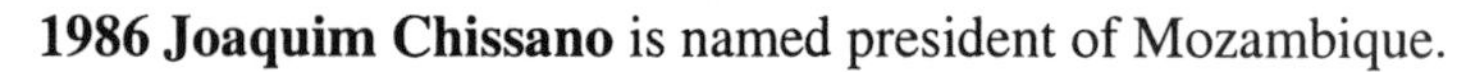

1986 Joaquim Chissano is named president of Mozambique.

1986 Yoweri Museveni takes over as the head of government in Uganda.

1990 Nelson Mandela is released from prison after 27 years.

1990 The first president of Namibia, **Sam Nujoma,** is sworn in.

1991 Nigerian writer **Ben Okri** wins the Booker Prize.

1991 South African fiction writer **Nadine Gordimer** wins the Nobel Prize for literature.

1992 President **Joaquim Chissano** helps to end the 16-year-long civil war in Mozambique and brings the rebel group headed by Afonso Dhlakama into the government through the country's first multiparty elections.

Nelson Mandela and Frederick Willem de Klerk.

1993 South Africans **Nelson Mandela** and **Frederick Willem de Klerk** are jointly awarded the Nobel Peace Prize for their efforts to form a democratic, representative government in South Africa.

1994 Nelson Mandela is inaugurated as the first black president of South Africa. His political party, the African National Congress, is elected as the majority in South Africa's parliament.

1996 Ghanaian diplomat **Kofi Annan** is named Secretary General of the United Nations.

1997 Nigerian Afro-Beat singer **Fela Kuti** dies of AIDS.

1998 U.S. embassies in Nairobi, Kenya, and Dar es Salaam, Tanzania, are bombed.

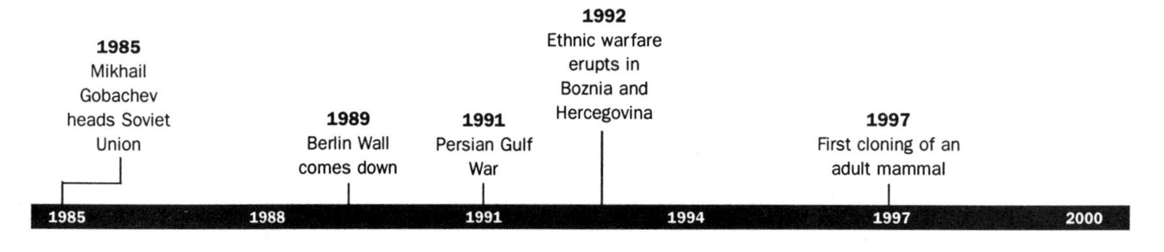
1985
Mikhail Gobachev heads Soviet Union
1989
Berlin Wall comes down
1991
Persian Gulf War
1992
Ethnic warfare erupts in Boznia and Hercegovina
1997
First cloning of an adult mammal
1985
1988
1991
1994
1997
2000

african BIOGRAPHY

Mutesa I

Born c. 1837
Buganda (Uganda)
Died 1884
Buganda (Uganda)

King of Buganda

Mutesa I (name in full, Mutesa Walugembe Mukaabya) was the king or *kabaka* of one of the most highly consolidated (or unified) kingdoms in eastern central Africa. During his reign he dealt with Arab slave traders, Muslim teachers, European explorers, and Christian missionaries. He was a keen statesman who balanced the demands of the outsiders against the needs of his people at home. Mutesa learned to read and speak Swahili (the language of the East Coast traders), and he welcomed new technology. But to the dismay of missionaries who thought he had adopted what they considered civilized ways, Mutesa used traditional ways when he was under pressure.

"[Mutesa] is a pagan . . . a heathen. All the faculties of lying, low cunning, hatred, pride and conceit, jealousy, cruelty . . . combined with extreme vanity . . . [are] concentrated in him. All is self, self, self. Uganda exists for him alone."

—Alexander Mackay, chief representative of the British Church Missionary Society, commenting on Mutesa

The East African kingdom of Buganda dates back to the 1400s; it grew to a large state in the 1700s and reached its height as an independent kingdom in the 1800s, with about 3 million subjects. Bugandan kings ruled for 22 generations until 1966, when Ugandan president Milton Obote abolished the kingdom and deposed the kabaka. Then, in 1993, President Yoweri Museveni (see entry) restored the son of the deposed king to the throne. At its peak, the kingdom stretched along the northwestern shore of Lake Victoria in a crescent shape for 150 miles. It was one of the wealthiest areas of what is now Uganda.

The wealth of the kingdom was based on bananas and slaves. Banana plantations provided the staple food and the basic ingredient for beer. Captives taken in wars furnished the labor for the plantations and were traded as slaves. The Bugandans were one of the largest slave-based societies in the region. Besides using the slave labor for agriculture, they also used slaves to develop their infrastructure (public works, government, and military systems). Each chief of a district constructed four-foot wide roads that ran from his district to the kabaka's center. On these roads leading to the capital, the slaves carried on their heads the chiefs' tribute or taxes to the kabaka. Slaves also gathered building materials for the elite and built huts. Later, when the Europeans arrived, the slaves built their schools and the mission centers from bricks.

Although Buganda was about 750 miles inland from the Indian Ocean coast (several months' travel time on foot), the kingdom had more contact with Europeans than most other African peoples in the region in early times. Kabaka Mutesa was the first Bugandan king to meet Europeans.

Isolation is no protection

European interest in East Africa did not emerge until the 1850s. Before then, during the sixteenth and seventeenth centuries, the Portuguese had controlled the Indian Ocean coast. In the early 1700s the Omani Arabs expelled the Portuguese north of central Mozambique and took over the slave trade. In their search for slaves, Arab traders penetrated the interior as far as Lake Tanganyika in the early 1840s. By 1843 they had established a permanent presence at the kabaka's court in Buganda on Lake Victoria. The Bugandans were proficient warriors and took many captives, which they then traded as slaves for guns, gunpowder, and beads from the Arabs.

Zanzibar, an island off the East Coast of Africa, developed as the major trading base for slaves brought out from the interior.

Zanzibar replaced the West African Atlantic Ocean depots in the 1800s, when Britain outlawed slavery and began patrolling the coastal waters for slave ships. In 1833 the sultan (king of a Muslim state) of Muscat, Omani Said, moved his court to Zanzibar. An estimated two-thirds of the island's 200,000 people were slaves. Half the slaves were exported in trade, and the others worked the clove plantations on the islands and the palm oil groves at Mombasa on the coast.

In 1841 the British consul at Zanzibar estimated that 40,000 slaves were brought onto the island each year. When reports of the Arab slave trade began to reach Europe, antislavery groups put pressure on the British government to stop it. In the 1860s Britain sent a naval squadron of seven or eight ships to patrol the western Indian Ocean. The British ships stopped and searched Arab ships sailing along the African coast, looking for captives being sent to Arabia. Still, an estimated 20,000 slaves were bought and sold each year.

Curiosity about the region and its geography prompted exploration of the area as well. The British Royal Geographic Society commissioned these early explorers. The 1850s saw only a few expeditions to central Africa, those led by British explorers Richard Francis Burton (1821-1890), John Hanning Speke (1827-1864), and James Grant (1827-1892). By the early 1860s many more explorers from different nations were crisscrossing the region.

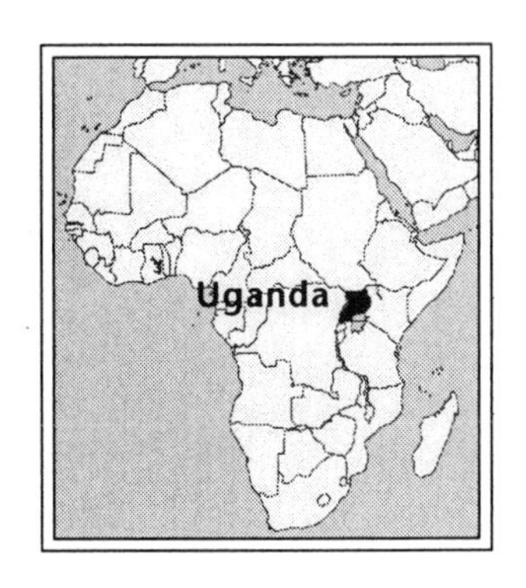

The kabaka's court

The earliest account of the splendor of Mutesa's court came from Speke, who was searching for the source of the White Nile, which he believed flowed from Lake Victoria. Speke spent five months in the kabaka's court, waiting for permission to travel through the kingdom. He kept detailed notes of his visit to the king and his court, reprinted in Margery Perham and J. Simmons's *African Discovery*:

> The palace or entrance quite surprised me by its extraordinary dimensions and the neatness with which it was kept. The whole brow and sides of the hill on which we stood were covered with gigantic grass huts, thatched as neatly as so many heads dressed by a London barber. . . . It is here most of [Mutesa]'s three or four hundred women are kept, the rest being quartered chiefly with his mother. . . .

> The king, a good-looking, well-figured, tall young man of twenty-five, was sitting on a red blanket spread upon a square platform of royal grass, encased in tiger-grass reeds, scrupulously well dressed in a new mbugu [cloth made of bark]. The hair of his head was cut short, except . . . on top, where it was combed up into a high ridge. . . . On his neck was a very neat ornament—a large ring of beautifully-worked small beads, forming elegant patterns by their various colours. On one arm was another bead ornament, prettily devised; and on the other a wooden charm, tied by string covered with snake-skin. On every finger and every toe he had alternate brass and copper rings; and above the ankles, half-way up to the calf, a stocking of very pretty beads. Everything was light, neat and elegant in its way.

His fine dressing style notwithstanding, the young Mutesa was an impulsive tyrant (an absolute ruler known for his harsh use of authority). He ruled his subjects through fear; suddenly and without warning he would order his executioners to put a man to death for speaking too loudly in his presence. On his succession as kabaka, Mutesa had 30 of his brothers burned alive to prevent any of them from scheming to take over his throne.

Changes over time

In 1869 the publisher of the *New York Herald* sent one of his young reporters, Henry Morton Stanley (1841-1904), to the Middle East and Africa. His orders to Stanley were to look for David Livingstone (1813-1873)—a devout Christian of Scottish descent, a veteran explorer of 22 years in Africa, and a dedicated abolitionist (antislavery advocate). Stanley tracked Livingstone down in central Africa in 1871 and reported back to his paper the famous greeting: "Dr. Livingstone, I presume." Livingstone died in 1873 and was buried in 1874 in Westminster Abbey in London. Stanley saw an opportunity to get back into the limelight, and he persuaded several newspaper publishers to fund him as he "completed Livingstone's work." (Like Speke, Livingstone had been seeking the source of the Nile River). Stanley arrived at Mutesa's court in 1875 and found conditions there quite changed from those described by Speke 13 years earlier.

Stanley described Mutesa as a "tall, clean-faced, large-eyed, nervous-looking thin man" wearing a Muslim robe, a white shirt belted with gold, and a red felt hat or *tarboosh.* Mutesa spoke to him in fluent Swahili, was a gracious host, and made Stanley comfortable. By this time in his early forties, Mutesa had acquired the polish and self-assurance of an African monarch. Stanley noted that there was no longer any evidence of murders and other atrocities taking place around the court. Mutesa had moved the capital to Rubaga, near present-day Kampala. The huts of the capital reached out over seven miles. Mutesa also had an army of 150,000 warriors and a large fleet of canoes.

In the intervening decade between Speke's visit and Stanley's, the kingdom had benefited from the opening up of trade. One of the factors promoting this change was the presence of Arab traders in the court. Stanley found that guns were commonplace. Manufactured goods were also available: cloth, wooden stools, steel knives and other tools, and Venetian glass beads. The Arabs had traded all of these manufactured goods for slaves taken by Mutesa's warriors.

Switches his allegiance

The traders had converted Mutesa to Islam (the religious faith of Muslims), teaching him about their culture, religion, and technology. In the late 1860s Mutesa's court adopted the Islamic calendar, practiced fasting (going without food as a symbol of sacrifice), and read the Koran (Muslim book of holy writings). The kabaka also held regular prayer services.

Mutesa grew dissatisfied with Islam when new, more traditional teachers came into the kingdom. The kabaka practiced a sort of "hybrid" Islam—a version of the faith that reflected and incorporated various African traditions. When it became clear to Mutesa that his followers respected the law of the Koran more than the king's law, he decided to tighten his reign over the kingdom by ridding the court of Islam's influence. In 1876 he began the first of Buganda's religious persecutions when he ordered the execution of all Muslims.

This was a year after Stanley had paid his visit. During that visit Stanley spent time reading the Bible to the kabaka and teaching him about Christianity. Stanley reported that the kabaka treated him well. He greeted his boat on the lake by sending out a fleet of six war canoes to escort him in. He was given a compound of grass huts to live in and many gifts. Mutesa even took him hunting for crocodiles accompanied by 200 riflemen. Stanley noted in his diary: "He has very intelligent and agreeable features. . . . He has . . . the general expression of amiability blended with dignity that pervades his face, and the large, lustrous, lambent eyes that lend it a strange beauty."

Later, when Stanley was in communication with his newspaper, he wrote an article exaggerating the Bugandan king's interest in the principles of Christian religion. Within three years, five missions from the British Church Missionary Society had established themselves in Buganda. Two years later the Catholic White Fathers formed a center in Buganda. Back in 1856 only one European missionary had been in East Africa. By the 1880s more than 100 had established themselves there.

The missionaries met with astonishing success in Buganda, particularly with the young men, the pages or courtiers in the king's court. Mutesa's willingness to entertain the Christians was motivated more by political interests than by religious ones. Islam had lost its appeal to Mutesa, and he had allowed Christian missionaries to enter his kingdom, hoping he might benefit from their presence and use them as allies against the powerful Muslim chiefs. In addition, Mutesa was fascinated with technology. From his previous exposure to Europeans he knew their technology, at least their firearms, were more advanced than what the Arabs had shown him.

One European missionary who answered the kabaka's invitation as reported by Stanley was Alexander Mackay, chief representative of the Church Missionary Society. He established a mission in the kingdom and came to admire the kabaka for his modernizing ways. Mackay was the last one to admit that Mutesa's embrace of Christianity was self-serving. In his journal Mackay angrily and vividly describes his despair when Mutesa turned his back on Christianity and resorted to his traditional ways. This turn of events occurred at the end of Mutesa's life, when he was afflicted with an incurable disease. He sought the advice of his traditional healers who told him to resume the practice of *kiwendo*—that is to sacrifice humans to appease the ancestors. Following this advice, Mutesa selected people at random for execution. Some nights 2,000 people were rounded up and held until morning for public sacrifice. Mackay was horrified to hear the executioners' drums and the victims' screams. He wrote, as quoted in Thomas Pakenham's *Scramble for Africa:*

> All this merely to gratify the blood thirstiness of this monster . . . this murderous maniac. Called by good people in England . . . the

In July 1973, 38-year old Ssabataka Ronald Muwenda Mutebi was installed as the 38th kabaka of Uganda. Mutebi is the son of Sir Edward Frederick Mutesa (also known as "King Freddie" and Mutesa II), who was deported (forced to flee from Uganda) by Prime Minister Milton Obote in 1966 and died in exile in 1971. Mutebi will preside over the cultural, customary, and traditional functions of the 4.4. million people of Uganda.

The Kabaka in the Late Twentieth Century

> humane king of Uganda [Buganda], [Mutesa] is a pagan . . . a heathen. All the faculties of lying, low cunning, hatred, pride and conceit, jealousy, cruelty . . . combined with extreme vanity . . . [are] concentrated in him. All is self, self, self. Uganda exists for him alone.

Mutesa was successful in balancing the interests of the various different religious groups—the Catholics, the Protestants, and the Muslims, as well as the pagans. Each of these groups, however, was building its own base of support within the royal court. When Mutesa died in 1884, his son, Mwanga, became the kabaka. He was only 20 years old and did not have the same ability to control and dominate as his father. Internal friction in the court overwhelmed Mwanga, and he made a series of bad decisions. Shortly after the British declared a protectorate (one power's authority over another state; in this case, Britain's power over Buganda) over the area in 1894, they deported Mwanga. He died in exile (meaning he was forced to leave his homeland) in the Seychelles, a group of islands in the Indian Ocean.

Further Reading

Forbath, Peter. *The River Congo.* New York: Harper, 1977.

Hallet, Robin. *Africa since 1875.* Ann Arbor: University of Michigan Press, 1974.

Moorehead, Alan. *The White Nile.* New York: Harper, 1971.

Oliver, Roland. *The African Experience.* Pimlico, 1991.

Pakenham, Thomas. *The Scramble for Africa.* Jonathan Ball, 1991.

Perham, Margery, and J. Simmons. *African Discovery: An Anthology of Exploration.*

The Travel Book Club, 1943.

Mwene Mutapa Negomo Mupunzagutu

Born c. 1550
Zambezi Valley (Zimbabwe)
Died c. 1586/9
Zambezi Valley (Zimbabwe)

King of the Mutapa

Caught up in court intrigue between Muslims and conservative members of the court, the Mwene Mutapa ordered the priest's death. The murder of Silveira became an enduring factor in setting Portuguese policy toward the Mutapa state.

About 100 years before Mwene Mutapa Negomo Mupunzagutu took the throne, a leader named Mutota founded the Mutapa dynasty in the mid-1400s. "Mwene Mutapa" was a praise name given to Mutota by his subjects. (The Portuguese thought the title referred to the whole empire and they called the land ruled by Mutota, Mwenemutapa or Munhumatapa.) The Mutapas ruled in northern and eastern Zimbabwe and the Zambezi River valley for about 500 years, from the 1400s to 1902. In the beginning of their rule, the area they controlled was vast, but by the death of the last Mwene Mutapa it had shrunk to a small chiefdom.

Negomo probably ruled from about 1560 to late in the 1580s. He was a young man when he became the Mutapa and his mother, aChiuyu, advised him about courtly matters. Historians have to be cautious when they try to link events and leaders of the Mutapa kingdom with specific events recorded by Portuguese traders or missionaries because the records are not always clear. Negomo was probably the king when the Portuguese Catholic priest Father Goncalvo da Silveira came to the kingdom and converted the royal court to Catholicism. Caught up in court intrigue between Muslims and conservative members of the court, the Mwene Mutapa ordered the priest's death. The murder of Silveira became an enduring factor in setting Portuguese policy toward the Mutapa state.

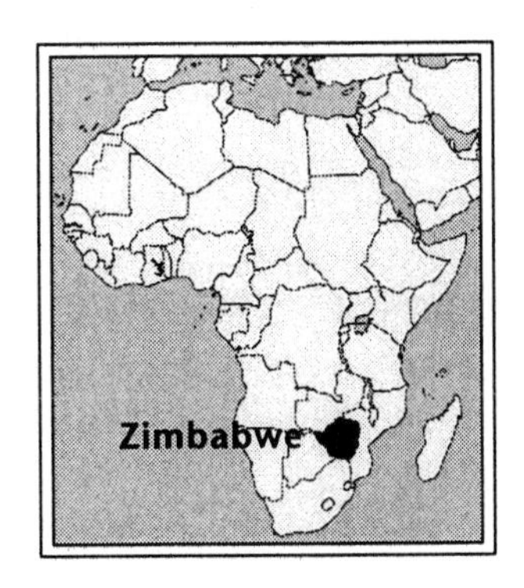

Great Zimbabwe breaks up

The Mutapa state started as a branch of Great Zimbabwe culture. Great Zimbabwe was the largest and strongest city of its time in central and southern Africa. Its stone ruins lie in the high plateau area of Zimbabwe and at its height in the 1300s, the population of Great Zimbabwe was about 18,000. Its rulers controlled an area about 60,000 square miles (about the size of the state of Washington), running between the Zambezi River and the Limpopo River. The country was rich in gold that could be panned easily from the rivers or mined near the surface. Elephants and game were plentiful.

The people at Great Zimbabwe traded with the Arabs who had established themselves along the Indian Ocean coast. Because of its location, Great Zimbabwe was also able to tax the people from further inland who traded with the Arabs. The Arab traders took the gold and ivory by boat to ports in East Africa. From there the monsoon winds took the boats to Arabia, India, and maybe even China. Great Zimbabwe dominated the trade from the interior to the coast for about 150 years. Glass beads, cotton, silk cloth, and ceramics are some of the items found in the ruins of Great Zimbabwe.

In the late 1300s and early 1400s, people began leaving Great Zimbabwe. Some took their cattle and moved to the south, to the Khami area, where they built new communities out of stone. Others moved to the north, and they settled along the Zambezi River Valley. The distance they traveled was not great, probably no more than 300 miles—about a month's journey. They probably already knew about the area because they had traded with the hunters and the gold panners from the valley. These people were called Karanga. The term "Shona" was later used to describe these people, but not until the 1800s.

The river valley provided the newcomers with an abundance of game, water, and even rock salt. The valley also was well

Selected Mutapa Dynasties until 1652

Mutota	c.1400-1450
Matope (Nebedza or Nyanhehwe)	c. 1450-1480
Nyahuma Mukombero	c. 1480-1490
Changamire [Torwa]	c. 1490-1494
Kakuyo (Chikuyo) Chisamarengu	c. 1494-1530
Neshangwe Munembire	c. 1530-1550
Chivere Nyasoro	c. 1550-1560
Negomo Mupunzagutu	c. 1550-1586/9
Gatsi Ruseri	c. 1586-1623
Nyambo Kapararidze	c. 1623-1629
Mavura Mhande (Felippe I)	c. 1629-1631
Nyambo Kapararidze	c. 1629-1631
Mavura Mhande (Felippe I)	c. 1632-1652

located for trade with the Arabs, who came in along the river route. Out of these newcomers a strong leader emerged. Nyatsimba Mutota is usually credited with being the founder of this new power bloc. Mutota conquered the people living there, the Tonga and the Tavara people, and made alliances with chiefs. He built his capital at Chitako Hill, above the valley, near the Utete River.

The Mutapa dynasty

Under Mutota's son, Matope, the empire reached its height. So great is his memory in Zimbabwe, that his spirit is invoked rather than the spirit of any other Mutapa. Matope controlled an area that reached between the Zambezi and the Limpopo Rivers and the Kalahari Desert to the Indian Ocean.

Historians do not know much about the early period of the Mutapa state. Matope ruled before the Portuguese made their way along the Zambezi River valley and, as a result, historians have little information on the early period. After 1490 historians rely on Portuguese sources for their information but this information is, of course, written from the Portuguese perspective. The first Mwene Mutapa to receive the Portuguese was Chikuyo (or Kakuyo) Chisamarengu in 1494.

The Portuguese had begun their explorations by sea in pursuit of the legendary Christian kingdom of Prester John in Ethiopia and they were trying to find a sea route to India. In the late 1400s they sailed around the Cape of Good Hope of South Africa and then began to explore the Indian Ocean coast line. They knew the interior of the continent held gold because they saw it traded in the markets along the coast. To gain control of this trade, the Portuguese forced the Arab traders out of the coastal areas along Mozambique and took over the trade themselves. They made their way inland, along the river routes—the Zambezi and Save.

The Mutapa state controlled the trade along the Zambezi River. The Mutapa appointed members of his family to act as governors of territories. Each governor had a standing army of between 200 and 500 men, whose responsibility it was to collect taxes and maintain the peace. The king, called the munhumutapa or mwenemutapa, had many advisers and some of his many wives also became officials of the court. The members of the court were wealthy and spent time and energy making themselves look prosperous. A Portuguese visitor to the Mutapa's court in 1518, as quoted in S. I. G. Mudenge's history of the dynasty, made these observations:

> They are black men, go about naked, and from the waist down they wear painted cotton cloths, and some cover themselves with animal skins, the skins they wear being of wild animals, and the leading citizens wear those skins trailing along the ground like tails, to shew quality and gallantry, making leaps and gestures that make those tails go from one side to the other. These latter carry swords in wooden sheaths, adorned with gold or other metals, they wear them on the left side like we do, on belts of painted cloth made for the purpose with four or five knots, with their tassels hanging; they weare these for gallantry; in their hands they carry bows and some spears. The bows they carry with their arrows are of middling size . . .; the shafts of the arrows are long and very well made; they are warriors, some of them merchants.

The royal court receives Father Silveira

Negomo Mupunzagutu was the ruling Mutapa when Father Silveira came to the royal court in January 1561. Silveira was a zealous Jesuit whose mission was to convert the Mutapa and reduce the influence of the Muslims in the court. He was an agent of both the Portuguese crown and the Church of Rome. Previously only the Muslims had sent their religious leaders to the court.

Negomo received Silveira and offered him the traditional gifts of welcome: gold, cattle, land, and women. When the priest refused to accept these gifts, he made a favorable impression on Negomo. The priest remained in the kingdom and introduced the young Negomo to a drawing of the Virgin Mary. Silveira told Negomo that the woman was the mother of God. Negomo hung the image in his bedroom and soon told the priest that the woman spoke to him in his dreams but that he could not understand her. Silveira reportedly told him it was because he was not a Christian that he could not understand her language. Infatuated with the female image and gullible to the craft of the priest, Negomo sent word that he was ready to become a Christian.

Negomo and his mother together took instruction from the priests for several weeks. When Silveira baptized him, Negomo took the name of Dom Sebastiao in honour of the Portuguese king. His mother took the name of Dona Maria. After the baptism, the priest's reputation and influence grew, so much so that the Muslim traders at the court worried about his popularity. The traditional spiritual leaders also worried about his influence on the young and impressionable king.

These different factions together began to undermine Negomo's trust in the priest. They told him the priest was a spy sent out by the Portuguese and that he was an ally of Negomo's enemy, Chipute. They also told Negomo that the baptismal water and all the paraphernalia used by the priest would make Negomo unable to resist his powers. The conspirators suggested to the Mutapa that the priest should not be allowed to go away alive, for if he did the Mutapa's people would begin to fight one another.

Negomo and his mother and some of the converted court members consulted a traditional diviner (someone who can foresee the future) who confirmed as true all the charges against the priest. With the charges confirmed, plans were made to get rid of the priest.

Even though he had been warned, Silveira made no plans to flee. Several nights later, on the evening of March 15, 1561, seven or eight men came into his room at night and strangled him with a rope. They dragged his body to the riverbanks and threw him into the crocodile-infested Musengezi River.

Fashion in Mutapa's court

Father Monclaro was one of the priests who visited at the Mutapa capital in the 1570s during the reign of Negomo. He left this description:

> All of them commonly wear loosely-woven cotton cloth . . . called *machiras*. . . . These machiras [may measure 41 feet in length and 24 feet across], being wound around the body and crosswise over the chest, the rest remaining uncovered. They wear horn-like headgear as an adornment, being made of their own hair turned back in a strange manner; these horns are in general use . . . and provide a good shade. In the middle of the head, they make one which draws the hair in . . . well-arranged fashion, first making the hair long by means of small pieces of copper or tin which they tie at the end of a few hairs brought together, so that the weight gradually makes them long and not crisp. . . .
>
> Once the hair has grown long, they bring it together in the middle of the head . . . to make a bigger horn, the hair being tied with a certain grass with which they make a very comely thread of a certain length; the tapering end is left untied. Then in a most regular fashion they do make other small horns . . .; and the women wear many copper rings in their arms and legs, being drawn very fine, and the same they make with gold, which is extremely fine and with this thread they make these rings.

From S. I. G. Mudenge's *A Political History of Munhumutapa: c. 1400-1902*, Zimbabwe Publishing House, 1988.

Portuguese warn the Mutapa

Portuguese traders came to Negomo several days after Silveira's death and warned him that Silveira was a Portuguese nobleman and that the crown would take its revenge on him. Negomo told them he was sorry about what had happened. To show his remorse, Negomo ordered the execution of several of the Muslims who had persuaded him to kill Silveira. Some reports say he even had his own mother killed. This satisfied the Portuguese for the time being but the repercussions of Silveira's death would be felt in years to come.

Silveira's death prodded the Portuguese to send more soldiers to invade the Mutapa's state and more missionaries to convert the people of his court. To avenge Silveira's death, the Portuguese king sent out Francisco Barreto, a nobleman and friend of Father Silveira and general of the Portuguese navy. Barreto's expedition also had greedy objectives. The Portuguese had heard of the rich deposits of gold in Mutapa and wanted to control the mines. In 1569 the king of Portugal appointed Barreto to lead the conquest of Mutapa. When Barreto arrived on the coast, he sent a messenger to the Mutapa's court informing the Mutapa of their arrival. He also requested that the Mutapa forego the traditional requirements of the court. Normally all visitors to the Mutapas were to approach them without shoes or arms and on their knees. They were to lie on their bellies when they were near the Mutapa.

Negomo reluctantly agreed and greeted the Portuguese delegation in European style: seated on chairs placed on a carpet. In his audience with the Mutapa, Barreto's messenger lied to him, saying he was there only for peaceful purposes. The messenger said they only wanted to avenge the death of Portuguese traders by Negomo's enemy, the Tonga led by Samungazi. In response, Negomo craftily offered to help them by providing 100,000 troops. This ploy put the Portuguese on notice that Negomo had plenty of warriors if the Portuguese entertained any ideas about attacking the Mutapa.

Wars begin

Barreto's forces did indeed attack the Tonga. Both parties suffered great loss of lives. The Tonga wisely covered their wells and hid their crops so the Portuguese could not get local food or fresh water. Eventually, however, the Tonga were outpowered by Barreto's superior firepower. The Tonga lost between 4,000 and 6,000 men; the Portuguese lost 40 men.

Barreto took his forces back to Sena, a Portuguese fort and trading post along the Zambezi River. Once the Portuguese had withdrawn, Negomo took advantage of his enemy's weakened position and sent his troops in to subdue the Tonga. Negomo also sent a delegation to talk with the Portuguese. Barreto died shortly after he returned to Sena, and Vasco Fernandes Homem had been sent out to replace him. Of the 650 men who had come out with Barreto, only 180 were still alive. Negomo told Homem that he wanted peace with the Portuguese and wanted to continue to trade. As a peace offering, he sent eight finely threaded gold bracelets and anklets to the Portuguese. In exchange, the Portuguese gave him valuable cloth and goods.

Portuguese revise their policy

Under Homem, the Portuguese policy changed. They no longer believed it was necessary or possible to dominate the kingdoms. They realized they could profit from the gold trade by taxing the traders. At strategic trading points, they set up official market places, called *feiras,* to tax the gold brought in from the mines before the traders from the interior sold it to the Arab and Portuguese traders.

To show their appreciation, the Portuguese gave Negomo a greyhound. Negomo died shortly after he was presented with the dog and, because he had grown so fond of the dog, he had it buried with him. At his death, his wife took poison and they buried her with him.

Gatsi Rusere succeeded Negomo with a long and eventful reign. The Portuguese eventually made inroads into the Mwene Mutapa's empire and by the late 1600s they had so much control that they appointed Mwene Mutapa Mavura Mhande, otherwise called Felippe I. Although the dynasty continued until the early 1900s, it never had the same power and authority over as many subjects as it had in the 1400s and 1500s.

Further Reading

Beach, D. N. *The Shona and Zimbabwe: 900-1850.* Mambo Press, 1980.

Bourdillon, Michael, *The Shona Peoples,* revised edition. Mambo Press, 1982.

Ellert H. *Rivers of Gold.* Mambo Press, 1993.

Mudenge, S. I. G. *A Political History of Munhumutapa: c. 1400-1902.* Zimbabwe Publishing House, 1988.

Joshua Nkomo

Born June 7, 1917
Semokwe, Matabeleland, Southern Rhodesia
(Zimbabwe)

Zimbabwean politician

Nkomo played a decisive role in the political and military battle for black-majority rule in Zimbabwe.

Often called the "Father of Zimbabwe," Joshua Mqabuko Nkomo (*en-KO-mo*) organized one of the earliest nationalist (independence-seeking) movements in Southern Rhodesia, which is now the south-central African republic of Zimbabwe. He got involved in nationalist politics in 1952, when he became president of the African National Congress (ANC) in Southern Rhodesia. (The ANC was the leading black organization opposed to white-minority rule in southern Africa.) As quickly as the Rhodesian authorities banned political organizations, new ones sprang up. In the early 1960s, after the government banned the National Democratic Party, Nkomo formed and headed the Zimbabwe African People's Union (ZAPU). ZAPU was one of the two main groups that successfully fought for the independence of Rhodesia. Nkomo played a decisive role in the political and military battle for black-majority rule in Zimbabwe, and after independence he became one of the nation's two vice presidents.

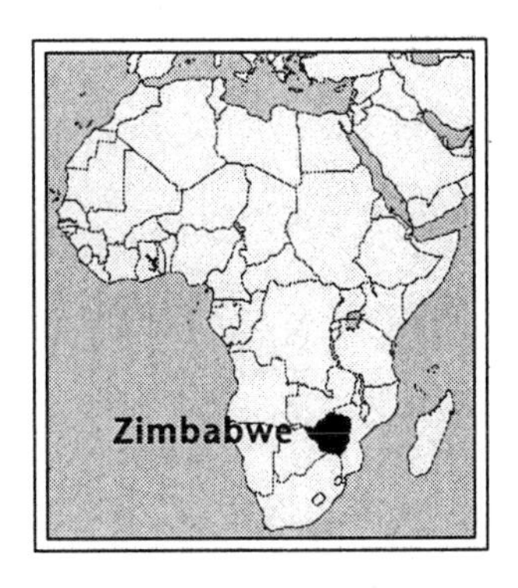

Growing up in Matabeleland

Nkomo was born June 7, 1917, to an African peasant family in rural Matabeleland. The Ndebele, an ethnic group living in Matabeleland, had pushed up from South Africa in the 1800s. They had been dislocated by the upheavals caused first by Zulu warrior Shaka (see entry) and second by expanding white settlements. The Ndebele have distinctive customs and speak a Nguni dialect, a language different from the Shona language spoken by the majority of the people of Zimbabwe. The Ndebele make up about 20 percent of the country's population.

Nkomo's father, Nyongolo, and his mother, Mlingo Hadebe, were born in the 1800s, when "my country was still free," Nkomo stated in his biography, *The Story of My Life.* At that point "the government was in the hands of the people, directed by custom and tradition." But the African people lost control of their land and their traditions in 1890, when the Pioneer Column of the British South Africa Company raised the British flag at Fort Salisbury, now called Harare, Zimbabwe's capital city. Within 10 years of the Pioneer Column's arrival, white settlers had claimed 16 million acres of land and had established large farms. They left the poor, dry lands to the black population.

Although Nkomo came from a large family of eight children, his parents were more prosperous than most and much better educated; both of them could read and write. Married in a Christian church, they refused to practice the Ndebele custom of a man taking several wives at one time. They did not eat traditional foods, and they taught Nkomo not to smoke or drink alcohol. Both parents worked for a mission settlement in Tshimale in Matabeleland. His father was a teacher; his mother was a cook. The mission sent his father to South Africa for three years to further his training. While he was away, the white settler community took over the mission land and uprooted the entire mission. Legislation enacted in 1931 allocated 49 million acres to the region's 50,000 whites and only 29 million acres to the million native Africans.

Nkomo's father sent several of his children to boarding schools, where they could learn a trade. At the age of 15, Nkomo was sent to Tjolotjo Government Industrial School in Matabeleland, where he learned carpentry and joinery (construction with wood). Since no secondary school for Africans existed in Southern Rhodesia at the time, Nkomo could not continue his education to qualify as a carpentry instructor. After trying for three years to make a decent living in Matabeleland, he went to South Africa and enrolled in Adams College in Durban. Nkomo was 25 years old, a large man, far older and bigger than his 17-year-old classmates. A white woman, Julia Hoskin, for whom he worked as a part-time driver, gave him money to pursue an advanced degree at the Jan Hofmeyr School of Social Work in Johannesburg, South Africa. In 1948 Nkomo graduated as a social worker and returned to Bulawayo, the major city in Matabeleland.

Next Nkomo went to work for the Rhodesian Railways, whose network extended from Northern Rhodesia (Zambia) through Southern Rhodesia and Bechuanaland (Botswana), connecting with the South African lines. The railway employed many migrant African workers from Mozambique, Nyasaland (Malawi), and Northern Rhodesia. The migrants lived in male-only barracks in enclosed compounds where the company provided for their basic needs. To protest their poor working and living conditions, the African workers formed a trade union and in 1946 staged a successful strike. Seeking to prevent further strikes, the railway employed Nkomo in its newly created Department of African Affairs to train assistants to help look after the welfare of the workers.

Represents railway workers

Nkomo identified not with the management of the railways but with the workers. He lived with them in the compound, ate the same food, and refused to take part in management meetings. In 1948 the railway workers asked him to help rebuild their African Railway Employee's Association, and they elected him president. Nkomo established an extensive membership of African workers—3,000 nationwide—in a well-organized structure consisting of 22 branches. Nkomo's leadership abilities brought him to the attention of the Southern Rhodesia African National Congress, founded in 1934, which asked him to be its president in 1952. Using his railway pass, he traveled the country by train, listening and talking to the working people. He wrote: "All we could do about people's grievances at that time was to find out what they were and formulate them, writing things down for the first time, organizing petitions and complaining about what was wrong."

Fighting the British federation

In the late 1940s white British settlers in south-central Africa began organizing attempts to secure their own political power in the region. After World War II the British government began a program to unite several of its African colonies—Nyasaland (Malawi), Northern Rhodesia, and Southern Rhodesia—into a federation. When negotiations among colony leaders began in 1952, Sir Godfrey Huggins, prime minister of Southern Rhodesia, asked Nkomo to attend the London conference as a representative of the African population. Huggins did not realize that Nkomo, like most other Africans, opposed federation. Nkomo surprised him when he announced to the conference that he and the Southern Rhodesian ANC were against federation—and then walked out. Nkomo's highly visible opposition to federation gave him an international reputation as a staunch African nationalist.

The government did not ask Nkomo to attend the second conference on federation. Instead, private individuals raised the money to finance his trip to London to lobby against the proposed white-dominated union. On his return to Bulawayo, police picked him up for having illegal pamphlets in his possession. Nkomo defended himself in court. His trial brought him and the antifederation movement more publicity than they could have received on their own.

In 1953, however, the demands of the white settler groups were met: Great Britain allowed the three territories to unite as the self-governing Federation of Rhodesia and Nyasaland. Black Africans strongly opposed the formation of the white-run federation, but it lasted for 10 years, from 1953 to 1963. In 1953 Nkomo ran unsuccessfully for one of two seats for candidates elected by the 450 eligible African voters in the federation. That same year he resigned from the welfare department of the railways to work for the Railway Employee's Association. He also set up a real estate agency and insurance firm in Bulawayo. Four years earlier, he had married Johanna Fuyana, the younger sister of his father's second wife.

The black-white rift widens

In Salisbury in 1955 young militants formed the African National Youth League. Its founders were opposed to federation and angered by the 1951 Native Husbandry Act, which had forced Africans to reduce the size of their herds. In 1956 the league staged mass demonstrations to protest increases in bus fares. A year later the Youth League merged with the ANC branch in Bulawayo to form the new ANC. They elected Nkomo president, partly in an effort to bring Ndebele supporters from Matabeleland in league with the Shona speakers from the northern part of the country.

As ANC president, Nkomo attended the World Assembly of Youth in New Delhi in late 1957, and the next year he went to the All-African People's Conference held in newly independent Ghana. Only four of the countries represented—Liberia, Ghana, Guinea, and Ethiopia—were independent; all the rest were represented by nationalist organizations seeking independence from their European colonizers. From this meeting, Nkomo came into contact with major figures in the anticolonialist movement.

While Nkomo was on a visit to Egypt following the conference, the Southern Rhodesian government banned the ANC. Rather than return home, Nkomo decided to stay in Cairo at the Egyptian government's invitation. In mid-1959 he moved to London, where he stayed until late 1960. He made many trips around Europe and the United States to raise funds for the liberation movement. Meanwhile, members of the banned African National Congress formed a new party, the National Democratic Party (NDP). They declared Nkomo its president even though he was not present for elections. He returned home in October 1960.

In 1961, when Nkomo attended a conference in Salisbury on a new constitution for Southern Rhodesia, a dispute erupted that had a long-lasting effect on his reputation in the nationalist movement. The British secretary for commonwealth relations, who was chairing the conference, announced to the press that Nkomo had accepted a specified number of reserved seats for blacks in the new white-dominated parliament. A howl of protest came from nationalists at home and in exile. At first, Nkomo defended his position; then, when he realized how much opposition he faced, he denied ever agreeing to the proposal. More radical supporters began to question his commitment to the nationalist movement.

They eventually broke away to form a rival group called the Zimbabwe African National Union (ZANU).

Heads African People's Union

White voters went to the polls in July 1961 to vote for a new constitution—one that would give whites even more power in Southern Rhodesia. In December 1961 the government banned the NDP. Activists immediately formed the Zimbabwe African People's Union (ZAPU) and elected Nkomo its first president. On December 20, 1962, the government banned ZAPU and restricted most of its leaders to their home areas for three months. On his release in early 1963, Nkomo flew to New York to address the United Nations (UN; an international organization formed after World War II to promote world peace). In April he called another meeting of ZAPU's executive committee in Dar es Salaam, but within a few months he returned to Rhodesia, determined this time to "fight the fight" inside the country.

Meanwhile, ZAPU members in exile—spearheaded by the Reverend Ndabaningi Sithole and Robert Mugabe (see entry), the future president of Zimbabwe—voted to oust Nkomo from the party's leadership position. Learning of the plan, Nkomo quashed it and dismissed the rebellious members. Then he firmed up his position at home by forming a People's Caretaker Council. About 90 of ZAPU's most radical members—those who wanted to engage in an armed struggle for independence—left ZAPU to form the Zimbabwe African National Union (ZANU) in August 1963. In the months that followed, supporters from the two parties fought it out on the streets of the townships to recruit new members.

Government arrests nationalist leaders

After the appointment of Ian Smith to the post of Rhodesian prime minister in April 1964, the Rhodesian government began a ruthless crusade against black nationalist leaders. In November, Nkomo was arrested and jailed. He would not be free for another ten and a half years. Nkomo spent much of this time restricted to a game reserve in a remote part of the country. Not until 1969, four years into his detention, did the authorities permit his wife to visit him.

The white-settler government in Southern Rhodesia feared interference by the British government in its racial laws. Smith called an election at the beginning of 1965, and his party won another large majority in parliament. On November 11, 1965, Smith made his party's Unilateral Declaration of Independence (UDI), declaring Southern Rhodesia independent of Great Britain. The British government did not recognize Rhodesia's independence and considered UDI an act of treason.

Guerrilla warfare

In 1966 the first military contact between the Rhodesian army and ZAPU guerrillas (independent fighting units) occurred. The next year South African ANC fighters joined the struggle, prompting agents of the South African government to enter the war on the Rhodesian side. The scope of the nationalists' struggle changed in 1974, with the military overthrow of the Portuguese government. The new government in Portugal immediately withdrew thousands of its troops from its African colonies. Within a short time African nationalist groups came to power in the southern African countries of Angola and Mozambique, aiding the black effort in Southern Rhodesia by opening the entire eastern border (its boundary with Mozambique) to guerrilla attack. Previously, the Zimbabwe nationalist guerrillas had been infiltrating through Zambia, across the Zambezi River and Lake Kariba. Nkomo's troops had borne the brunt of the fighting until the front opened in Mozambique.

The international community put pressure on Smith to reach an agreement with the black majority in Southern Rhodesia. Bowing to South African pressure, Smith brought the nationalist leaders out of detention to attend a conference in Lusaka in November 1974. Smith, however, refused to make concessions. By 1976 the African leaders set up a united front called the Patriotic Front. With the opening of Mozambique, ZANU's Zimbabwe National Liberation Army (ZANLA) forces concentrated on the eastern front. ZAPU's Zimbabwe People's Revolutionary Army (ZIPRA) remained in Zambia.

Nkomo based himself in Lusaka where he directed ZAPU's military, political, and diplomatic activities. In Nkomo's early years of exile, he sought assistance for the liberation movement from the Cubans and the Soviets, and they had provided training, equipment, and supplies. When Mugabe split from ZAPU, he turned to China for assistance. He was impressed by the Chinese style of guerrilla warfare and the importance of getting help from the rural people. Influenced by the East Europeans, Nkomo's tactics were limited and calculated armed attacks. Most of Nkomo's troops were in Zambia and Botswana. He did not recruit inside Zimbabwe until 1977.

Peace talks fail

Even international negotiators failed to make headway with the Rhodesian government. Unwilling to give in to demands for black majority rule, Smith thought he could settle things by establishing a black transitional government headed by a handpicked candidate. Smith's so-called "Internal Settlement" put Bishop Abel Muzorewa into the presidency of the new country called Zimbabwe-Rhodesia until 1979 elections. No major international power recognized this new government, and the African people rejected it because it could not stop the war.

Finally, in December 1979 a groundbreaking constitutional conference was held at Lancaster House in London with Smith, Nkomo, and Mugabe serving as its three main delegates. By the end of the conference the leaders had hammered out a new constitution and electoral procedures for independent Zimbabwe. British-supervised elections were held in March 1980 and Nkomo's PF-ZAPU lost badly to Mugabe's ZANU-PF. Mugabe offered Nkomo the position of ceremonial president of the new republic. Nkomo refused, although he did accept the cabinet position of minister of home affairs, in charge of the police. The accord between Nkomo and Mugabe lasted only a short time, though. In 1982 government security people unearthed arms hidden on farms owned by Nkomo and ZAPU. Nkomo was accused of working with the South Africans to destabilize Zimbabwe's government.

Because security people threatened his safety and that of his family, Nkomo left the country for a few months. Fighting between ZAPU and ZANU supporters escalated. Persistent, low-level attacks began taking place in Matabeleland against government-owned property and targets likely to get publicity—mainly white farmers and tourists. Prime Minister Mugabe sent in specially trained troops to put down the disturbances. The rough treatment his troops dealt to the people further inflamed the situation.

In 1987 Mugabe and Nkomo put an end to their long-running feud and agreed to merge their two parties and called for an end to the fighting. As part of the deal, Nkomo was brought back into the cabinet in 1988 as a senior minister. In 1990 ZANU-PF and PF-ZAPU formed a single party, taking the name of Mugabe's party, ZANU-PF. Following the actual merger in December 1990, Nkomo became one of two vice presidents in Zimbabwe. Until his health failed, he traveled widely on government business. He also owned several farms and served on the board of government-owned corporations.

Further Reading

Cary, Robert, and Diana Mitchell. *African Nationalist Leaders in Rhodesia: Who's Who 1980.* Books of Rhodesia, 1980.

Contemporary Black Biography. Vol. 4. Detroit: Gale, 1993.

Historic World Leaders. Edited by Anne Commire. Vol. 1. Detroit: Gale, 1994.

Martin, David, and Phyllis Johnson. *The Struggle for Zimbabwe: The Chimurenga War.* Winchester, MA: Faber, 1981.

Meredith, Martin. *The Past Is Another Country: Rhodesia UDI to Zimbabwe.* London: Pan Books, 1980.

Nkomo, Joshua. *Nkomo: The Story of My Life.* New York: Methuen, 1984.

Nyagumbo, Maurice. *With the People.* Akron, OH: Graham Publishing, 1980.

Verrier, Anthony. *The Road to Zimbabwe: 1890-1980.* North Pomfret, VT: J. Cape, 1986.

Kwame Nkrumah

Born September 21, 1909
Nkrofro, Gold Coast (Ghana)
Died April 27, 1972
Bucharest, Romania

First prime minister and president of Ghana

Ghana was the first British colony in Africa to achieve independence after World War II (1939-45). African statesman Kwame Nkrumah (*en-KROO-ma*) was Ghana's first president. An ambitious politician with a magnetic personality, Nkrumah led the way for other African leaders in the chaotic tidal wave of postwar independence on the continent. His most famous proclamation to fellow African revolutionaries was: "Seek ye first the political kingdom and all else will follow." Unfortunately, what followed was a storm of economic disaster and political dictatorship in Ghana and across the continent that would impoverish and oppress Africans for the next 50 years.

Nkrumah's radical approach to politics may have been his greatest contribution to African freedom movements.

Ghana lies along the Atlantic Coast of West Africa on the Gulf of Guinea. The area became known to European traders as the Gold Coast because of the huge amounts of gold being traded by

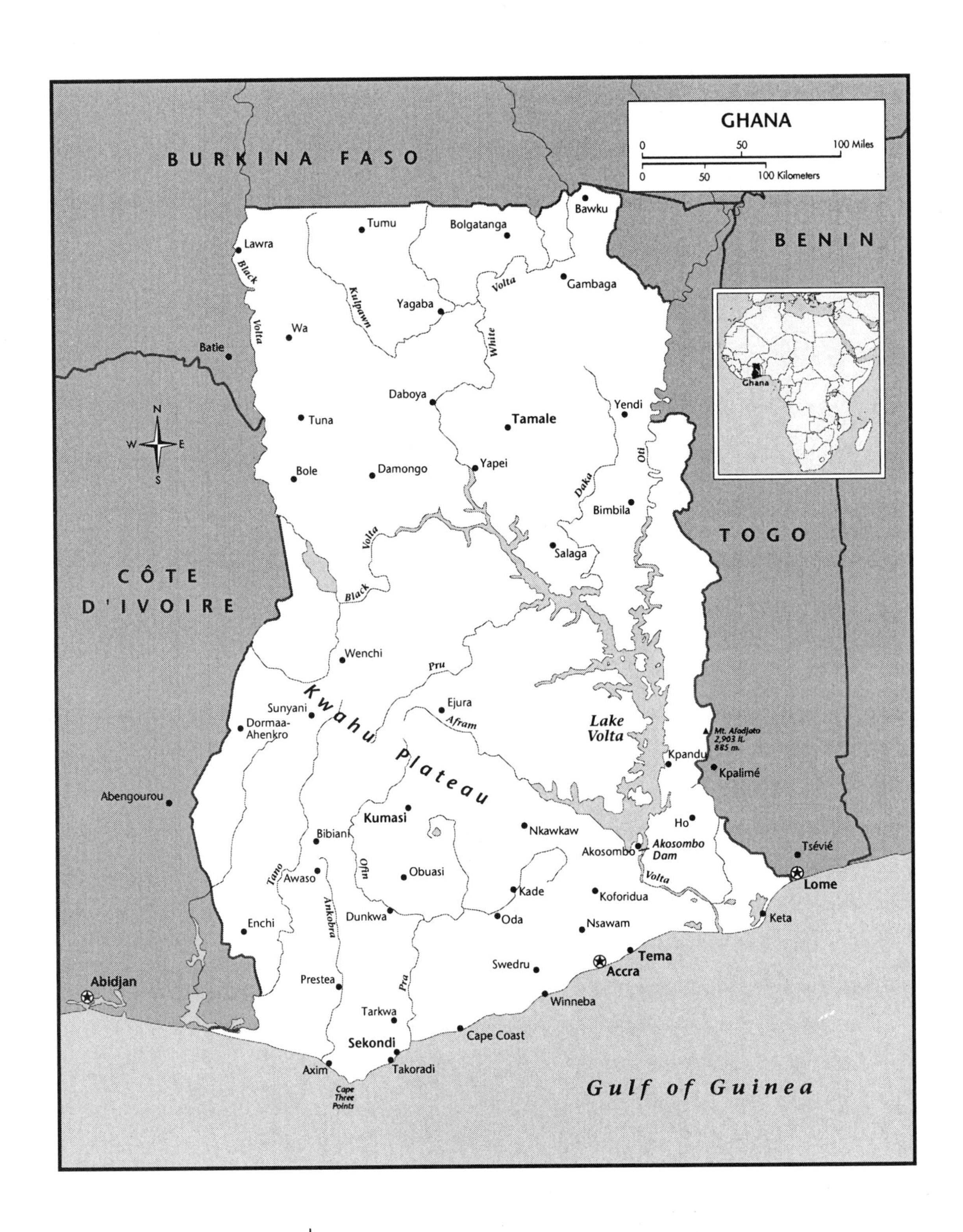
GHANA
0
50
100 Miles
0
50
100 Kilometers
BURKINA FASO
BENIN
TOGO
CÔTE D'IVOIRE
Ghana
Bawku
Tumu
Bolgatanga
Lawra
Gambaga
Yagaba
Wa
Batie
Daboya
Yendi
Tuna
Tamale
Yapei
Bole
Damongo
Bimbila
Salaga
Wenchi
Sunyani
Dormaa-Ahenkro
Ejura
Kwahu Plateau
Lake Volta
Mt. Afadjato 2,903 ft. 885 m.
Kpandu
Kpalimé
Abengourou
Kumasi
Ho
Nkawkaw
Bibiani
Akosombo
Akosombo Dam
Tsévié
Awaso
Obuasi
Lome
Kade
Koforidua
Dunkwa
Oda
Keta
Enchi
Nsawam
Tema
Swedru
Accra
Abidjan
Prestea
Winneba
Tarkwa
Cape Coast
Sekondi
Axim
Takoradi
Cape Three Points
Gulf of Guinea
Black Volta
Kulpawn
Volta
White
Oti
Daka
Volta
Black
Pru
Afram
Tano
Ofin
Ankobra
Pra
Volta
N
S
E
W

the people in the interior. Between the fifteenth and nineteenth centuries, first the Portuguese and then Dutch, Danish, French, and British companies set up trading posts along the coast. Later, European traders used these posts, or forts and castles, in the slave trade. In 1874 Great Britain claimed the Gold Coast as a crown colony. The region brought much profit to European investors and was in many ways the greatest British success story in West Africa. For the native African population of the colony in the early 1900s, however, even the name Gold Coast had a distasteful sound. It represented what the Europeans had made of their country—or rather what they had taken from it.

The gifted student

Nkrumah was born in 1909 in the village of Nkrofro, near the coastline in the southwest corner of the colony. As a young boy, he became obsessed with books. Although his parents were illiterate, they saw to it that their son was educated. Nkrumah's father, though not one of the traditional Nzima elite (meaning he was not extremely wealthy or of noble background), was well respected as the finest goldsmith in the community. His mother, Elizabeth Nyanibah, was an important trader in Nkrofro and added to the family's income by selling rice and sugar. She visited distant markets regularly and often took along her young son. Later in his political career, Nkrumah would appeal to and get the support of the women traders.

Nkrumah went to a Roman Catholic elementary school at Half Assini, a marketplace frequented by his mother. He was said to have been popular with his schoolmates and his teachers, and when he finished his studies the school hired him as a student-teacher. Nkrumah turned out to be such a gifted instructor that the principal of Accra's prestigious Achimota College recruited him for further study at Achimota, which at the time was considered the most progressive school in West Africa. Achimota's British founder believed that the betterment of social conditions for Africans was only possible with the direct participation of the Africans themselves. Not surprisingly, this approach appealed to Nkrumah, who for the first time encountered a body of young African men willing to discuss self-rule openly.

Accra was not a sleepy town like Half Assini. Nkrumah took quickly to the hustle and bustle of urban life. During his four years at Achimota, he met people from other regions of the continent who spoke different languages. He soon began to think of Africa as single nation. In 1930 Nkrumah graduated from Achimota and took teaching positions at several Roman Catholic institutions in the colony. Though a brilliant instructor, he became a rather controversial figure, especially when he helped establish a trade union for Gold Coast teachers.

Studies in the United States

Unlike his traditional-minded opponents in the Gold Coast, Nkrumah was educated in the United States. He was urged to study there, rather than in Britain, by an older African nationalist (freedom-seeker), Nnamdi Azikiwe (1904-1996; see entry). Since the United States had no African colonies, young African nationalists who studied there were able to break European ties that often held back European-educated African intellectuals.

In 1935 Nkrumah arrived in New York, bewildered by much of what he saw. Close to penniless, he accepted a scholarship to Lincoln University in Pennsylvania. He also did graduate work at the University of Pennsylvania in Philadelphia. In his free time and during the summer months he took what work he could find. He had one job in a shipbuilding yard in Chester, Pennsylvania, another in a soap factory in New York, and sometimes worked as a dishwasher and waiter on ships traveling between the United States and Latin America. As he studied philosophy and history, he became convinced that Africans had the right to form their own nations or federations (unions) of states. Nkrumah was profoundly influenced by the works of German political philosopher Karl Marx (1818-1883), who championed a classless society, and by the views of black nationalists such as Marcus Garvey (1887-1940) and W. E. B. Du Bois (1868-1963).

In May 1945 Nkrumah moved to Britain to study law. George Padmore, a Trinidadian political writer, involved Nkrumah in preparations for the sixth Pan-African Congress held in Manchester. (Pan-Africanism, a movement toward African unity, is discussed in the box on facing page.) The Congress elected Nkrumah general-secretary for a two-year term. He also got involved with the West African Students' Union and participated in other African-centered organizations. Eventually Nkrumah dropped out of law school and enrolled in the London School of Economics and Political Science.

The Pan-Africanist movement gained popularity in the first half of the twentieth century, before European colonies in Africa started to achieve independence. A general term representing a commitment to the solidarity, or unity, of all black peoples, Pan-Africanism advocated the merging of smaller African states into one huge African nation. But as more and more African states became independent in the 1960s and 1970s, internal political and ethnic rivalries took over, ending any thought of a continent-wide union.

Pan-Africanism

In 1947 he wrote a pamphlet that would be published 15 years later as *Towards Colonial Freedom.* A compilation of his political and philosophical ideas, the work reflects a wide variety of revolutionary influences and denounces British colonial rule in Africa.

Returns home as political leader

In 1947 Dr. J. B. Danquah (1895-1965) and other nationalists formed the United Gold Coast Convention (UGCC), a party dedicated to African self-rule through constitutional means. Danquah offered Nkrumah the new organization's key position of general-secretary and paid his ship fare home to the Gold Coast. From the start Nkrumah found himself immersed in controversy. Unlike the party's conservative leaders, Nkrumah wanted to create a massive base for the organization to confront the British directly. When rioting and looting took place in Accra, Kumasi, and other Ghana towns in February 1948, British authorities jailed Nkrumah and other party leaders for a short time.

Nkrumah soon broke with the UGCC over the pace of change in the colony. He favored a less structured, more radical approach to overcoming British authority. In June 1949 he founded the Convention People's Party (CPP). A few months later he initiated a campaign of "positive action," involving nonviolent protests and strikes against the authorities. The party demanded immediate self-government for Ghana. "If we get self-government, we'll transform the Gold Coast into a paradise in ten years," he promised.

Nkrumah shaped himself as a man of the people. He spoke for the unemployed, the market women, the dispossessed. His party rallies—always staged with flare—were highlighted by bands and dancing in the streets. Nkrumah became known as the "Star of

Nkrumah's legacy

Nkrumah set a pattern for African nationalists that sped up independence for their countries. His radical approach to politics may have been his greatest contribution to African freedom movements. Africa's educated leaders had never been able to engage the African majority in a broad mass movement to force the minority Europeans out of power. But Nkrumah did just that. He led an uprising by the black population of the Gold Coast against British rule, establishing himself as the clear choice to lead Ghana at independence in 1957. But as the post-independence history of many African countries has shown, good revolutionaries do not necessarily make good administrators. While Nkrumah was an articulate activist, he lacked patience and a willingness to compromise—two qualities that were vital to the successful management of so many different ethnic groups and clashing interests.

Africa" and even the "Great Leader of Street Boys." As American writer John Gunther commented in *Inside Africa:*

> Nkrumah's first quality is, people say, his animal spark, his magnetism and vitality. You can feel this across a room. Second, his ability and resilience. He . . . can bounce back from almost any blow. He works by intuition . . . and is a highly skilled negotiator. Third [is his] confidence. . . . Fourth, his charm and sense of humor. . . . He is a gentleman. . . . But do not forget that the hub of his character is nationalism.

Becomes prime minister

The Nkrumah-led political agitation, work stoppages, and strikes in the Gold Coast nearly brought the colony's economy to a standstill. Again in 1950, the authorities arrested Nkrumah. But soon the British rulers began to yield to African demands, adopting a new constitution that allowed for limited self-government. Elections were held in 1951 in most parts of the country. When the CPP won the most seats in the new parliament, the government released Nkrumah and asked him to form a new government. In 1952 he became prime minister—the first African-born prime minister of a sub-Saharan British dependency—but the real power in the Gold Coast was still in European hands.

While continuing to press for independence, Nkrumah created an all-African cabinet. In 1954 colonial authorities held elections for an enlarged parliament. This time the CPP won 79 out of 104 seats; in 1956 it won 71 seats. Finally convinced that Nkrumah's party represented the majority of the people, the British set the

Nkrumah in ceremonial robes, with his sword-bearer in front of him and accompanied by his wife, on his way to open the republic's second Parliament, 1965.

date for independence and asked Nkrumah to head the new government. On the eve of independence the country was badly divided between two political groups. Nevertheless, the Gold Coast achieved its independence on March 6, 1957, endowed with a good economy, a well-developed educational system, and an efficient administration.

Seeks liberation of the African continent

The independence government renamed the country Ghana, after the ancient empire of West Africa. Nkrumah helped design the national flag, opting for a variation of the Pan-African colors—red, yellow, and green—set off by a gleaming black star to signify that Ghana was the beacon for all of Africa. Nkrumah had grand plans for the newly independent nation. His government constructed some of the most modern roads in Africa. It built the Volta Dam, a massive hydroelectric facility, and spent lavishly on monumental architecture and heroic statuary.

Perhaps the most striking expense involved foreign relations. From the day of Ghanaian independence onward, Nkrumah pledged his country—and a good portion of its national budget—to the total liberation of the African continent. In 1958 Ghana held two major conferences: one included all of the then-independent African states; the other concerned nationalist organizations seeking freedom from colonial rule. Freedom fighters from Angola, South Africa, and other areas found refuge in Accra. Nkrumah also committed troops to the Belgian Congo (later known as Zaire; now the Democratic Republic of the Congo) as part of the United Nations Emergency Force in 1960 and planned to send them to Rhodesia in 1966.

Nkrumah forged a political union with the republic of Guinea. That nation's radical leader, Sékou Touré (see entry), had earlier rejected French president Charles de Gaulle's proposal to join a federal French Community of West African states and instead demanded full independence for Guinea. He and Nkrumah entered a partnership they hoped would provide the kernel for complete African unity.

The dream of unification, however, proved both expensive and impractical. In his preoccupation with foreign affairs, Nkrumah badly mismanaged matters at home. Local opposition to his policies began growing early in the 1950s. By 1960 his opponents were engineering his overthrow. At this point Nkrumah had scrapped the parliament and replaced it with his own constitution—one that empowered him to proclaim laws without consulting parliament or anyone else. He curbed all political debate and dissent, even to the point of stifling the publication of opposing views in Ghana's newspapers. Nkrumah still had a small base of support—a kind of cult that had grown around him. His faithful followers called him the *Osagyefo* (the "Hero" or "Warrior").

But a growing number of Ghanaians felt that Nkrumah had failed them. Despite the magnificence of the Volta Dam and the Black Star Monument, the average Ghanaian felt disillusioned about any future under the Osagyefo. Their once-prosperous country had become crippled with foreign debt, and food was becoming scarce. Labor unrest spread, particularly throughout the cacao sector. (The cacao tree produces cocoa beans used in the manufacture of chocolate; cocoa is Ghana's main agricultural product.)

In September 1961 union leaders organized a general strike among the nation's laborers. Nkrumah broke the strike using the full power of the police and army. He arrested his old allies and left them to die in prisons. He also turned increasingly to Communist countries for support and even let the former Soviet Union's notorious secret police, the KGB, organize his security forces. (Communism is a system of government in which the state controls property and jobs.)

These moves angered the people of Ghana. They resented Nkrumah's isolation from the realities of everyday life. The president became even more secluded after becoming the target of an August 1962 assassination attempt in the northeastern part of the country. Other attempts followed, driving Nkrumah farther and farther away from the mainstream of life in Ghana. Besides giving the KGB full rein over the security police, he established the President's Own Guard Regiment, a move that angered some army regulars who, up to that point, had remained loyal to him.

Clearly, Ghana's stability had crumbled. Rather than mend the political damage he caused, Nkrumah gave himself over to the study and preparation of new Pan-African ventures. In 1964, as the economy passed from bad to worse, he proclaimed Ghana a one-party state and himself life-president of both nation and party. His reign reached its lowest point two years later, when economic conditions deteriorated so much as to cause real hunger among the country's people.

Ghanaian army seizes power

Political experts agree that excessive government spending, corruption within the ruling party, and repression of opposition parties were the key sources of unrest and violence among Ghana's people. On February 24, 1966, the Ghanaian army seized power. Nkrumah was out of the country, on his way to Hanoi, North Vietnam, where he intended to work on a solution to Vietnam's civil war (1954-1975). Breaking into the presidential palace, the soldiers discovered Soviet KGB agents operating the national radio and police communications. They also discovered considerable documentation linking Nkrumah and his party officials with stolen funds and other wrongdoings.

When the smoke cleared from the 1966 coup, the depth of Nkrumah's unpopularity became obvious even to his closest supporters. Foreign observers noted that they had not seen such rejoicing in the streets since the independence celebrations in 1957.

One of the leaders of the overthrow, Colonel Akwasi Amankwa, summed up Nkrumah's downfall in David Lamb's book *The Africans:*

> Nkrumah could have been such a great man. He started well, led the independence movement and became, on behalf of Ghana, the symbol of emerging Africa. Somewhere down the line, however, he became ambitious, built a cult of personality and ruthlessly used the powers invested in him by his own constitution. He developed a strange love for absolute power.

Unable to return home, Nkrumah went to Guinea to stay with his old friend Sékou Touré. Touré made him co-president of Guinea—essentially an honorary position. Nkrumah dedicated the rest of his life to writing theoretical works that still find an audience among African Marxists. He died of cancer in a hospital in Bucharest, Romania, in 1972. Recognizing his important place in the history of their country, the Ghanaian authorities allowed his body to be returned for burial in his homeland. Nkrumah was married to Helen Ritz Fattiah and they had three children.

Further Reading

Ayittey, George B. N. *Africa Betrayed.* New York: St. Martin's Press, 1992.

Bretton, Henry. *The Rise and Fall of Kwame Nkrumah.* New York: Praeger, 1966.

Contemporary Black Biography. Vol. 3. Detroit: Gale, 1993.

Crowder, Michael. *The Story of Nigeria.* Winchester, MA: Faber, 1978.

Dictionary of African Biography. Algonac, MI: Reference Publications, 1979.

Friedland, W. H., and Carl G. Rosberg, eds. *African Socialism.* Stanford, CA: Stanford University Press, 1964.

Gunther, John. *Inside Africa.* North Pomfret, VT: Hamish Hamilton, 1955.

Hallet, Robin. *Africa since 1875.* Ann Arbor: University of Michigan Press, 1974.

Historic World Leaders. Edited by Anne Commire. Vol. 1. Detroit: Gale, 1994.

Lamb, David. *The Africans.* New York: Random House, 1984.

Maier, Karl. *Into the House of the Ancestors.* Chichester, W. Sussex, U.K.: John Wiley, 1998.

Newsweek, May 8, 1972.

Nkrumah, Kwame. *Autobiography.* Sunbury-on-Thames, Middx., U.K.: Thomas Nelson, 1957.

Omari, T. Peter. *Kwame Nkrumah: An Anatomy of African Dictatorship.* Accra, 1970.

Time, May 8, 1972.

Sam Nujoma

Born May 12, 1929
Ovamboland, South West Africa (now Namibia)

First president of independent Namibia

On March 21, 1990, Shafilshuna Samuel (popularly known as "Sam") Nujoma (*new-YOOH-mah*) was sworn in as the first president of Namibia. For more than two decades he kept the issue of Namibian independence alive through his negotiating and fundraising efforts. From 1915 to 1968, when it was known as South West Africa, Namibia was governed by South Africa. By the early 1960s nationalist (or independence-seeking) movements began taking shape in Namibia. At first the nationalists functioned mainly as nonviolent political rights groups, pushing South Africa to change its policy of apartheid. (Apartheid, which in English means "apartness" or "separateness," is a system of segregation based on race in which a white minority dominates politically and economically.) In 1966, however, Namibian nationalists took up arms against South Africa. For 23 years the South West Africa People's Organization

Nujoma's greatest triumph was in the diplomatic field, when the United Nations gave SWAPO official "observer status" and recognized it as the "sole and authentic representative" of the Namibian people.

(SWAPO) under the presidency of Sam Nujoma, waged a low-scale war against South Africa's occupying forces. With political pressure mounting at home and abroad, the South African government finally agreed in 1988 to accept the results of elections leading to the region's independence.

The role of the United Nations in Namibia

Namibia is a long narrow stretch of rocky desert along Africa's southern Atlantic Coast. German missionaries and farmers first settled there in the mid-1800s. In the division of Africa among European powers in 1884, Germany declared South West Africa its colony, meaning Germany then began to manage the political affairs of this southwestern African region. In 1904 Germany launched an ambitious white settler policy, using German troops to solidify the white population's hold on the area. More than 75,000 African people—about 60 percent of the population of central and southern Namibia—died over the next three years as the Germans attempted to claim the region for the whites.

After Germany was defeated in World War I (1914-18), the League of Nations (an international peacekeeping organization later replaced by the United Nations) assumed responsibility for Germany's colonies. In 1920 the League asked South Africa to administer the former German colony "for the people's well being and development." Five years later a new constitution gave the whites of South West Africa limited self-rule, but South Africa continued to have control over customs, defense, foreign affairs, transport, justice, and nonwhite affairs. The South African government appointed a white administrator general to look after its interests there.

In 1946 South Africa asked the United Nations for permission to claim South West Africa as a province (a dependent political unit). The UN refused. But when the white-run Nationalist party won the 1948 elections in South Africa, party leaders defied the UN and gave South West Africa representation in the South African parliament. South Africa maintained its control over the region by sheer force.

Joins the nationalists

Sam Nujoma was born on May 12, 1929, in Ovamboland, a vast and highly populated area in the north of South West Africa.

His parents, Daniel Utoma Nujoma and Mpingana Kondombola, were peasant farmers. Nujoma went to a Finnish mission school for nine years in the late 1930s and 1940s and then continued his education at night school in Windhoek, the colony's capital. After school he took a job as a steward on the South African Railways for two years. In 1957, however, the railway authorities fired him because of his involvement in controversial political activities.

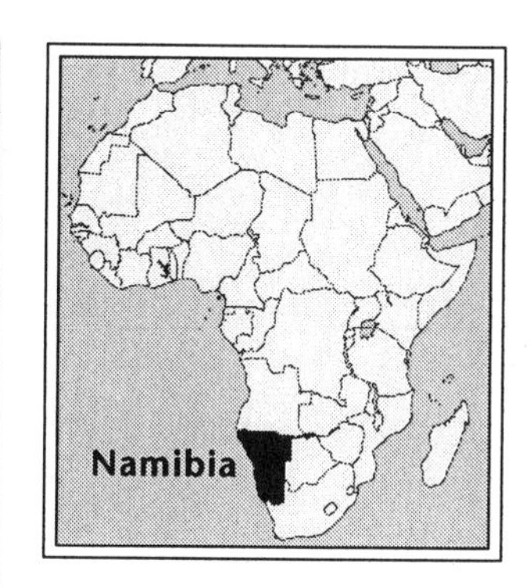

While working for the railway line, Nujoma traveled to some of the bigger cities of South Africa. There he met Andimba Toivo ja Toivo, an African nationalist from South West Africa. (African nationalism is the struggle for self rule for African nations.) Toivo and other expatriate (people who leave their native country to live elsewhere) students from South West Africa had founded the Ovamboland People's Organization (OPO; originally called the Ovamboland People's Congress) in 1958. Nearly half the population of South West Africa were living in Ovamboland because the white European settlers had no desire for the tsetse fly-infested land in that section of the colony. Cattle and horses cannot live in tsetse areas.

In 1959 Nujoma joined the OPO and became the Windhoek branch president that same year. In December he helped organize a massive campaign of black resistance. The white administration wanted to move black residents of a Windhoek township to a new location far outside the city. Black opposition to the removals led to a massacre in which police killed 13 demonstrators. Nujoma was arrested and then released for trial for his role in the operation. Rather than face trial, he fled South West Africa in March 1960, crossing the Kalahari Desert on foot. He made his way to the western African nation of Ghana by way of Botswana and Tanzania. On his way to Botswana he was aided, fed, and supplied with horses by local Herero chiefs. Nujoma assumed a false name and obtained false papers. With help from many supporters along the way, he ended up in New York City, where he joined other Namibian exiles petitioning the United Nations to end South Africa's control over the territory.

Nationalists take up arms

In 1960 OPO was renamed SWAPO (the South West Africa People's Organization) and Nujoma became its president. He traveled throughout Africa, Europe, and the United States to raise funds for the movement and to explain his country's plight. He testified before the UN, gained Organization of African Unity support, and established a network of offices with provisional headquarters in Dar es Salaam, Tanzania. Nujoma's greatest triumph was in the diplomatic field, when the United Nations gave SWAPO official "observer status" and recognized it as the "sole and authentic representative" of the Namibian people.

Originally a nonviolent anti-apartheid pressure group, SWAPO began a guerrilla war against South Africa's occupation in the late 1960s. In 1966 the United Nations denied South Africa's right to control South West Africa. But the UN had no way to enforce its decision, and South Africa simply refused to abide by it. SWAPO leaders realized that they could not rely on international goodwill; they had to take up arms against the South Africans. SWAPO turned to Cuba, East Europe, the Nordic countries (Germanic countries of Northern Europe), and the Soviet Union for funds and arms. Many Western nations would not help a liberation movement against South Africa because they were afraid of jeopardizing their own economic interests.

SWAPO is stricken from inside and out

SWAPO fighters first made contact with the South African police in August 1966. With neighboring Zambia's independence in 1964 and a sympathetic government in power, SWAPO set up bases in Zambia and from there sent its fighters into northern Namibia. South Africa quickly clamped down on SWAPO activities. Unable to operate at home, more and more political leaders fled the country to join SWAPO in exile. In the 1970s the freedom-fighting organization was nearly torn apart by internal conflicts. SWAPO's traditional-minded older leaders clashed with the group's younger members, who wanted to hold elections for SWAPO's leadership positions. Nearly 2,000 SWAPO members were tortured and jailed by SWAPO leaders over the next decade.

SWAPO's military wing—called PLAN, or the People's Liberation Army of Namibia—was not a particularly effective liberation army. During the guerrilla war, SWAPO lost an estimated 20,000 soldiers. Contact with South African troops was limited mainly to the northern part of the country, although SWAPO conducted bombings and acts of terrorism in agricultural and urban centers, including the capital city of Windhoek.

Nujoma gives a black power salute in Windhoek after winning in the 1989 elections.

The tangled politics of Namibia in the 1970s was further complicated by political events that were occurring in neighboring countries. The fiercely anti-Communist South African government stationed about 100,000 troops in northern Namibia because of the threat posed by nearly 35,000 Cuban troops based in nearby Angola, a former colony of Portugal. (Communism is a system of government in which the state controls the means of production and the distribution of goods.) The former Soviet Union's Communist government was the primary economic backer of Cuba. In the mid-1970s the southwestern African state of Angola—still reeling from internal fighting after the departure of the Portuguese—was taken over by a pro-Soviet nationalist group. At this point, the United States and other Western countries had extremely tense political relations with the Soviet Union. The Cubans came to the aid of the Angolan government when the United States funded and supplied an opposition group to resist the spread of communism in Angola.

In brief, the costly presence of South African troops in Namibia and the Cuban presence in Angola were among the main reasons South Africa finally agreed in 1988 to UN-supervised elections—elections that would lead to independence for Namibia. SWAPO did not take part in the negotiations.

Nujoma returns home

Nujoma returned to Namibia in 1989 after 29 years in exile and attracted large crowds to his political rallies. For many he was the living symbol of the struggle for independence in Namibia. But the UN-aided peace process between Namibia and South Africa almost came to a halt on April 1, 1989. On that day SWAPO sent nearly 1,000 heavily armed guerrillas into Namibia from Angola. (Nujoma had previously promised to keep his forces well inside Angolan borders.) Fighting resumed for a short time, and within several weeks South African troops had killed approximately 300 SWAPO guerrillas.

UN-supervised elections for a government assembly in Namibia went ahead in November 1989. SWAPO won 57 percent of the seats, and the following March the new government was sworn in with Nujoma as the first president of independent Namibia. Initially Nujoma supported a multiparty system with a limited presidency of two five-year terms. He now favors amending the constitution so he can serve a third term.

Nujoma is married to Kowambo Katjimunia. The couple has 11 children.

Further Reading

Lunn, John, and Christopher Saunders. "Recent History of Namibia." In *Africa South of the Sahara: 1994.* 23rd ed. London: Europa, 1994.

Putz, J. H. von Egidy, and P. Caplan. *Namibia Handbook and Who's Who.* Magus, 1989.

Flora Nwapa

Born January 13, 1931
Oguta, Nigeria
Died October 1993
Enugu, Nigeria

Nigerian writer and publisher

Nigerian author Flora Nwapa was one of the first African women to write and publish a novel in English. Although early critics of African literature did not recognize the significance of her work, experts in the field now widely praise her ability to capture the essence of her Ibo dialect in English. (The Ibo, or Igbo, are culturally united communities of people who live in the southeastern part of Nigeria. They speak the Ibo language, one of the major language groups in the country.) Nwapa offered readers a fresh perspective on traditional West African culture and modern Nigeria by exploring each from a woman's point of view. She is acknowledged as the key literary voice of the African woman during a period when men dominated African literature.

Nwapa is acknowledged as the key literary voice of the African woman during a period when men dominated African literature.

Selected Writings of Flora Nwapa

- *Efuru* (1966, Heinemann), novel.
- *Idu* (1970, Heinemann), novel.
- *This Is Lagos and Other Stories* (1971, Nwankwo-Ifejika), short stories.
- *Emeka, Driver's Guard* (1972, University of London Press), children's book.
- *Never Again* (1975, Nwamife), autobiography.
- *Mammywater* (1979, Tana Press), children's book.
- *Wives at War and Other Stories* (1980, Tana Press), short stories.
- *Journey to Space* (1980, Tana Press), children's book.
- *The Miracle Kittens* (1980, Tana Press), children's book.
- *The Adventures of Deke* (1980, Tana Press), children's book.
- *One Is Enough* (1981, Tana Press), novel.
- *Women Are Different* (1986, Tana Press), novel.
- *Cassava Song and Rice Song* (1986, Tana Press), poetry.

Women's stories and songs

Flora Nwanzuruahu Nkiru Nwapa was born in Oguta, in eastern Nigeria, the eldest of six children. Both her parents were schoolteachers. As a child she was surrounded by women who told tales and sang songs, and she freely admitted that these women, including her mother, influenced her art. Nwapa left Oguta to finish her schooling, going first to the coastal town of Port Harcourt and later to Lagos, then the capital of Nigeria. She was one of the earliest graduates of Nigeria's prestigious University College (now the University of Ibadan), receiving her bachelor's degree in 1957. She later studied at Edinburgh University in Scotland for her diploma in education, which she earned in 1958.

Nigeria gained its independence from Great Britain in October 1960. When Nwapa left Europe and returned to Nigeria, the country was in the midst of a major transition to democracy. Nwapa held a variety of teaching and administrative positions but consistently pursued a career in writing. During stints as a teacher of English and geography at Queen's College in Enugu and as the public relations head for the University of Lagos, she completed work on her first novel, *Efuru,* published in 1966. Nwapa was forced to return to eastern Nigeria during the nation's bloody civil war from 1967 to 1970, when the Christians in the South broke away from the central government and formed a separate nation called Biafra. The Nigerian government sent its troops into Biafra to put down the rebellion, and in January 1970 Biafra fell to federal forces. The next year Nwapa published her second novel *Idu.* Around this time she also married Gogo Nwakuche, an industrialist, and they had one son.

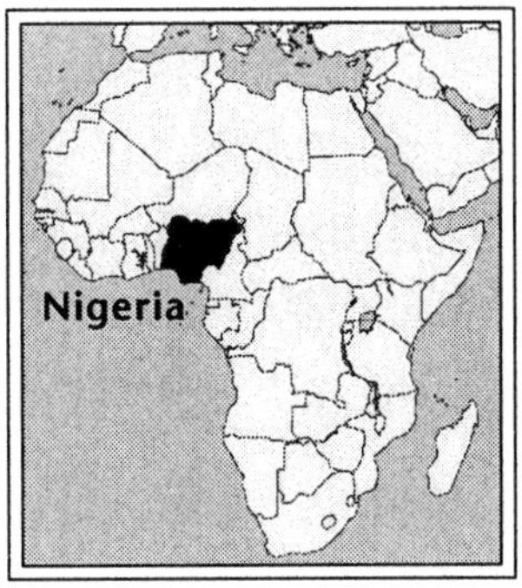

Writes about women

All Nwapa's fiction for adults centers on the role of women in Nigerian society. Her earliest works are based in the rural village of her childhood, but later works branched out into life in the hectic urban world of Lagos. Nwapa wrote about women's rights and their postion in a society controlled by men. Women were powerful figures in traditional culture, economically secure and socially vibrant, yet bound to a system of male dominance that limited their choices. In facing this dilemma, Nwapa's women are forced to confront the confines of their culture.

The author's focus on women's lives, particularly in the villages, gave an oral quality to her writing. Like many of her male contemporaries, Nwapa relied on African oral tradition in the form of proverbs, parables, songs, and tales, thus creating a distinctly African sound to her works in English. Her writing also reflected oral tradition in another way. Nwapa rarely described an event or scene in prose; instead, she passed on information through dialogue. As in an oral culture, the characters in her novels and short stories find out important news and gossip through contacts at the marketplace, at the farm, in town, or around the family compound.

Efuru, Nwapa's first novel, is set in the village community of Oguta, where the author was raised. The title character is a remarkable woman of great beauty, intelligence, and success. Her inability to have a child, though, is viewed by the people of the village as her one major flaw. Efuru respects her society's traditions but does not always follow them. She chooses both of her husbands without her family's approval, and both marriages end disastrously. But even though Efuru does not meet the conventional requirements of the village society as a wife and a mother, the people give her another chance to serve the community—she becomes the worshipper of the lake goddess Uhamiri. Stories of Uhamiri fascinated Nwapa as a child, and it is through this powerful female god that Efuru takes her place as a full citizen of her society.

Critical response to *Efuru* in 1966 was negative or indifferent at best. Reviewers saw Nwapa as a mere imitator of fellow Ibo writer Chinua Achebe (see entry) and faulted her for writing exclusively about women and their lives. By the 1990s, though, a majority of critics regarded *Efuru* as an early classic of African literature, a book that explored a traditional world untouched by European influence and examined the varying roles of women in that world.

Heinemann's African Writers Series published both *Efuru* and *Idu.* Nwapa's next book was a short story collection titled *This Is Lagos.* In this 1971 publication the author changed her approach and her material: she moved her setting from the rural village to the urban capital. She also broke with her British publisher and had her work published by a Nigerian company. Although this helped bolster Nigerian readership and the Nigerian publishing industry, Nwapa was denied the critical response she normally received. Most critical writing on African literature at that time focused on materials published in the United States or Great Britain.

The East goes to war

Like Achebe and other Nigerian writers, Nwapa turned away from writing novels at the time of the Biafran War (1967-70), a fierce conflict that left more than a million Ibo civilians dead from starvation. During the war Nwapa (who was then assistant registrar at the University of Lagos), her husband, and their family were forced to leave Lagos and return to Iboland. Nwapa reflects on the war and the disaster that followed in *Never Again,* a novella published in 1975. Nwapa was uniquely suited to write this novella not only because of her past career as a writer and her personal experience as an Ibo during the fighting, but also because of her postwar role in the administration of the former Biafra. (She was a member of the East Central State Executive Council.) Though probably more important for its historical documentation than for its literary merit, *Never Again* clearly reflects Nwapa's antiwar sentiments.

Becomes a publisher

After the release of *Never Again,* Nwapa made a big change in her writing career: she became a publisher. Early in 1975 she had left her position as government commissioner to devote her time to writing. She found, however, that she was unable to write in the isolation of her home; she needed interaction with others. Unhappy with her publishers, Nwapa decided to set up her own publishing house, which she called Tana Press. The relative freedom of publishing her own works and the works of others was spoiled somewhat by the problems inherent in the publishing business. Import duty and currency changes often left her newly published books stranded at the docks, and her small editorial staff did not have the resources to produce error-free publications. As a result the books contained considerable numbers of typographical errors and suffered overall from a lack of careful editing. Finally, because of Nigeria's isolation from the West, the books were not distributed widely and did not receive the critical attention her earlier novels had.

Besides her writing and publishing ventures, Nwapa continued her career as an educator. She taught at colleges and universities around the world, including New York University, Trinity College, and the universities of Minnesota and Michigan. She died in October 1993 after having completed a tour of the United States.

Of the early writers in English African literature, Flora Nwapa was perhaps the least acknowledged. With new approaches to African literature and with more women critics in the literary field, Nwapa's works—particularly her first two novels, *Efuru* and *Idu*—are receiving more of the recognition they deserve. For most contemporary critics of African literature, Nwapa's position as a forerunner of modern African women's writings is secure. Through the voices of *Efuru* and Nwapa's other female characters, the previously undocumented stories of African village women are heard.

Further Reading

Wilentz, Gay. *Binding Cultures: Black Women Writers in Africa and the Diaspora.* Bloomington: Indiana University Press, 1992.

Wilentz, Gay. "Flora Nwapa." In *Dictionary of Literary Biography.* Volume 125. Detroit: Gale, 1993.

Julius K. Nyerere

Born March 1922
Butima, Tanganyika (Tanzania)

President of Tanzania

"The family to which we all belong must be extended yet further—beyond the tribe, the community, the nation, or even the continent—to embrace the whole of mankind."

—Nyerere, explaining the principle of African socialism based on *ujamaa*

Julius K. Nyerere (*nigh-AIR-ree*) was an early African nationalist fighting for his people's independence after World War II (1939-45). He attempted to blend the Marxist-socialist economic theory—one in which the government takes control of all businesses and corporations in the country—with traditional African customs. (Marxist doctrine, based on the philosophy of German intellectual Karl Marx, centers on the belief that a revolution by the working class would lead eventually to a classless society.) As the first president of Tanzania (formerly Tanganyika and Zanzibar) in the early 1960s, Nyerere sought to instill a sense of self-help (*ujamaa*) in the newly independent nation. He succeeded in introducing some social reforms based on *ujamaa,* but his economic policies brought disaster to the country. Nyerere was one of the few presidents in the post-war period to resign voluntarily from office. He is regarded by the African and international communities as an elder statesman and is consulted regularly on regional issues.

European colonization

With the division of African territories among European countries after 1885, Germany had control over vast areas of Tanganyika, a region lying along Africa's Indian Ocean Coast. The Germans invested heavily in northern Tanganyika, hoping to develop the area for coffee and tea plantations. Africans resented European influence: the Germans tried to force the people of Tanganyika to pay hut taxes and work as cheap laborers on the plantations. Resistance culminated in the bloody anti-white Maji Maji rebellion, which occurred in the South between 1905 and 1906. As many as 300,000 Africans are believed to have died in the rebellion or as a result of the subsequent famine caused intentionally by the Germans.

During World War I (1914-18) Tanganyika probably suffered more destruction and loss of life than any other African territory. The Germans recruited Africans as soldiers and a small German African force tied down about 250,000 British and colonial troops for four years. In the aftermath of the war and Germany's defeat, the League of Nations gave Great Britain control over the former German territory and gave it the name Tanganyika. Britain introduced Western education in Tanganyika and brought in agricultural innovations but did not develop the region as a white settler colony. Instead, the British government chose to rule indirectly by maintaining the traditional structure of chiefs and adding only a few British administrators to keep an eye on developments in each kingdom.

A good student

Nyerere's father, Chief Nyerere Burito, was a sub-chief of the Zanaki under the Germans. The Zanakis are one of the smallest groups in the country, made up of only about 40,000 people living in a remote area of northwestern Tanganyika. Chief Burito was 61 years old when he took a young woman, Mugaya, as his fifth wife. Mugaya bore him eight children. Julius was the second of their four sons, born in 1922. His father died in 1942 at the age of 82.

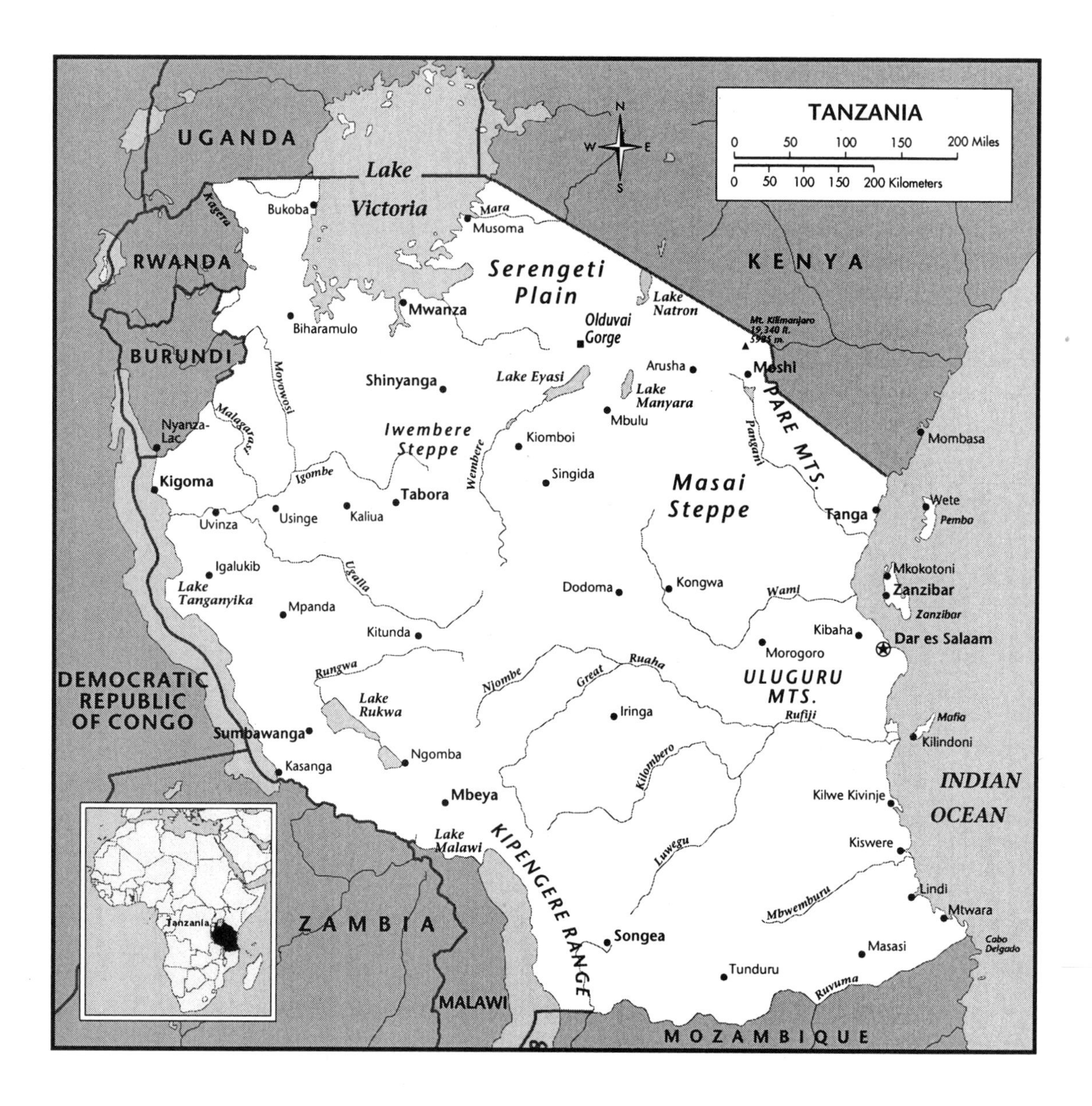

In his lifetime, the chief had married 22 women and fathered 26 children. (In many African societies, both in the past and in recent times, men have practiced polygyny—taking more than one wife. Each wife and her children are thought of as a separate "house," either a right-hand or a left-hand house, depending upon their relation to the main house. This arrangement regulates inheritance.)

Nyerere's parents gave him the name "Kambarage" because of the violent rain that fell in Butima, Tanganyika, on the day of his birth. He took the name "Julius" later in life, when he converted to Catholicism. When Nyerere was growing up, his people still used traditional fighting weapons against their neighbors, the Maasai. Their bows and arrows were hardly a match for the Maasai and their long spears.

An older brother of Nyerere's persuaded their father to send Nyerere away to school to get a superior education. At the age of 12, young Nyerere went off to a boarding school in Musoma, on the shores of Lake Victoria. The elder Nyerere realized the ways of the Zanaki were dying, and he wished to prepare his son for the changes by giving him an adequate education. At the Native Authority Boarding School, Nyerere led his class.

Nyerere later transferred to the only secondary school in Tanganyika at Tabora. The Tabora Government Secondary School was modeled after an English private school. Named a prefect or leader of his residence, Nyerere was entitled to special dining and disciplinary privileges. But he hated the injustice of the system and agitated to have the special privileges of his office abolished.

From teaching to politics

After graduating from Tabora in 1943 and securing financial help from his family and Tabora's headmaster, Nyerere entered Makerere College, a teacher's college in Uganda. Here he first came into contact with other young African scholars and developed his own theory of nationalism (the belief that Africans should form independent, self-governing nations on the African continent).

Following his graduation in 1945, Nyerere accepted a teaching position at St. Mary's Catholic Boys School, a school in Tabora run by white missionaries. Known as the White Fathers, these priests and the Maryknoll missionaries exerted a tremendous influence on him. In December 1945 Nyerere became a Christian and was baptized into the Roman Catholic faith. He fell in love with another convert, Maria Gabriel Magige of the Msinditi tribe, who had been educated by the White Sisters. Magige and Nyerere became engaged before Nyerere left for Edinburgh University in Scotland.

During his three years at Edinburgh, Nyerere studied history and economics. Gradually he developed a plan for his future: he decided to get involved in politics and work for the independence of Tanganyika. In 1953, after receiving his master of arts degree and returning to Tanganyika, Nyerere married his fiancée. Later that year, he took a job teaching history at St. Francis College at Pugu, near the eastern city of Dar es Salaam.

While in Uganda in the early 1940s, Nyerere had learned of a defunct (no longer functioning) African social study group, the Tanganyika African Association (TAA). He revived it when he was teaching in Tabora. Later on, while at St. Francis College, a local branch of the TAA elected him secretary. This position brought him into contact with some prominent and influential Tanganyikan thinkers.

"Africa for Africans"

In 1953 the TAA elected Nyerere its president by a narrow margin. He immediately began to reshape the organization into an active political party. By July 1954 he had spearheaded the formation of a new and independent party, the Tanganyika African National Union (TANU), with a platform calling for "Africa for the Africans." TANU was extremely well-organized, with active branches in almost every district. Setting up a national party in Tanzania had some advantages. None of the country's 120 tribal groups was large enough to be considered dominant, and almost everybody in the country spoke the same language—the unofficial national language of Swahili. The Arabs from Zanzibar and the Arabian peninsula had introduced Swahili in the nineteenth century, when they cut trade routes to the region's interior.

In March 1955 Nyerere told the United Nations (UN; an international organization set up after World War II to promote world peace) that TANU's political goal was to prepare the people of Tanganyika for self-government and independence. The prospect of black majority rule in Tanganyika frightened the region's whites. Nevertheless, the United Nations recommended that a date be set for independence from British rule. Conflict developed, pitting Nyerere and his nationalist group against British district officers stationed in Tanganyika.

The nation's first prime minister

With the 1958 appointment of a new British governor named Sir Richard Turnbull, the prospects for Tanganyika's independence

Mau Mau was a violent rebellion by the Kikuyu people that broke out in 1951 in the European farming area of Kenya. It began with the murder of several British farmers and the destruction of their cattle. The Kikuyu wanted their land back and hoped to scare the Europeans out of the country. The British government responded by arresting nationalist leader Jomo Kenyatta (see entry) and other well-known Kikuyu leaders and rounding up Kikuyu farmers and forcing them to live in guarded compounds. By the end of 1955 the revolt had been put down. About 100 British settlers had been killed in the uprising; nearly 3,000 Kikuyu had died in the civil war that pitted Kenyan rebels against blacks who were suspected of supporting the white regime.

The Terror of Mau Mau

seemed much brighter. Turnbull had seen the worst of racial antagonism during the violent Mau Mau rebellion in Kenya, and he admired Nyerere's peaceful brand of African nationalism. TANU even won the support of a significant portion of the Asian and European segments of Tanganyikan society by promoting a policy of nonracial Tanganyikan citizenship. This contrasted sharply with the racial divisions that plagued neighboring countries' politics.

TANU won sweeping electoral victories in 1958 and 1960. Nyerere took office as the chief minister during the peaceful transition to self-government. Later, in December 1961, Tanganyika gained complete independence and Nyerere became its first prime minister.

In a move that surprised his supporters, Nyerere resigned his post as prime minister only a little more than six weeks after Tanganyika had achieved self rule. Debate raged over the reasons for his resignation. In actuality, his retreat from the spotlight afforded him the necessary time to formulate his social and economic plan for Tanganyika, a plan known as "*Ujamaa*—the Basis of African Socialism."

Two decades of power

Nyerere's principle of *ujamaa* or "familyhood" was central to his understanding of socialism. He was opposed to capitalism, an economic system based on private ownership of property and a free, competitive market, because he felt it sought "to build a

Nyerere (left) with President Aseid Karume signing agreement uniting Tanganyika and Zanzibar to create the Republic of Tanzania, 1964.

happy society" at the expense of the workers. He was also wary of the "inevitable conflict" that could be generated between people in a socialistic system. African socialism, based on *ujamaa,* held that "the family to which we all belong must be extended yet further—beyond the tribe, the community, the nation, or even the continent—to embrace the whole of mankind." With this principle guiding his politics, Nyerere reentered the political arena late in 1962 when Tanganyika became a republic. He won the federal election by an overwhelming majority to become the nation's first president, a position he would hold until 1984.

Meanwhile, trouble was brewing on the nearby island of Zanzibar, located in the Indian Ocean less than 25 miles off the coast of Tanganyika. In December 1963 the British granted independence to Zanzibar. A month later the island's African majority population revolted, seizing power from the traditional ruling Arab minority. Then, within a few days, Tanganyikan armed forces, led by younger officers, staged an uprising and went on a looting spree in the streets of Dar es Salaam. The army revolts spread to Uganda and Kenya. All three governments called on

Great Britain for military assistance against their own armies. Order was reestablished, but Nyerere was concerned by the threat of renewed instability in Zanzibar. In April 1964 Zanzibar and Tanganyika joined together to form a new country, the United Republic of Tanzania, with Nyerere as its president.

A home-grown brand of socialism

As a consequence of the troubles on Zanzibar and in Tanganyika, Nyerere became a more radical and militant (willing to fight) politician. By 1967 Nyerere had formulated his Arusha Declaration, a new policy that blended African traditional ideas with socialist principles of economics. (It was named after the town of Arusha, where Nyerere first revealed the fine points of the plan.) The declaration was rooted in the socialist belief that redistributing wealth among a nation's people is more important than creating new wealth for its own sake. The government would redistribute the country's wealth largely by spending it to expand social services.

Nyerere had undertaken a massive program of reorganization with an emphasis on economic cooperation, racial and tribal harmony, and self-sacrifice. To achieve his goals he established a one-party democracy (government by the people), outlawing all political parties other than TANU. (In Western nations like the United States, the idea of "democracy" hinges on a multiparty system that gives voters distinct choices.) Tanzania was a largely rural, impoverished country—a country with an economy built on peasant farming. President Nyerere sought to build the nation into a self-sufficient socialist society based on cooperative agriculture—farms owned by and operated for the benefit of their workers. His plan would unite the nation's farmworkers on nationalized (government-owned) land, and all farming operations would be conducted under government supervision.

Village collectives were set up—by force in many instances—throughout the nation's rural areas. Whole villages of people were packed up in the backs of trucks and carted to new areas, where they were expected to settle and work with people from other villages. In such a situation, a clash in customs and traditions was inevitable. The rationale for uprooting and resettling so many people was practicality: providing medical services, water, and school facilities to the people of Tanzania would be easier if the workers were concentrated in large settlements. By 1976 more than 90 percent of the 11 million rural Tanzanians lived in more than 8,000 *ujamaa* villages. Peasant farmers were never really able to accept the new collective farms, and within a decade nearly 85 percent of them had returned to independent subsistence farming (feeding their own families with the crops they grew). Government had also taken control of all industries and services, marketing, production, and distribution systems. Nationalizing industry (placing it in the control of the government) and creating artificial villages required a large bureaucracy. (A bureaucracy is a system of administration or government that is often considered inefficient because it makes accomplishing things more difficult with official processes and rules, red-tape, and hierarchies.) The growth of an intricate and snarled bureaucracy in turn created widespread corruption and dissatisfaction. It took $10 billion in foreign aid just to keep Tanzania's economy afloat.

Sets a foreign policy with integrity

In foreign policy Nyerere was guided by his strong opposition to racism in any form. He organized African nations to officially oppose white-minority rule in Rhodesia, South Africa, Namibia, Mozambique, and Angola. Though it was a disadvantage to his own country, he made Tanzania the home base for nationalist freedom movements in those lands. He was also one of the first to condemn the atrocities in Idi Amin's (see entry) oppressive Ugandan government, denouncing the dictator's attempts to expel all Asians from that country.

Tanzania has always been a safe haven for refugees from neighboring countries. In early 1973 tens of thousands of Hutus from Burundi sought protection within Tanzania's borders. This same scene was to be repeated in 1994, when thousands of Hutu refugees from Rwanda took shelter in Tanzania.

Nyerere steps down

In the presidential and parliamentary elections in October 1980, Nyerere was reelected for another five-year term. Later, he announced that he would not seek another term in 1985. (In 1984 parliament passed a constitutional amendment limiting the term of presidency to two five-year terms.) Nyerere's vice president, Ali Hassan Mwinyi (the former president of Zanzibar), succeeded him.

Nyerere stepped down gracefully to a life of semiretirement. He chaired the Chama Cha Mapinduzi-Revolutionary party

Nyerere vs. Amin

From the early 1970s Nyerere had been a persistent critic of Uganda's military dictator, Idi Amin, charging him with racism and inhumanity for his harsh treatment of Uganda's Asian population. But because Amin was not a Communist, Western nations allowed him to carry out his discriminatory, anti-Asian policies without much objection. In fact, Nyerere's opposition to Amin actually aggravated Tanzania's relations with Western powers. The friction between Nyerere and Amin also wrecked the regional attempt to create an East African Common Market, which was to include Tanzania, Uganda, and Kenya.

Although Nyerere had given former Ugandan president Milton Obote a base in Tanzania from which to operate, he had not taken part in Obote's plan to overthrow Amin in 1972. Six years later, when Amin sent Ugandan troops into Tanzania, Nyerere responded by invading Uganda with 20,000 Tanzanian troops alongside members of the Uganda National Liberation Front. The united force chased Amin from the country and took the capital city of Kampala. Tanzanian troops remained in Uganda in support of the liberation forces until 1981. This venture reportedly cost the Tanzania government an estimated $1 million a day, a high price for one of the poorest countries in the world.

(CCM) until 1990. (The CCM was created in the late 1970s when TANU merged with Zanzibar's o-Shirazi party.) Nyerere has, however, remained active in regional politics, chairing a committee to maintain sanctions, or economic boycotts, against an illegal government formed in the central African nation of Burundi in 1996. Most political observers agree that Nyerere sought power with one goal in mind: to better the conditions of Tanzania's people. Neither he nor his family members have ever been accused of enriching themselves at the expense of the people. His economic policies, however, failed miserably, and even Nyerere admits it. In 1992, Nyerere himself demanded change and *Ujamaa* has been allowed to die a slow death. The new government is selling the previously nationalized industries and businesses and the only political party, the CCM, has recommended that opposition parties be allowed to function.

Further Reading

Contemporary Black Biography. Volume 5. Detroit: Gale, 1994.

Current History, April 1985; May 1988.

Duggan, William Redman, and John R. Civille. *Tanzania and Nyerere: A Study of Ujamaa and Nationhood.* London: Orbis Books, 1976.

Graham, Shirley. *Julius K. Nyerere: Teacher of Africa.* New York: Messner, 1975.

Hatch, John. *Tanzania: A Profile.* New York: Praeger, 1972.

Historic World Leaders. Edited by Anne Commire. Detroit: Gale, 1994.

Nyerere, Julius K. *Freedom and Development* New York/UK: Oxford University Press, 1974.

Pratt, Cranford. *The Critical Phase in Tanzania, 1945-1968: Nyerere and the Emergence of a Socialist Strategy.* New York/UK: Cambridge University Press, 1976.

Smith, William Edgett. *Nyerere of Tanzania.* London: Victor Gollancz, 1973.

Anna Nzinga

Born c. 1581
Ndongo (Angola)
Died December 17, 1663
Matamba (Angola)

Queen of the Mbundu kingdom of the Ndongo and Matamba

As the Portuguese expanded their influence in central Africa in the sixteenth century, resistance among black Africans increased. When the Kongo kingdom of Afonso I (c. 1461-c. 1543; see entry) collapsed, Portuguese slave traders and adventurers moved south into the kingdom of the Ndongo. The Ndongo were Mbundu-speaking people living along the coast of today's northern Angola. They controlled all the land up to the Cuanza, Lukala, and Dande rivers. The Portuguese mistook the Ndongo name *ngola,* meaning "king," for the name of the people, so the territory came to be called Angola. When the Ndongo ngola Kiluanji first encountered the Portuguese, he welcomed them and carried on business dealings with them. The king soon grew rich by providing the foreigners with slaves. With development of the South American land of Brazil as a Portuguese colony and the resulting

"Everyone fell to their knees and kissed the ground at her approach, a strange sight [since] women did not usually hold power."

—Dutch military attaché Captain Füller describing support for Nzinga as she battled the Portuguese

need for slaves, however, the Portuguese stepped up their slaving raids and moved inland. The Portuguese also were motivated by the belief that the mountains in Africa's interior held rich silver mines. As they moved farther inland in search of slaves and the fabled mines of Cambambe, they ran into conflict with the Ndongo over territory and boundaries. In 1581, led by Ngola Kiluanji, the Ndongo went to war against the Portuguese.

Anna Nzinga (sometimes spelled Njinja; pronounced *nuh-ZHING-uh*), the daughter of Kiluanji, was born the year the war started. In 1623, when she was in her early forties, she succeeded her half-brother, Mbandi, to the throne. As queen of the Ndongo and later the Matamba, Nzinga dominated the history of central Africa for 40 years. She sharpened her diplomatic skills by playing European powers against each other and protected her people using whatever tactics she felt necessary. Nzinga made alliances by marrying powerful chiefs and struck hard bargains with Portuguese officials. When her deals with the Europeans failed, she led a guerrilla (independent fighting unit) army against them.

The kingdom in ruins

As a young woman, Nzinga followed the traditional role laid out for her as the daughter of the royal court: she married and had a child, a son. Although her father was a powerful ruler, as he aged he became oppressive and unreasonable—acting like a dictator who had sole and absolute authority over his kingdom. As a result, he lost the support of his people. Around 1618 his son Mbandi took advantage of the discontent among the king's followers. He overthrew the royal court and killed his father. But Mbandi lacked the leadership skills of his father, and within four years the Ndongo kingdom crumbled.

Mbandi was a cruel and tyrannical man—very similar to his father in his old age. He eliminated any potential threat to the throne by ordering the murder of both his younger brother and Nzinga's only child. He also executed the chiefs who had helped him gain power. Nzinga, her husband, and her sisters left the capital, Mbamba, and went to the neighboring area of Matamba.

The Portuguese slave traders took advantage of the disorder in the kingdom and looted what they could. They also ravaged the

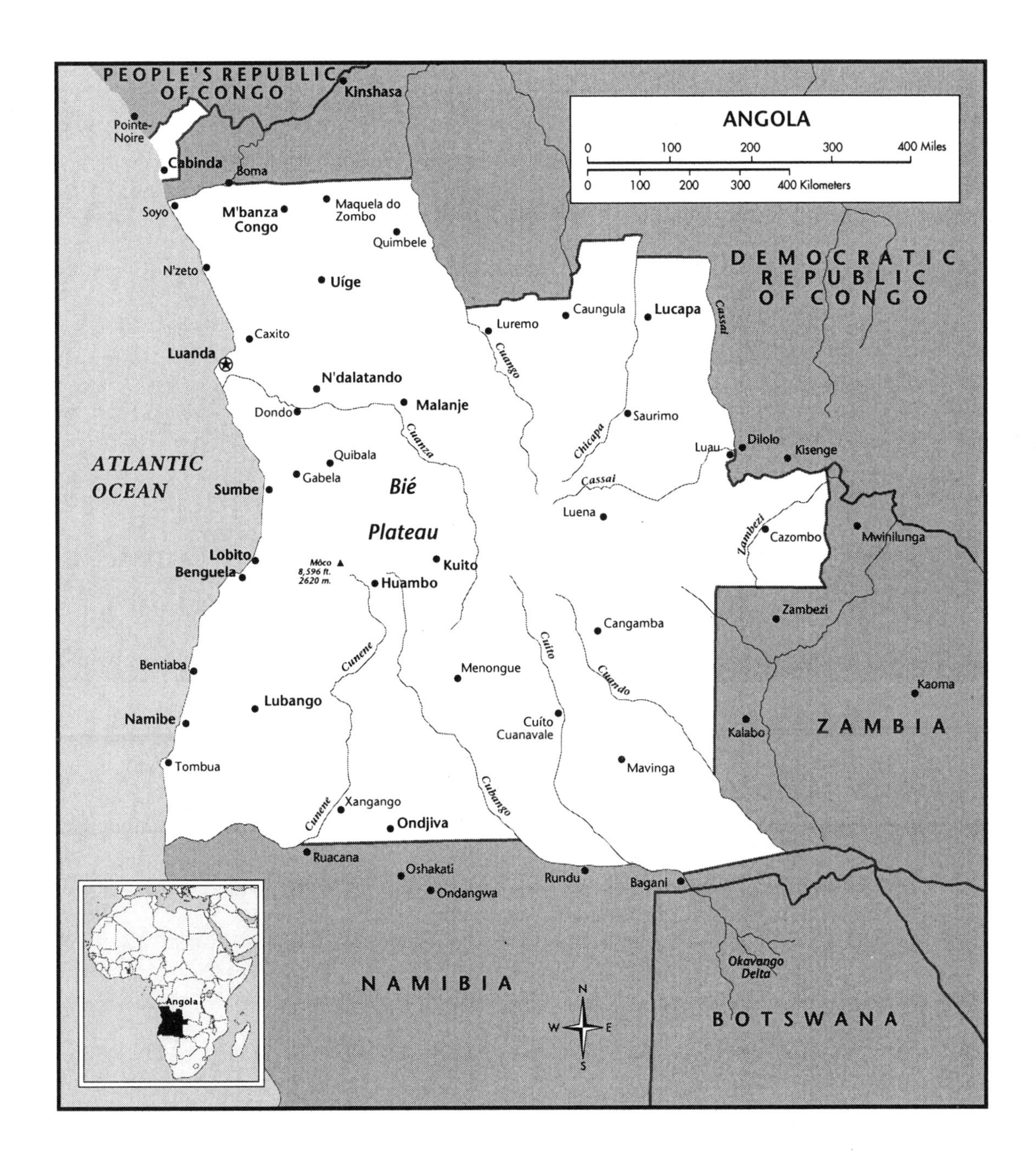

population by taking as many slaves as possible. The Portuguese sought help in their slave hunts from the Jaga, a fierce roaming band of warriors whose only loyalty was to the people who hired them. Mbandi fled the capital and took refuge on an island in the Cuanza River.

The situation was so chaotic and disruptive that even the Portuguese wanted to settle matters and restore peace. In 1622 they invited Mbandi back to Luanda to negotiate for peace. Mbandi sent word to his sister asking her to represent him at the peace talks. Despite his earlier cruelty toward her, she agreed to represent him because she was anxious to protect her people and territory from the Portuguese.

A display of power

A drawing by a Dutch artist attending the peace talks immortalized the story of Anna Nzinga in the history of Africa. A member of the negotiating team made a sketch of her sitting on the back of her kneeling maid. Determined to put on a show of strength, Nzinga had arranged her arrival at the Portuguese governor's mansion with as much pomp and circumstance as she could summon. She had to rely on a symbolic show of power, though, because her brother had already surrendered everything, leaving her little room for bargaining. Arriving at the governor's residence and escorted into the meeting room, she apparently found only one chair in the room—the governor's chair. Not wishing to be at a disadvantage, she ordered one of her female attendants to kneel down on all fours, then seated herself on the servant's back. Thus, when the governor entered the room, he found her already seated and was forced to negotiate with her as an equal.

Nzinga's negotiations with the Portuguese were quite successful. The Europeans agreed to withdraw their troops and to recognize her brother's rule of an independent Ndongo kingdom. In exchange, Nzinga agreed to release the Portuguese captives taken by her brother, to assist in the slave trade, and to help rid the area of the Jaga, who had by this time become a menace.

While in Luanda, Nzinga was baptized into the Christian faith. She took the name Dona Anna de Souza, after the name of the Portuguese governor. Politics probably motivated her acceptance of Christianity more than religion. She hoped that if European powers regarded her as a Christian, they would help her kingdom by providing European missionaries and access to Western technology. But, despite her compliance with Portuguese demands, when she returned to her brother's capital in the Cuanza River she discovered that the Portuguese had not kept their promises. Realizing that her brother did not have the courage to fight the Portuguese for the restoration of the Ndongo kingdom, she had him and his son killed. Nzinga became queen and in 1623 renewed the war with the Portuguese because they had not honored the terms of the 1622 treaty.

Challenges the Portuguese

This time Nzinga made alliances with neighboring groups and with a Jaga group, the Imbangala, from the south of the Cuanza River. She also allied her kingdom with Dutch traders who had established themselves as rivals to the Portuguese. By now the Portuguese had figured out that the mountains of Cambambe did not hold the legendary silver deposits. Still, the slave traders realized the great potential of Africa's interior as a source of slaves. The Portuguese sent a large army eastward and mounted several attacks on Nzinga's forces. They forced her to flee the capital but twice failed to capture her. Eventually the Portuguese took the capital and appointed a new ruler, Philip I. A relative of Nzinga, Philip functioned only as a puppet king, meaning his actions were controlled by an outside force—the Portuguese. Having evaded the Portuguese, Nzinga sought the assistance of the Imbangala (Jaga group) of Kasanje and conquered the Matamba in 1630. She then became the queen of the Matamba.

Nzinga immediately consolidated her allies. (The Imbangala of Kasanje, however, withdrew their support and remained neutral.) Nzinga harassed the puppet government of the Portuguese at the Ndongo capital. By 1639 she and her followers had become so much of a nuisance that the Portuguese again requested peace talks to stop the fighting. The talks did not result in any agreement, though, and the Portuguese soon found themselves fighting on three separate fronts: to the north, the Kongo king Garcia II began resisting Portuguese occupation; to the south, Nzinga's armies confronted them; and to the west, the Dutch took Luanda. As of 1641 the Portuguese held only a fortress at Masangano and the surrounding territory.

In 1648 reinforcements arrived from the Portuguese colony of Brazil, and within a short time the Portuguese regained their advantage. The Dutch fled Luanda. Without her Dutch allies and with the increasing desertion of her African allies, Nzinga was vulnerable and could not continue the siege at Masangano. Absolutely unwilling to give in, she established peace talks with the Portuguese and managed to draw them out for six years. Finally, the Portuguese forced her to recognize the puppet king Philip as the ngola and Portugal's sovereignty over the Ndongo kingdom. Nzinga, however, remained the queen of independent Matamba until her death in 1663. She was about 82 years old.

Independent till the end

A Dutch military attaché named Captain Füller accompanied Nzinga in battle against the Portuguese. According to David Sweetman in *Women Leaders in African History:*

> [Füller] describes how everyone fell to their knees and kissed the ground at her approach, a strange sight for women did not usually hold power. She was obliged to dress as a man and kept a 'harem' of young men dressed as women who were her 'wives.' Although she was advised by a council of elders, Füller makes it clear that she was the military strategist and although past sixty led her warriors herself.

As the queen of Matamba, Nzinga allowed Christian missionaries to work in her kingdom, but she never accepted Portuguese authority. She made a token gesture to the Portuguese and was rebaptized; in exchange, the Portuguese released her sister, whom they had held captive for 11 years. Sweetman noted that she abandoned her harem when she was about 75 years old and formally married one of her younger so-called wives. She also arranged for her sister, Dona Barbara, to succeed her. In anticipation of her sister's succession, she arranged Dona Barbara's marriage to the general of the army.

Even with Nzinga's sister as queen, however, the days of an independent Matamba and other African kingdoms in central Africa were limited. Once the Portuguese regained control of the territory in 1648, they would not face another challenge to their authority until 1974, when a military takeover in Portugal forced the government to withdraw its troops from its African colonies.

Further Reading

Bender, Gerald J. *Angola under the Portuguese: The Myth and the Reality.* Berkeley: University of California Press, 1978.

Curtin, Philip, and others, eds. *African History: From Earliest Times to Independence.* 2nd ed. New York: Longman, 1995.

Davidson, Basil. *Africa in History.* New York: Collier, 1974.

Murphy, E. Jefferson. *The Bantu Civilization of Southern Africa.* New York: Thomas Crowell, 1974.

Sweetman, David. *Women Leaders in African History.* Portsmouth, NH: Heinemann Educational, 1984.

Wilson, Derek. *A History of South and Central Africa.* New York/UK: Cambridge University Press, 1975.

Ben Okri

Born March 15, 1959
Minna, Nigeria

Nigerian writer

"I just knew that writing was where my own river flowed."

—Okri, commenting on his decision to become a writer

Novelist and short story writer Ben Okri uses nightmarish images and fantastic twists of reality to portray the bizarre social and political conditions inside his native Nigeria. Nigeria has the largest population of any country in Africa and earns billions of dollars annually from its off-shore oil, but it has not had a stable government for more than 30 years. The Nigeria Okri describes is dark and often violent and chaotic. Drawing on his childhood memories and imagination, he creates an atmosphere of an African village that lingers in the reader's mind. In his works such as *Incidents at the Shrine, Stars of the New Curfew,* and 1991's Booker-McConnell prizewinner *The Famished Road,* his characters become mixed up with supernatural elements to the extent that the real is indistinguishable from the imaginary. Okri insists that the supernatural is a real part of the world of Nigerians.

He was quoted as saying: "All I'm trying to do is write about the world from the world view of that place so that it is true to the characters."

Influences on his writing

Okri was born in Minna, in central Nigeria, in 1959. When he was 18 months old his parents, Silver and Grace Okri, moved to England because his father had won a scholarship to study law. Okri lived in England until he was seven and attended primary school in Peckham. After his father qualified as a lawyer, the family moved back to Nigeria. Okri claims that he said goodbye to his childhood when he left England.

Okri talks about himself with much reluctance. He prefers to discuss the influence that reading has had on his writing. His father had an extensive library that he brought back from England, and Okri read the classics not knowing they were supposed to be great literature, "but just absorbed in the stories they told."

As with many African children of his generation, storytelling was a basic component of Okri's upbringing in Nigeria. He noted in an interview for *Contemporary Authors:*

> We are a people who are massaged by fictions; we grow up in a sea of narratives and myths, the perpetual invention of stories. When I was growing up, you sat with your age mates in the evenings and the elders would come out and tell you stories, if you asked them; or your mother would tell you stories to illustrate a hundred different points, lessons, morals she wanted to get across to you. Or you'd tell stories to one another as a way of making the moonlight more intoxicating, more beautiful. You invented stories; you were encouraged to take existing stories and weave your own variation of them.

Okri's extensive reading inspired him to write stories and essays while he was in secondary school. Later he attended Urhobo College in Warri, but only for a short time. Some sources say he took a job at a paint store during the day and began writing for Nigerian newspapers and women's magazines at night.

Returns to London

Around 1977, when he was 18 years old, Okri returned to London and stayed with his uncle. He had already completed his first novel, *Flowers and Shadows.* Not long after his arrival in London, though, the urban authorities tore his uncle's house down. Okri—now homeless—was forced to lived in subway stations and on the streets. His difficulties were eased when the Nigerian government came through with a grant for him to study at the University of Essex. Longman Publishers had already agreed to publish his book.

An acquaintance of his at the time, Alan Taylor, recalled his friend's situation. He says that Okri dropped out of Essex in 1983, after two years of study:

> [He was] broke. . . . It was a tough time but he responded with *Incidents at the Shrine,* a stunning collection of short stories, which captured the glorious horror of life in Nigeria. I recall meeting him back then, when I invited him to Edinburgh to give a reading. He was lean and very hungry—you should have seen him wolf down a pizza—but with an air of self-assurance and a voice as rich as [stage and screen actor] Richard Burton's. When he spoke in public he was mesmeric.

Wins the Booker Prize

After Essex, Okri held a number of jobs. He was the poetry editor for *West Africa* from 1983 to 1986 and a broadcaster and presenter for the British Broadcasting Corporation (BBC) from 1983 to 1985. Okri's breakthrough came in 1991, when his book *The Famished Road* won the prestigious British Booker-McConnell Prize. The story's main character is Azaro, an *abiku* child torn between the spirit world and the natural world. In the Yoruba belief system, which Okri has used for his imagery, an *abiku* is a spirit-child who resists being born because of his love for the world of the unborn. Azaro struggles to free himself from the spirit realm as his father becomes increasingly involved in the political fight against poverty and oppression in Nigeria. By the end of the novel Azaro recognizes the similarities between the nation and the abiku; each is forced to make sacrifices to reach maturity and a new state of being.

Okri told *Contemporary Authors* that the role of Azaro, the spirit-child, is a natural part of his world:

> If you accept the basic premise that this kid is an abiku, a spirit-child, it's not unnatural that he would see spirits. If all the characters were to see spirits, that would be pushing it a bit, as far as Western thinking is concerned. But from this kid's point of view, it's completely

Selected Writings of Ben Okri

- ***Flowers and Shadows*** **(1980), novel.**
- ***The Landscapes Within*** **(1981), novel.**
- ***Incidents at the Shrine*** **(1986), short stories.**
- ***Stars of the New Curfew*** **(1988), short stories.**
- ***The Famished Road*** **(1991), novel.**
- ***An African Elegy*** **(1992), poetry.**
- ***Songs of Enchantment*** **(1993), novel.**
- ***Birds of Heaven*****, novel.**
- ***Astonishing the Gods*** **(1995), novel.**

> natural. . . . I'm looking at the world in *The Famished Road* from the inside of the African world view. . . . This is just the way the world is seen: the dead are not really dead, the ancestors are still part of the living community and there are innumerable gradations of reality, and so on. It's quite simple and straightforward. I'm treating it naturally. It's a kind of realism, but a realism with many more dimensions.

After publication of *The Famished Road,* Okri wrote a sequel to it, *Songs of Enchantment.* Besides his several new novels, he has returned to his first love—poetry:

> I can remember the first moment I became aware that I was going to be a writer. Things had taken a tumble in our lives. We were living in the ghetto in Lagos with my dad, and there were many kids. On a particular day, everyone else was out, and it rained. I was in the living room alone. I think it was because it was the first time in a long, long time that I was actually alone in the house, and I knew the rain would keep the others from getting home, that I took out a piece of paper and drew what was on the mantelpiece and then wrote a poem. I looked at the drawing and I looked at the poem. The drawing was not particularly good and the poem was tolerable. It was a simple decision after that. I just knew that writing was where my own river flowed more naturally.

Okri lives in London and continues to write novels and poetry. He is among the new generation of African writers who are more personal and introspective and less concerned with historical and political subjects. Okri says it has taken him a long time to be able "to write about home simply and clearly. It's because of the enormous effort it takes to actually see what's in front of you. We don't actually look at what's in front of us."

Further Reading

Contemporary Authors. Volume 138. Detroit: Gale, 1993.

Ousby, Ian. *The Cambridge Guide to Literature in English.* New York/UK: Cambridge University Press, 1993.

Taylor, Alan. "Magical Mysteries: Ben Okri—Lyrical Prose Has Entranced Readers with Images of Africa." Edinburgh Festival, August 11, 1997.

Who's Who 1997: An Annual Biographical Dictionary. A & C Black, 1997.

Alan Paton

Born January 11, 1903
Pietermaritzburg, Natal, South Africa
Died April 12, 1988
Natal, South Africa

Writer, educator, social reformer, and leader of the Liberal party

Alan Stewart Paton (*PAY-ton*) is probably best remembered as the author of *Cry, the Beloved Country,* the classic story of race relations in South Africa in the 1940s. Even 50 years after its initial publication, the book was still selling about 100,000 copies a year. *Cry, the Beloved Country* helped turn world attention toward the injustices of a government system that favored whites and turned blacks into a faceless laborers. The notoriety and income from his bestselling novel allowed Paton to leave his job as principal of a reformatory for black juveniles and turn to writing and politics. In May 1948, a few months after his book was first published, the National party of D. F. Malan won control of the South African government. As the Nationalists began enacting legislation to create its race-based society, which it called apartheid or separateness, Paton formed and headed an opposition

"I grew up with an abhorrence of authoritarianism, especially the authoritarianism of the State, and a love of liberty, especially within the State."

—Alan Paton, in *Towards the Mountain*

party called the Liberal party. In 1968 the Nationalists outlawed mixed-raced political associations. Rather than exclude its non-white members as the government demanded, the Liberal party was dissolved that same year.

In the first volume of his autobiography, *Towards the Mountain,* Paton says that the story that emerged in *Cry, the Beloved Country* was unplanned. While on a trip to Europe visiting prisons, he became homesick and jotted down a description of a small town surrounded by the hills and valleys of Natal province. "But the tenor of the following paragraphs was quite different," he claimed. "It became clear that the story was to be not so much about the beauties of the land, but about its men and women, and about the gross inequalities that so disfigured our national life."

Christian upbringing

Paton grew up in a frugal and deeply religious Christian household in the British town of Pietermaritzburg in Natal, South Africa. His parents were of Scottish and English descent. Paton's father, James, was from Glasgow, Scotland, and went to South Africa in 1901 during the Boer War (1899-1902). (The Boers were Afrikaans-speaking European farmers. The Boer War was fought by the British and the Boers for control over two of South Africa's provinces.) The elder Paton did not fight in the war because he was a member of the Christadelphians, a religious sect that did not allow its members to take up arms. Rather, he worked as a stenographer or court reporter for the Natal Supreme Court, and he occasionally wrote poems that the local newspaper published. Alan's mother, Eunice Warder James, was a schoolteacher. Her father, Thomas Warder James, had come from Bristol, England, to South Africa in 1850. He was a Methodist and worked as a wagon maker. James Paton and Eunice James were married in March 1902. Alan was born on January 11, 1903, the first of their four children.

Paton's father bullied his children, using force to make them obey him. Paton says that his father's mean-spiritedness had "two important consequences. One was that my feelings towards him were almost those of hate. The other was that I grew up with an abhorrence [hatred] of authoritarianism, especially the authoritarianism of the State, and a love of liberty, especially within the State."

Paton began his elementary schooling at the Berg Street Girls' School, which took small boys in the early classes. In 1909 he transferred to the Havelock Road Boys' School and studied there until 1913, at which point he passed exams that enabled him to attend a college-prep high school. At the age of 16 Paton entered Natal University College located in a suburb of Pietermaritzburg. Although he wanted to major in liberal arts, he enrolled in a student-teaching program because of finances. The Natal Education Department needed science and mathematics teachers, and it offered full scholarships and paid expenses for students in the education program. Paton graduated in 1923 with a degree in mathematics and physics and a diploma in education.

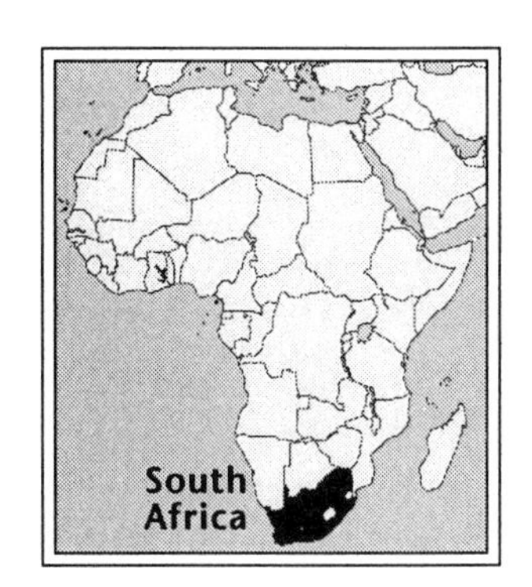

Challenging work in education

After meeting all his requirements for teaching, Paton took a trip to England in 1924 to represent Natal University College at the first Imperial Conference of Students. On his return he took a temporary teaching post at Newcastle and then went to teach at a co-ed high school in Ixopo, a small village in the center of a white farming community in Natal.

In 1925 Paton met and fell in love with Dorrie Lusted. She was married at the time to Bernard Lusted, the owner of an Ixopo garage and service station. He died of advanced tuberculosis later in 1925, and Paton and Dorrie Lusted were married in July 1928. Paton transferred from the Ixopo secondary school in 1928 to head the physics department at Pietermaritzburg College. He taught at the school for seven years while he and Dorrie raised their young son, David.

With help from a high-ranking friend in the government, Paton applied for and got one of four openings for the post of headmaster or principal of a reformatory. South African reformatories were state institutions for juvenile delinquents. The inmates ranged from 7 to 21 years of age. Paton claimed in his autobiography that he applied for the job because he was restless, ambitious, and felt that working with troubled youth would be a rewarding and challenging endeavor. In 1935 he began his work as principal of the Diepkloof Reformatory for African boys, located on farmland just outside Johannesburg, South Africa's largest city. When Paton first arrived at the reformatory, four hundred boys lived there. During the 13 years he served as principal, the number increased to nearly seven hundred.

Paton stayed at the reformatory until 1948, all the while fighting its strict authoritarian policies. Slowly he made changes, reducing the punishing aspects of Diepkloof and emphasizing learning and training opportunities for the young boys. He gave them more freedom and responsibility and taught them useful job-related skills. As his innovative program became known, officials and students from around the world visited Diepkloof. At the end of World War II (1939-45), Paton traveled abroad to study foreign prisons, reformatories, and institutions for boys and girls. His trip included visits to Britain, Sweden, the United States, and Canada, with a side trip to Norway.

While on his travels Paton began writing *Cry, the Beloved Country.* The spark for the book was an accumulation of many experiences and emotions. One specific event was the 1938 celebration of the 100th anniversary of the Great Trek. (Trekboers embarked on the "Great Trek" from the Cape Colony to land north of the Orange River, seeking freedom from British domination.) Before the celebration, Paton had admired the Afrikaner spirit and had learned to speak the language. But he realized that day that racist Afrikaner leaders (D. H. Malan and Dr. H. F. Verwoerd; see entry) had replaced their more moderate predecessors (Afrikaners like General Jan Smuts and General J.B. Hertzog). Paton claimed the celebration "was a lonely and terrible experience for any English-speaking South African who had gone there to rejoice in the Afrikaner festival."

The emergence of Adolf Hitler's (1889-45) anti-Jewish Nazi party in Germany in the 1930s forced many white South Africans to look closely at their own society. Some identified with the German movement; many others did not. Religious, political, and social leaders began looking within and demanding a restructuring of South African society. To this end the Anglican church appointed several commissions to investigate ways to improve the situation for the nation's black population. Paton sat on two of these commissions—Education and Social Welfare—for two years. He says this was "one of the seminal events of my life, after which I was never the same again. I had to open my eyes and look at South Africa as I had never looked at it before."

Selected Writings of Alan Paton

- *Cry, the Beloved Country* (1948), novel.
- *Cry, the Beloved Country* (1951), screenplay based on novel.
- *Too Late the Phalarope* (1953), novel.
- *The Land and the People of South Africa* (1955).
- *South Africa in Transition* (1956).
- *Hope for South Africa* (1959).
- *Tales from a Troubled Land* (1961; published in England as *Debbie Go Home*), short stories.
- *Hofmeyr* (1964), biography.
- *Sponono*, a play written with Krishna Shah based on three short stories from *Tales from a Troubled Land*; first produced on Broadway at Cort Theater, 1964.
- *Instrument of Thy Peace: The Prayer of St. Francis* (1968).
- *For You Departed*, (1969; published in England as *Kontakion for You Departed*).
- *Apartheid and the Archbishop: The Life and Times of Geoffrey Clayton, Archbishop of Cape Town* (1973).
- *Knocking on the Door: Alan Paton/Shorter Writings* (1975; edited by Colin Gardner).
- *Towards the Mountain: An Autobiography* (1980), first volume of autobiography.
- *Ah, But Your Land Is Beautiful!* (1981), novel.
- *Journey Continued* (1988), second volume of autobiography.

Becomes active in politics

Paton completed his book on his trip overseas, and some friends in California helped him find a publisher while he was still in the United States. The book was highly successful and was soon adapted for film (*Lost in the Stars,* 1949) and the stage.

With the economic freedom provided by the sale of the book, Paton resigned from Diepkloof to devote himself to writing and politics. In 1953 he published a second novel, *Too Late the Phalarope,* about two lovers of different races. The book was banned by South African authorities. That same year Paton became active in politics and resurrected the Liberal party of

A scene from the film Cry, the Beloved Country.

South Africa, becoming its president in 1955. The Liberal party was a multiracial party that participated in anti-apartheid protests. In 1960 Paton went to the United States to receive the Freedom Award. On his return, the South African authorities withdrew his passport for 10 years, preventing him from leaving the country.

Paton continued his writing. He published a series of short stories called *Debbie Go Home* in 1961 and *Instrument of Thy Peace* in 1968. In between he completed a biography of his friend Jan Hofmeyr. (Hofmeyr was the minister of education and finance in the Union government of Smuts. He was the friend who had helped Paton get the job as headmaster of the Diepkloof Reformatory.) In 1967 Paton's wife, Dorrie, died, leaving him with two grown sons. Two years later he married his secretary, Anne Hopkins. He continued his writing until his death from cancer in 1988, having completed the second volume of his autobiography, *Journey Continued.*

In the early years of the struggle against apartheid, Alan Paton was considered one of the most liberal (supportive of change) politicians in South Africa. But in his last years Paton was criticized by many anti-apartheid activists because he rejected the use of violence in the racial struggle and he opposed the West's establishment of an economic boycott against South Africa. The discouragement of foreign investment in South Africa, Paton argued, would unduly punish the nation's poorest blacks, and he criticized even Nobel Prize-winning clergyman Desmond Tutu (see entry) for supporting such a strategy. Though controversial, Paton saw his actions as being consistent with a lifelong belief in progress through moderation and mutual understanding. Many of his friends and allies were disappointed in his final stand, and the younger generation of blacks and many liberal whites rejected his views completely. But, regardless of the conflict, in *Cry, the Beloved Country* Paton passionately and eloquently drew attention to the plight of South African blacks just as the apartheid Nationalist government came to power.

Further Reading

Paton, Alan. *Towards the Mountain: An Autobiography.* David Philip, 1980.

Paton, Anne. *Some Sort of a Job: My Life with Alan Paton.* New York: Viking, 1992.

Prempeh I

Born 1872
Gold Coast (Ghana)
Died 1931
Kumasi, Gold Coast (Ghana)

Ashanti king

"It is I you want, take me and leave my people alone."

—Prempeh I, to British military leaders in Kumasi, January 1896

Amid late nineteenth century colonial greed and violence, King Prempeh I (*PREM-peh*) kept alive one of Africa's strongest and proudest empires, the Ashanti kingdom. (Colonialism is the extension of a nation's power beyond its own borders, usually for economic gain.) The king held his West African kingdom together despite military force, near disgrace, and exile imposed on him by British colonial authorities.

In an effort to resist British takeover of his kingdom, which was based at Kumasi in the central region of today's Ghana, Prempeh I began by using diplomatic means. When the British ignored his pleas for peace and threatened to wipe out the Ashanti people, he counseled his eager-to-fight army to avoid war in order to preserve the Ashanti nation. The Ashanti had a long, proud military history, and they were accustomed to winning wars. Only his sacred status as *asantehene,* or king of the Ashanti people, and his rank of commander in chief of the military gave Prempeh I enough authority to keep his soldiers from battling with the British at Kumasi in 1896. There was nothing more noble for an Ashanti than to die in battle—thus the Ashanti saying, "It is the coward who narrates stories of the battles."

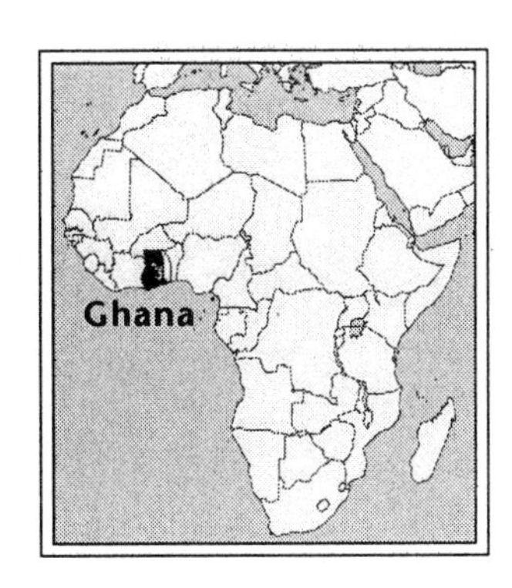

Wisdom of the king

But Prempeh I understood the odds against his people. The British military, armed with newly invented Maxim heavy machine guns, could easily destroy the kingdom that had existed for more than 200 years. He also knew the wisdom of living to fight another day in another way. "It is I you want, take me and leave my people alone," Prempeh I was quoted as saying to the leaders of the British expeditionary force that marched into Kumasi in January 1896. Among the British officers was Major Robert Baden-Powell, who would later found the Boy Scout movement. The Ashanti accused Baden-Powell of, among other things, robbing them of large buckets full of gold dust.

Prempeh tried to pacify the British by offering them 700 ounces of gold as an installment on 50,000 ounces that the British had demanded as payment more than 20 years earlier at the end of a war against the Ashanti (the war of 1874). For centuries gold had been abundant in territory controlled by the Ashanti. Shortly after the British took over the kingdom, the Ashanti Goldfields Corporation financed by English money established a gold mine near Kumasi, at the town of Obuasi. Rightfully, Obuasi earned the reputation of the "richest square mile in Africa." At the dawn of the twenty-first century, Ashanti Goldfields' deep gold mine at Obuasi remained one of the richest and most profitable in the world.

Garnet Wolseley, Britain's most celebrated general of the nineteenth century, led the 1874 expedition against the Ashanti. He described the Ashanti war as the worst of the many colonial conflicts he had fought. In the end Wolseley's force occupied, sacked (raided and robbed), and burned Kumasi, then withdrew from the Ashanti capital. The British demanded the 50,000 ounces of gold to pay for the enormous cost of Wolseley's expedition. The Ashanti ignored the claim until 1896, when Prempeh I pledged to satisfy the huge demand in installment payments if the British would again withdraw and leave his kingdom in peace.

Face down in the dust

But Prempeh's offer was not good enough for the British in 1896. Colonial officials required the Ashanti king to submit (or acknowledge British authority over his kingdom) formally in a public ceremony, humiliating himself before his people. The British forced Prempeh I to lie face down at the feet of colonial Governor William Maxwell and ask for protection from Victoria, the Queen of Great Britain and Ireland. This act brought great shame to the king. Traditionally, the asantehene's royal feet never touched the ground—they were supported by a stool wrapped in leopard skins. He dressed in elaborate silken kente cloth reserved solely for the king, carried a golden fly whisk, and wore heavy golden bracelets and necklaces. None of the lower-ranking Ashanti—not even the chiefs—could speak to him directly. Instead, they addressed a royal linguist, who then related their questions and comments to the asantehene. And when Prempeh was transported through the streets of Kumasi in a royal carriage on the shoulders of court bearers, other members of his court ran alongside holding large, colorful umbrellas over him to insure the sun never damaged his skin.

The king ruled over a nation whose emblem was the porcupine—an animal the Ashanti admired because it never gave in to aggressors until death. The asantehene was viewed as a black mamba, the most aggressive and poisonous of snakes, and was said to possess the wisdom of a parrot, regarded as the most intelligent of birds. From such a lofty position Prempeh I dropped down to lie in the dust before the British governor. Perhaps it was the respect of his people for his intelligence that led them to obey his orders not to fight the British at that time.

The British took Prempeh I, along with his relatives and Ashanti nobles and chiefs, to prison at the slave fort of Elmina, on the Atlantic Coast of present-day Ghana. A short time later they were transferred to the Seychelles Islands, located about a thousand miles off the northeast African coast in the Indian Ocean. In 1924, the British allowed Prempeh I to return home to Kumasi where his people never ceased to honor him as their asantehene.

Because of the actions taken by Prempeh I at a crucial point in European colonialism, the Ashanti people today retain much of their ancient culture. The modern Ashanti king holds a standing among his people equal to royalty anywhere in the world, includ-

Kente Cloth

At home and abroad the Ashanti's best-known product is the fabric of kings—brilliantly colored, tightly woven kente cloth. Historically, the asantehene ("Ashanti king") held copyright to kente designs. He would assign kente patterns exclusively to men and women of influence in his court. These designs became family tartans or trademarks.

Centuries ago, the Ashanti wove cloth from raffia, strips of bark from a palm tree called *kyenkyen.* This material also was used for making baskets. The Ashanti weavers called the basket cloth *kenten toma.* When the weavers substituted cotton for raffia, they named it kente. Later, as trade expanded via the Atlantic coast, the Ashanti imported silk garments, unraveled them into threads, and rewove the thread into kente cloth so expensive only royalty could afford it. When silk threads became easily available at a cheaper price, the use of kente cloth spread among the Ashanti. Using hand looms, weavers produced the cloth in 4-inch strips. The strips were then sewn together to make a larger piece of fabric. (The king, however, was entitled to a kente cloth of a special width, design, and colors reserved for him alone.)

Before the cloth became a global commodity, each kente pattern had a name and represented a clan, social status, or proverb. Sometimes symbols reminded chiefs of their responsibilities to the people and the risk of being ousted from their lofty positions if they failed to perform their duties.

Today, genuine kente cloth remains expensive, even if bought directly from the weavers.

ing the current queen of the greatly shrunken empire of Great Britain and Northern Ireland. And the asantehene's power still rests on the legendary golden stool that unified the Ashanti kingdom in the early seventeenth century.

Ashanti increase in numbers

Historians estimate that at its precolonial peak the Ashanti kingdom covered an area nearly the size of today's Ghana and had a population of about 2.2 million. By the late 1990s, as the largest ethnic group in Ghana, the Ashanti numbered about 8 million.

Prempeh I is believed to have been born in 1872, the grandson of Kwaku Dua I, the asantehene from 1834 to 1867. Kwaku Dua I's successor had been Asantehene Kofi Kakari (1837–1884), who served as Ashanti king from 1867 to 1874. Kofi Kakari's armies

Osei Tutu and the Golden Stool

Osei Tutu is said to have founded the Ashanti kingdom based on a golden stool descended from Heaven, a symbol powerful enough to sustain the nation for three centuries. At the dawn of the twenty-first century, the Ashanti numbered about 8 million. Their capital remains at Kumasi, in central Ghana, where Tutu established it around the turn of the seventeenth century. Myths and traditions created by Tutu and his chiefs endure among the Ashanti today.

Helped by a priest with extraordinary powers, Tutu united six clans. He and the priest, Okomfo Anokye (c. 1660-1712), trained a strong military and created a constitutional government that included 77 laws governing the Ashanti empire fairly. In 1923 R. S. Rattray researched Ashanti history. By that time, the legend of the golden stool had been fixed firmly in Ashanti memory. As told, Priest Anokye and Tutu called an assembly of the clans under a Kuma tree in Kumasi. The priest summoned his spiritual powers "and brought down from the sky, in a black cloud and among rumblings, and in air thick with white dust, a wooden stool with three supports and partly covered with gold." The spellbound crowd watched the stool settle on Tutu's knees, a divine sign Tutu had been chosen as the asantehene, or Ashanti king.

Rattray was told that the priest informed "Osei Tutu and all the people that the stool contained the *sunsum* (soul or spirit) of the Ashante nation, and that their power, their health, their bravery, their welfare were all in this stool." Anokye became one of the Ashanti's most influential chiefs. The priest's descendants served as diviners or fortune-tellers for the Ashanti kings.

conquered the southern Gold Coast (now the southern region of Ghana). But the Ashanti expansion provoked the anger of Great Britain, then trying to establish itself as the leading colonial power in the Gold Coast. The British sent Wolseley's expedition to Kumasi in 1874 to raid and burn Kumasi. In the wake of the destruction, Ashanti chiefs blamed Kofi Kakari for the British victory. They forced him to resign as asantehene and give up the golden stool in 1874.

A period of instability followed among Ashanti rulers until Prempeh I was anointed asantehene in 1888. At the time Prempeh I was only 16 years old. His supporters, Ashanti's most distinguished chiefs, had triumphed in a civil war over Yaw Atwereboana, a member of the royal family who claimed the throne. With the guidance of the Ashanti ruling class, Prempeh I expanded the kingdom through warfare and political alliances with other African chiefs in the North (now northern Ghana) and the Southwest (Côte d'Ivoire [Ivory Coast]). His army also was preparing to move to the East toward today's Togo.

But Prempeh I's plans for further expansion were stifled by circumstances beyond his control. At the Berlin Conference of 1885, Europe's top powers decided to divide Africa into colonies according to the simple rules of "finders, keepers." If a European country could occupy and defend the borders it carved out of an African area, the occupier was allowed to declare a protectorate over the region and, in effect, rule it as a colony. This became known as the "Scramble for Africa." As a result, the French pushed from the West (now Côte d'Ivoire) and the North (now Burkina Faso) down toward the Ashanti kingdom's capital in Kumasi. The Germans pressed in from the East (an area that is now known as Togo). And the British moved up from the southern Gold Coast (now Ghana's Atlantic coastal region). The three European powers squeezed Prempeh I's territory like a huge lobster claw.

In 1894 the British asked Prempeh I to make a deal to allow a British resident in Kumasi to oversee the kingdom. In keeping with the European practice of bribing African leaders, the British offered to pay money to the asantehene and his chiefs if they surrendered control over their kingdom. Prempeh I knew that if he gave in to the British he would be replaced by his people; on the other hand, he realized that refusing to cooperate with the British would result in a military confrontation.

Golden squeeze by the Europeans

"Ashanti must remain independent as of old, at the same time being friendly with all white men," the king stated in response to the British offer. At the same time, Prempeh I sent an Ashanti delegation (representatives) to London to negotiate a settlement with the British colonial secretary. The British, however, were concerned that the French or the Germans might beat them to the gold-rich Ashanti region. Before the Ashanti delegation reached England, Maxwell (colonial governor from 1895 to 1896) issued an ultimatum, or final demand, that Prempeh I accept a British resident; then he sent the military force to Kumasi to declare the Ashanti kingdom a British-controlled territory.

Soon the British realized that in order to administer the Kumasi area, they would need to show a greater respect for the Ashanti people and their beliefs. The Ashanti began to adapt to the new Western ways of commerce and civil service, while retaining the essence of their culture. In 1924 the British allowed Prempeh I to return to Kumasi, but only to assume the title of Kumasihene, ruler of Kumasi. The Ashanti celebrated his return as "sweet sunshine after dark clouds." Prempeh I had remained their asantehene for the 28 years he had been away. And he remained so until his death in 1931. Even then his people said: "A king of Ashanti never dies."

Further Reading

Arhin, Kwame. *Traditional Rule in Ghana, Past and Present.* Sedco Publishing Ltd., 1985.

Davidson, Basil. *Africa History, Themes and Outlines.* New rev. ed. New York: Collier Books, 1974.

Davidson, Basil, *The Black Man's Burden: Africa and the Curse of the Nation-State.* James Curry, 1992.

Dictionary of African Biography. Algonac, MI: Reference Publications, 1977.

Gunther, John. *Inside Africa.* North Pomfret, VT: Hamish Hamilton, 1955.

Hallett, Robin. *Africa since 1875.* Ann Arbor: University of Michigan Press, 1974.

Obeng, Ernest E. *Ancient Ashanti Chieftaincy.* Ghana Publishing Corporation, 1988.

Oliver, Roland. *The African Experience.* Pimlico, 1994.

Rattray, R. S. *Ashanti.* New York/UK: Oxford University Press, 1923.

Tufuo, J. W., and C. E. Donkor. *Ashantis of Ghana: People with a Soul.* Anowou Educational Publications, 1989.

Warren, Dennis M. *The Akan of Ghana.* Rev. ed. Pointer Limited, 1986.

Ranavalona I

Born c. 1788
Madagascar
Died August 16, 1861
Madagascar

Queen of Madagascar

Ranavalona I (*ran-ah-vuh-LOW-nah*) ruled over the island nation of Madagascar from 1828 until her death in 1861. Madagascar is a 1,000-mile-long island lying 250 miles off the East Coast of Africa in the Indian Ocean. At the end of her 33-year rule, Ranavalona had eliminated most foreign influence from the country and in doing so preserved the traditional culture of her people. As a result of this prolonged period of isolation, ancestral values and customs survived in Madagascar; many, in fact, were still in practice at the turn of the twenty-first century. Some historians regard her reign as the greatest period of independence the country ever knew.

Ranavalona eliminated most foreign influence from Madagascar and in doing so preserved the traditional culture of her people.

Madagascar is unique among African countries because Ranavalona kept Christian missionaries out of the country for several decades. In their absence traditional cultural practices

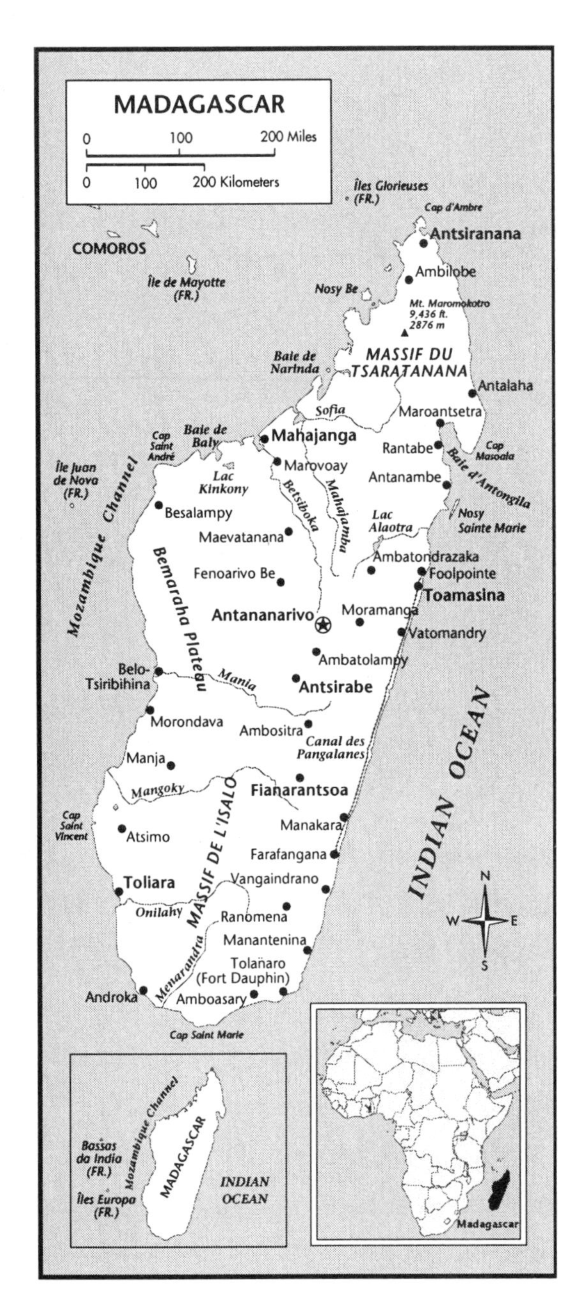

flourished. Without a doubt, the missionaries and their converts suffered badly at the hands of Ranavalona. Her treatment of them earned her the nickname "the cruel queen" or "the wicked queen." In time, however, the missionaries prevailed. In 1869 Ranavalona's daughter-in-law (her son's wife, Ranavalona II) ordered all traditional objects of worship to be burned and made Protestant Christianity the official religion of the state.

A question of politics

According to some historical observers, Ranavalona's anti-missionary policy was motivated more by political reasons than by religious ones. By 1806, more than 20 years before Ranavalona became Madagascar's queen, King Nampoina (reigned 1806-10; the name is short for Andrianampoinimerina) had unified the region's individual Merina kingdoms of the central highlands. His strong centralized state regulated the rice cultivation on which the economy was built. Public works projects were established to build and maintain the all-important irrigation systems. The central government also controlled the ritual objects—the symbols of power called the *sampy.* The people believed the *sampy* possessed the power to bring fertility to the land, increase the harvests, prevent epidemics (widespread outbreak of disease), and ensure good relations between the king and his subjects.

The ruling elite grew rich under the policies of Nampoina and his successor, Radama I (1810-28), and it sought to diminish the powers of the sampy and the authority of the ritual leaders. To weaken the authority of the traditional nobles, Radama I invited missionaries belonging to the London Missionary Society to convert the Merina people to Christianity, thereby giving the Christian court more control in

Because Ranavalona I was a widowed woman, court authorities appointed a male guardian or official consort (partner) for her. His name was Andriamihaja, and he is believed to have been the father of her only son, who would succeed her as Radama II (reigned 1861-63)

In a Man's World

the kingdom. He also established a highly organized 35,000-man army, appointed a French military sergeant as general in command, and made an Englishman his personal advisor. In 1820 Britain recognized Madagascar as an independent state. The churches set up schools and wrote down the Malagasy language. In 1835 the church printed the first version of the Bible in Malagasy. (The people of Madagascar and their language are both called Malagasy. The Malagasy people are of African and Indonesian origin, and their language is of the Malayo-Polynesian family spoken in the southern Pacific region.)

Ramavo becomes Queen Ranavalona I

In 1827 Radama I was suddenly taken ill. He came down with a serious fever and lingered on for seven months before killing himself in 1828. Radama died without designating a successor, as he had no sons to take over the throne. His first wife, 40-year-old Ramavo, schemed with certain members of the court and announced that the sampy had chosen her to succeed Radama. She became Queen Ranavalona I of Madagascar.

On taking power, Ranavalona had her husband's daughter, a nephew, and other influential people killed so that no one could threaten her position. In 1829 she canceled all treaties with Britain and France, and both countries withdrew all their traders. During her rise to power Ranavalona sought the support of the wealthy traditional families, not the Christian families of the royal court. To fulfill her obligation to her wealthy supporters, she tried to decrease the role of the missionaries in Madagascar. The most conservative (traditional) elements in society wanted to free the land of all Christian influences, but Ranavalona realized that the court needed the missionaries for their skills, especially in manufacturing.

The Christian problem

As a compromise, Ranavalona agreed to allow the missionaries to baptize people into the Christian faith if they continued to manufacture goods such as soap. She was apparently surprised and shaken when thousands of her people flocked to the missionaries for a Christian baptism. In 1835 she called the missionaries to a meeting and informed them that henceforth she would be following "the traditions of the ancestors." All religious teaching, therefore, was forbidden. All those who had been baptized were required to confess. Furthermore, all known Christians would lose their jobs or be removed from positions of authority. In response to these new policies, the missionaries left Madagascar.

Two years later, in 1837, a Christian woman named Rasalama was publicly executed—speared to death because she refused to deny her faith. She became the country's first Christian martyr (one who is willing to die for belief in a cause) and served to strengthen Christian resistance in Madagascar. Hundreds of other believers followed her example, and when they refused to deny their faith they were thrown to their deaths from a high cliff overlooking the rice paddies.

Rather than ease up on the Christians, Ranavalona became even more conservative in ensuing years and announced that she was restoring the old methods of execution and trial by *tangena. Tangena* is a nut that causes vomiting. Traditional practitioners used it to determine a person's guilt or innocence. A person on trial would be given some of the nut to eat along with three pieces of chicken skin. If the person vomited all three pieces of skin, he or she was considered innocent. If fewer than three pieces were vomited, the person was found guilty and either put to death or enslaved. Rather than subject themselves to this ordeal, many people fled to the South and became outlaws.

Selected foreign influence

But not all foreigners left Madagascar. Several Europeans had gained favor with the queen, and they rewarded her for their special status. Prominent among them was Napoléon de Lastelle, who had arrived on the island back in 1829. He operated a sugar plantation and shared his rum-production profits with the queen and the ruling elite. The other European of note was Jean-Baptiste

A group of Malagasy people, around 1864.

Laborde, the 25-year-old son of a blacksmith and an escaped convict, who was shipwrecked off the coast of Madagascar in 1831. He became acquainted with the queen through de Lastelle. Laborde was an exceptionally clever man and began what author David Sweetman calls a "one-man revolution."

In the absence of the French and British traders, the kingdom was soon in desperate need of manufactured goods. In 1835 Laborde set up a factory complex, including an iron foundry, at Mantasao, about 50 miles from the capital of Antananarivo. There he manufactured muskets and gunpowder. Using only local resources, he produced many items the kingdom could no longer obtain from foreign suppliers—goods like porcelain, silk, soap, cement, and candles. At the time of peak production, he is said to have employed about 1,200 people in his factories and on his experimental farm. Laborde also built the queen's palace, which stood on the highest hill of Antananarivo until fire destroyed it in 1995.

With local production of many goods formerly imported, Ranavalona felt confident enough to take an uncompromising stand against the remaining traders in Madagascar. She told them they would have to submit to Malagasy law, which meant they would have to perform compulsory labor on the irrigation projects. Rather than agree to these conditions, the foreigners left, and in revenge the French and British bombed the port city of Tamatave in 1845. This officially ended all foreign contacts with Madagascar.

The end of an era

In the absence of the Protestant British missionaries, the French Catholic church on Réunion (an island located east of Madagascar) saw an opportunity to influence the court. And Laborde became a significant source of influence on the queen's son and heir, Prince Rakoto. He exposed the prince to the ideas and events that were shaping the outside world and instilled a sense of curiosity in the young man. With Laborde as his guide, the prince developed a decidedly European perspective. When the queen agreed to a visit by a French shipowner named Lambert and his companion in 1855, Rakoto conspired with them to remove her from power. After finding out about the conspiracy in 1857, she refused to believe her son was involved. Instead, she blamed the foreigners and expelled Laborde, de Lastelle, and Lambert from Madagascar. Without Laborde, the government could not manage the factories. The workers did not get paid, and in retaliation they destroyed the foundry, the factories, the machinery, and all the tools.

By this time Ranavalona was growing old, but she continued to rule for a few more years. She would not accept the fact that her son stood for everything she had opposed during her reign. On her death in 1861, Prince Rakoto became King Radama II. He reversed all of his mother's political alliances and invited the exiled missionaries and Frenchmen to return to Madagascar. Radama II ruled for only two years before high officials in the government ordered his assassination. Ranavalona's fear of outside influences was justified when, in 1896, the French conquered the country and ended the monarchy. French officials sent the then-reigning queen, Ranavalona III (reigned 1883-97), into exile in Algeria, where she died in 1938.

Further Reading

Bradt, Hilary. *Guide to Madagascar.* Bradt Publications, 1988.

Curtin, Philip, and others, eds. *African History: From Earliest Times to Independence.* 2nd ed. New York: Longman, 1995.

Mack, John. *Madagascar: Island of the Ancestors.* British Museums Publications, 1986.

Makers of Modern Africa: Profiles in History. 3rd ed. Africa Books, 1996.

Sweetman, David. *Women Leaders in African History.* Portsmouth, NH: Heinemann Educational, 1984.

Olufunmilayo Ransome-Kuti

Born October 25, 1900
Abeokuta, Nigeria
Died April 13, 1978
Lagos, Nigeria

Nigerian women's rights leader, educator, politician

"[Being] unwanted in the political circle then largely dominated by men, . . . I decided I would fight to force a change of attitude towards women [in Nigeria]."

—Ransome-Kuti, on her efforts to advance the cause of women's rights in Nigeria after World War II

A champion of women's rights, Olufunmilayo (or Funmilayo) Ransome-Kuti fought British colonial rule and a series of military dictators after her native Nigeria gained independence in 1960. (Colonialism is a nation's control of a territory that lies beyond its own borders—in this case, Britain's control over Nigeria.) She pushed her way into Nigeria's previously male-only political arena and campaigned for socialism, a political and economic system based on government control of the production and distribution of goods. (Socialists champion the removal of private property in a quest to attain a classless society.) She also raised four children who became leading medical, musical, and human rights figures in Nigeria—including the flamboyant international Afro-Beat star Fela Kuti (1938-97; see entry).

Learned rebellion early

Ransome-Kuti was born to Chief Thomas and his wife on October 25, 1900, in Abeokuta, a town about 30 miles northwest of Lagos, the country's former capital. At the turn of the twentieth century the area was ruled by the independent Egba United Government, which was modeled on the British system. Abeokuta had a proud, peculiar history that seemed to influence Ransome-Kuti's strong-willed actions. The town was settled around 1830 by Yoruba people of the Egba clan. Among the early settlers were Yoruba rescued by British warships from slave vessels sailing to the Americas. Britain's Royal Navy returned the Yoruba as free Africans to British-sponsored Sierra Leone on the West African coast. Strongly influenced by Christian missionaries and educators, these Egba made their way back home and settled in what is today's southwestern Nigeria.

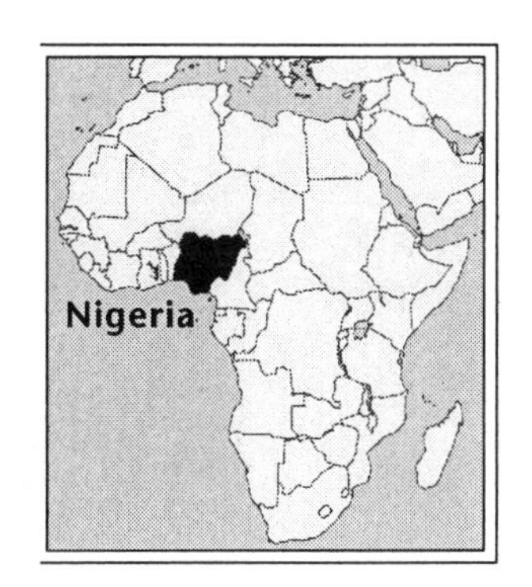

In the 1860s the Christian-educated elite and Yoruba chiefs came together to set up an autonomous (self-ruling and self-sufficient) government that served the interests of the Egba people as a whole. According to Karl Maier in *Into the House of the Ancestors,* this mix "of African and Western ideas, Christianity and traditional Yoruba religion . . . had carried Abeokuta and its favorite sons to the forefront of the anticolonial struggle. For many historians, that moment marked the beginning of West African political thought of the modern, post-colonial era."

When Frederick Lugard became British governor in Lagos in 1912, he frowned on Abeokuta's independence. Still, he was unable to bring Abeokuta under the degree of British colonial rule imposed in other Yoruba areas—the town's independence had been guaranteed by an 1893 treaty signed by the British. In 1914 Lugard finally found an excuse to send British troops into Abeokuta. He sought to put down demonstrations by the Egba United Government against civil rights violations. The troops fired on demonstrators, massacring a large number of protesters. When Lugard imposed British rule on the region, the Egba rebelled in 1918, tearing up railway lines and stations. The British rushed in 1,000 more troops to put down the uprising. More than 500 Egba rebels were killed before the British triumphed.

Model for her sons

Ransome-Kuti was a teenager during this turbulent, bloody chapter in Nigeria's history. She attended the Anglican Church

Much-Honored Woman

Ransome-Kuti had the distinction of becoming one of the first women chiefs in Nigeria. She was also the recipient of two prominent awards: 1) an honorary doctorate of laws degree from Nigeria's top institution of higher learning, the University of Ibadan, and 2) the Lenin Peace Prize from the former Soviet Union.

Primary School in Abeokuta and Abeokuta Girls' Grammar School before heading to Manchester, England, in 1920 to study domestic science and music at Wincham Hall College. Having qualified to work as a teacher in England, she returned home in 1923 to teach at Abeokuta Girls' Grammar School. Soon after, she married the Reverend Josiah Ransome-Kuti, a prominent Anglican church leader and educator from Abeokuta.

Ransome-Kuti and her husband had four children: Afro-Beat creator and activist Fela Kuti; Dolupo Ransome-Kuti, a nurse; Dr. Olikoye Ransome-Kuti, a pediatrician; and Dr. Beko Ransome-Kuti, a general physician. The sons followed in their mother's footsteps in opposing authoritarian rule. Through his music Fela berated Nigeria's military rulers for their corrupt and oppressive ways. Nigeria's dictatorial governments continually harassed and repeatedly jailed Fela and Beko for their unabashedly outspoken criticism. Even now, Beko and Olikoye (the two doctors) support democratic rule (government by the people) in Nigeria and strongly oppose human rights violations committed by the series of military governments that have ruled Nigeria on and off for more than two and a half decades. (Nigeria achieved independence in 1960, but its brief experiments in civilian [or nonmilitary] government control have failed.)

Growing political activism

Ransome-Kuti first entered the political arena in the 1940s by setting up a Ladies' Club for educated women. The club later branched out to organize market women and provide adult education for them. Eventually the two groups merged into the Egba Women's Union. During World War II (1939-45) the Women's Union protested food regulations imposed by the British-appointed Oba Ademola II, who held the position of *alake* ("king" in Yoruba language). The women accused the king of abuse of

Others well-known Nigerians who hail from Abeokuta include author-activist Wole Soyinka (1934—; see entry), the only black African to win the Nobel Prize for Literature, and Olusegun Obasanjo (1937—), a Nigerian army general and military head of state. Ironically, Ransome-Kuti would later encounter violent—some would say deadly—repressive action at the hands of Obasanjo's government.

In the Company of Leaders

power, protested taxes and discriminatory wages, and demanded the right to vote. With Ransome-Kuti at the helm, the Abeokuta women's campaign forced the British to send the alake to the distant town of Oshogbo in 1948 in order to maintain peace. The market women won major tax relief.

Prominence in a male-dominated circle

As the post-World War II movement for independence gained momentum, Ransome-Kuti joined in the fight. She became a member of the National Council of Nigerian Citizens, which at the time was Nigeria's major African political party. (It was headed by Dr. Nnamdi Azikiwe [1904-96; see entry].) Ransome-Kuti rose to positions of prominence within the party and was the only woman to attend a 1947 constitutional conference called by the British in London. She lashed out against both British colonialism and Nigerian male chauvinism (discrimination against women). As quoted in *Makers of Modern Africa: Profiles in History,* she found herself "unwanted in the political circle then largely dominated by men. . . . This made me unhappy and I decided I would fight to force a change of attitude towards women."

Ransome-Kuti said she also joined Azikiwe's party because she judged it to be "more liberal" (more supportive of change) than the others. But the party wasn't quite liberal enough for her. Widowed in 1955, Ransome-Kuti journeyed to the Soviet Union, which bestowed honors on her, and to China, where she met Communist party leader Mao Tse-tung. When she returned home, Nigerian authorities seized her passport. Ransome-Kuti also sent her son Fela on vacation to East Berlin, East Germany (now Germany), to expose him to socialist ideas. "She turned Communist Party member," Fela said in a 1986 radio interview. "She was the sixth vice president of the Women's International Democratic Federation in Russia."

Ransome-Kuti, behind the center of the table, speaks to the Abeokuta Women's Union at a meeting in the 1940s.

A tragic end

Ransome-Kuti lived to see women gain the right to vote in Nigeria at independence, but not to see the end of dictatorship in her country. On February 18, 1977, General Obasanjo's troops surrounded Fela's compound in a Lagos suburb. Fela had put up an electric fence around his nightclub and residence, The Shrine, and declared the compound the independent state of Kalakuta Republic. The soldiers raided the compound, burned down the house, beat Fela and others found inside, and tossed Ransome-Kuti out a second-floor window. Maier quoted Beko's recollection of the incident:

> They attacked the house, and they threw my mother out of the window. She broke her leg. She just never recovered from it. She could not eat or drink. They had to put her on [intravenous] drips and so on for months. I think probably what might have affected her was the fact that after all her hopes to achieve independence the country could degenerate to such a point where people might just come, surround your house, set it on fire, and throw you out the window.

Unable to regain her strength and recover from her injuries, Ransome-Kuti died April 13, 1978.

Further Reading

Crowder, Michael. *The Story of Nigeria.* Winchester, MA: Faber, 1978.

Johnson-Odin, Cheryl. *For Women and the Nation: Funmilayo Ransome-Kuti of Nigeria.* University of Illinois Press, 1997.

Maier, Karl. *Into the House of the Ancestors.* New York: John Wiley & Sons, 1998.

Makers of Modern Africa: Profiles in History. 3rd. ed. Africa Books, 1996.

Additional information for this entry was taken from a WUSB 90.1 FM (Stony Brook, NY) radio broadcast featuring Lister Hewan-Lowe, June 21, 1986.

Jerry Rawlings

Born June 22, 1947
Accra, Gold Coast (Ghana)

President of Ghana

Rawlings emerged as a spokesperson for the nation's common people.

Jerry Rawlings has been a key figure in Ghanaian politics since the late 1970s, when he led a military overthrow of the nation's ruling government. In November 1992 he won Ghana's first multiparty presidential election in 11 years by a large margin. Rawlings has found himself at the center of political controversy over the years due to his extremely tight grasp on the reins of power in Ghana. Opposition leaders accuse him of making every effort to curb democracy (government by the people) and freedom of speech throughout the country. But his supporters claim that he has steered Ghana's economy in the right direction, decreased poverty and debt, and successfully led local efforts to feed and educate the nation's people.

The West African nation of Ghana is situated on the Gulf of Guinea along Africa's Atlantic Coast. Before achieving independence from Great Britain in 1957, Ghana was known as the Gold Coast. As the first sub-Saharan (south of the Sahara desert region) African nation to become independent after World War II (1939-45), Ghana was held up as the model for the continent's future independent states. It had achieved freedom without a war and had developed a solid economic foundation based in gold and cocoa trade. It also had an educated, professional class ready to take over government operations. But nine years after independence, Ghana's stability began to crumble. Excessive government spending, corruption within the nation's ruling political party, and repression of opposition parties (political parties that disagreed with the ruling party's philosophy) led to unrest and violence among Ghana's people. In 1966 the country's first president, Kwame Nkrumah (see entry), was removed from office in a military coup (the overthrow of an existing government). Throughout the rest of the 1960s and into the early 1980s, Ghana experienced frequent changes in government; a series of civilian (nonmilitary) and military regimes took turns seizing—and later losing—power through coups.

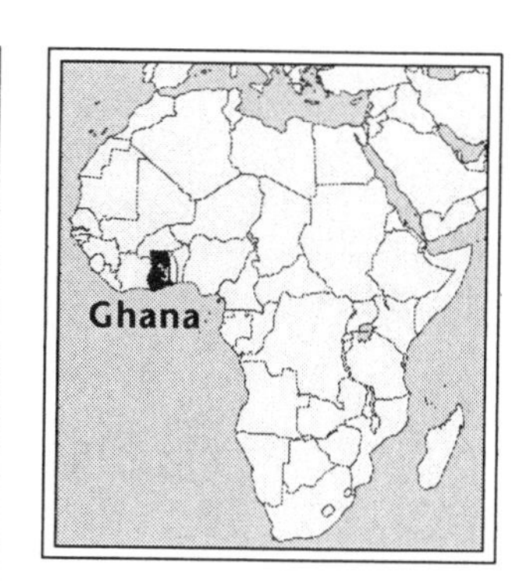

Joins the air force

Rawlings was born in Accra, the country's capital, on June 22, 1947. His name at birth was Jerry Rawlings John. Little is known about his family background, except that Rawlings is of mixed racial heritage—his mother, Victoria Abbotoi, was a Ghanaian of the Ewe ethnic group, and his father was from Scotland. Rawlings's father and mother never wed because his father was already married to another woman. Initially baptized as a Christian by the Bremen Mission, Rawlings later joined the Roman Catholic church. Though sometimes jokingly described as "a rusty white man" because of his European facial features, he has never lost touch with his black African ancestry and remains popular with the Accra-based Ewe people in Ghana.

Rawlings's mother raised him by herself, and she knew the value of a good education. She managed to raise enough money to send her son to the prestigious Achimota secondary school. At Achimota, he earned the equivalent of a high school diploma in 1966.

After a year on his own, Rawlings enlisted as a flight cadet at Takoradi Air Force Station. He claims that on his application he wrote his name—Jerry Rawlings John—out in full, but a secretary apparently recorded "Rawlings," not "John," as his last name. Rawlings never corrected the error and has used the name Jerry Rawlings ever since. Qualifying for flight training school, he was commissioned as a pilot officer in 1969, then promoted to flight officer and later to flight lieutenant. In 1969 he won the Speed Bird Trophy for being the best cadet in flying and airmanship. He married a high school friend, Nana Konadu Agyeman, in 1977. They have two daughters.

Jailed for speaking out

All these accomplishments came during a period of relative prosperity in Ghana. As the 1970s progressed, however, Rawlings and other young military officers began to lose faith in their government. Corruption was suspected in the government's highest ranks, and the Ghanaian economy was declining rapidly. When the ruling military regime of General Frederick Akuffo legalized political parties in early 1979, Rawlings emerged as a spokesperson for the nation's common people. He quickly earned a wide following—especially among the poor and the lower ranks of the military.

Rawlings and some of his fellow air force officers made their first major antigovernment move in May 1979, seizing weapons from the military's supply warehouse to force their senior officers to meet their demands. Overpowered and forced to surrender, Rawlings and the other officers went to jail. The government decided to make an example of the men and tried them in public. At his court hearing, Rawlings's lawyer openly criticized the ruling government. Rawlings emerged from the trial as a folk hero to the military's ordinary soldiers.

Rawlings did not stay in prison long. On June 4 his supporters helped him escape. Rawlings went immediately to the local radio station and broadcast an appeal to his supporters to take control of Ghana's government. He announced the formation of an Armed Forces Revolutionary Council to replace Akuffo. He also promised that the council would return the country to civilian (nonmilitary) rule as soon as it could hold general elections. Some units in the armed forces remained loyal to their commanding officers and resisted the overthrow, but within 24 hours Rawlings and his men had effectively taken control of the government.

A second coup

The 1979 coup was not bloodless. Several generals and other senior officers were charged with corruption, convicted, and then executed. Rawlings, however, kept his promise to turn power over to a civilian government. The government held elections in September 1979, and Dr. Hilla Limann won the presidency. Rawlings returned to the military and his duties as a flight lieutenant.

Within a short time, however, tension grew between Rawlings and the Limann administration. As the Ghanaian economy continued deteriorating, Rawlings put more and more pressure on the government, declaring himself guardian of the people's "revolution" he had initiated in June 1979. In response, the Limann administration forced Rawlings to resign his military post. He was kept under the watchful eye of the Ghanaian government because officials feared he was planning another coup.

Convinced that the new civilian rulers would not be able to reverse Ghana's declining standard of living, Rawlings did stage another coup—this one on December 31, 1981. This time Rawlings abolished the nation's existing constitution, dissolved parliament, and outlawed the formation and operation of opposition parties. He also founded and led a Provisional National Defence Council (PNDC) to serve as the country's only political party. Rawlings seems to have viewed the PNDC not as a military dictatorship (a form of government in which absolute power is held by a single, and often oppressive, ruler), but rather as a stable alliance of civilians and soldiers who would help return prosperity to Ghana before allowing multiparty elections.

Rawlings did his best to reverse Ghana's staggering inflation and drastic declines in public school enrollment. When the former Soviet Union failed to give him assistance, he looked to the West (the United States and Western European countries) for help.

Many of the economic measures Rawlings put in place were unpopular, and the PNDC faced repeated coup attempts and growing domestic unrest. Between 1983 and 1987 the PNDC was challenged by opposition groups inside and outside the country. Opposition came mainly from the military, where factions (groups) based on tribal affiliation had formed. Students also protested against the government's seeming inability to turn the economy around and its international relations with Libya and Cuba.

Rawlings strolls through the White House with President Bill Clinton, 1995.

The PNDC's preoccupation with security led to the detention (holding in custody or under guard) of members of the political opposition and the execution of more than one person convicted of conspiring to overthrow the government. Ghanaian citizens outside the country brought the PNDC's violent tactics to the attention of Amnesty International, a human rights group, which in turn publicized the plight of political prisoners in Ghana.

Rawlings continued to head a one-party state, but he did provide for district assembly elections in 1988, allowing regional government bodies to help people solve their problems at a local, grass-roots level. While some observers hailed this step as the first in a trend toward multiparty politics in Ghana, others complained that all the assembly candidates were subsidized (or partially funded) by—and therefore sympathetic to—the PNDC.

Moves to multiparty system

Responding to demands for a more open society in the 1990s, Rawlings formed the National Commission for Democracy

(NCD). He asked the commission to hold regional debates to get a feel for what changes the people wanted. Once done, they could figure out how to make the transition to multiparty democracy. Although opposition groups complained that the NCD was too closely associated with the PNDC, the commission continued its work through 1991. In March of that year the NCD recommended elections for the office of president, the establishment of a national assembly (a body of lawmakers), and creation of the post of prime minister (the head of the president's advisers). The PNDC agreed, and the next year the government legalized political parties—with the provision that none could use titles that had been used before—and set a timetable for presidential elections.

Rawlings retired from the armed forces and stood as a civilian, or nonmilitary, candidate for the National Democratic Congress, the successor party to the PNDC. Although his opponents had access to television and newspaper coverage—and the government had lifted its restrictions on the press—no single candidate could match the popularity of Rawlings. Election returns on November 3, 1992, gave him 58.3 percent of the vote, a landslide victory. Foreign observers declared the voting to be "free and fair." Almost immediately, however, the leaders of the country's opposition parties claimed that the election had been rigged and that widespread abuses had occurred at the polls. The leaders encouraged their followers to boycott (refuse to get involved with in any way) subsequent parliamentary elections. As a result the National Democratic Congress candidates won 189 of 200 seats in the new parliament. This gave Rawlings a four-year term and nearly an entire assembly filled with his party's supporters.

In the 1996 elections Rawlings's appeal to the voters—particularly the rural voters—remained strong, but he and his party lost in most of the major cities. Nevertheless, 70 percent of Ghana's people live in rural areas, so Rawlings and his party easily retained their majority in parliament. Outside election observers claimed this election was, indeed, free and fair. In January 1997 Rawlings was again sworn in as president of Ghana.

Further Reading

Contemporary Black Biography. Volume 9. Detroit: Gale, 199 .

Rake, Alan. *Who's Who in Africa: Leaders for the 1990s.* Metuchen, NJ: Scarecrow Press, 1992.

Shillington, Kevin. *Ghana and the Rawlings Factor.* New York: Macmillan, 1992.

Léopold Sédar Senghor

Born October 9, 1906
Joal, Senegal

Senegalese poet and politician

Senghor "is as African as he is European, as much a poet as a politician, . . . as much a revolutionary as a traditionalist."

—Jacques Louis Hymans, in *Léopold Sédar Senghor: An Intellectual Biography*

Léopold Sédar Senghor will be remembered for his wide-ranging contributions to world literature and African politics. He was the first president of independent Senegal in French West Africa. He was also the first black member of the prestigious Académie Française, a 300-year-old organization honoring the most respected French-speaking intellectuals. According to Jacques Louis Hymans in *Léopold Sédar Senghor: An Intellectual Biography,* Senghor is responsible for "setting in motion a whole series of African ideological movements." Commenting on Senghor's ability to embrace clashing views and cultures, Hymans noted, "He is as African as he is European, as much a poet as a politician, . . . as much a revolutionary as a traditionalist."

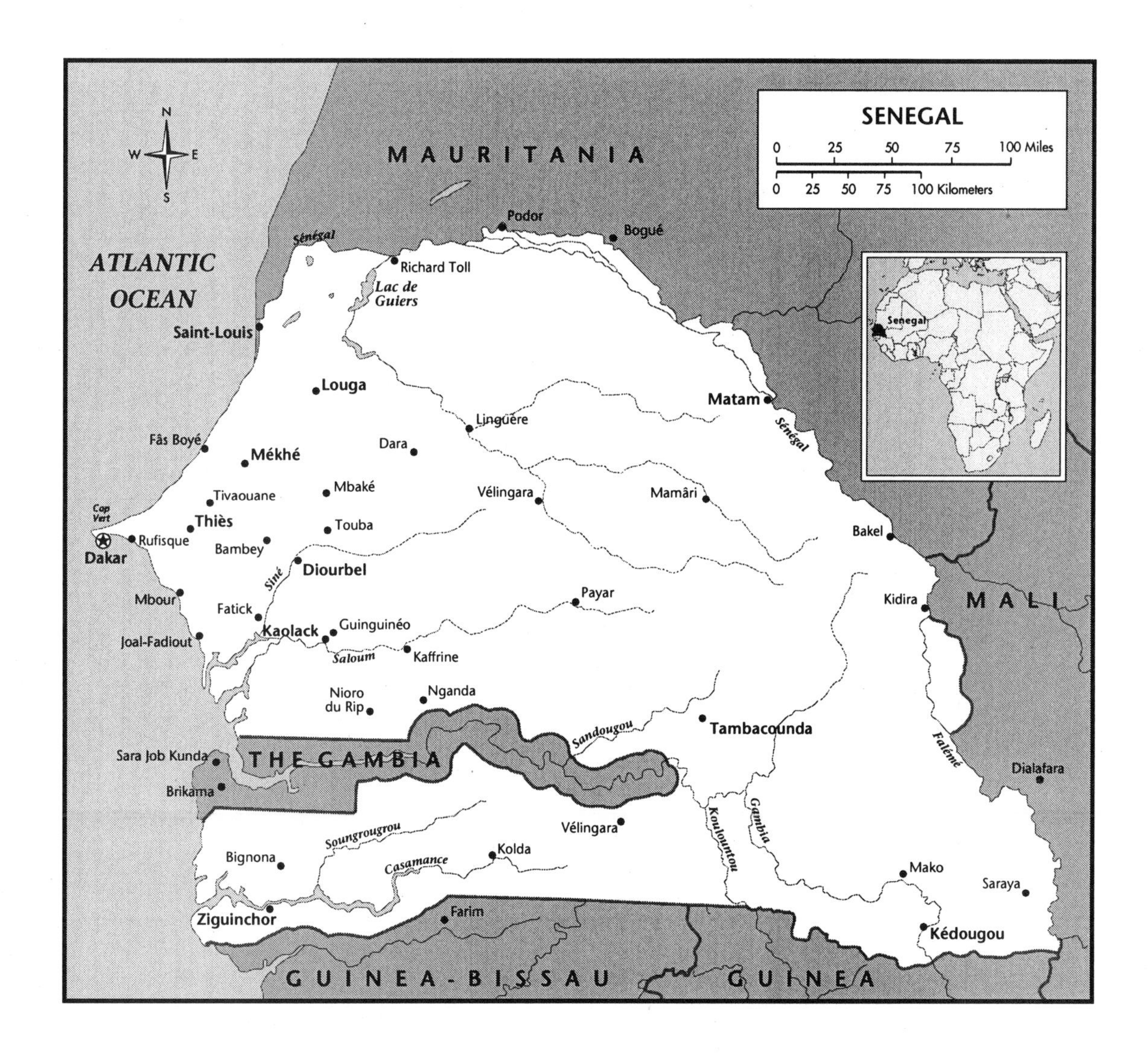

Born at the height of French influence in Senegal

Senghor was born in French-controlled Senegal on October 9, 1906. Of the French possessions in West Africa, Senegal was the most closely aligned with France. Since the 1800s, citizens of the major cities in Senegal had been given a form of French citizenship and were represented in the French national assembly. Senghor's father was a wealthy trader, supplying agricultural products to the French. The elder Senghor sent his young son to the Catholic Mission school so that he might learn the ways of Europe, tearing him, as Senghor says, "away from the mother tongue, from the ancestor's skull, from the tom-tom of My soul."

Senghor claimed that his first seven years were the only happy ones of his early life, until he rediscovered traditional Africa in books and formulated his theory of negritude, a celebration of African heritage. The mid-twentieth century negritude movement had an impact on black consciousness and culture throughout the world. Throughout his life, Senghor longed for the happiness of his childhood, which he says kept him innocent of Europe.

Described by his brother as a bookworm, Senghor worked hard to be a successful student. He was endowed with a superb memory and a lively intelligence, but he was not by nature outgoing. At the age of 13, Senghor felt he had been called to the religious life and began preparing for Catholic priesthood. In 1922 in Dakar, the administrative center of French West Africa, he entered the seminary and immersed himself in the study of Catholic theology and philosophy. Although he believed firmly in his calling to the church, his African pride made him protest against the racism of the seminary's head priest, who one day called Senghor's parents "primitives" and "savages."

Asked to leave the seminary in 1926, the adolescent Senghor entered the public secondary school in Dakar, earning his high school degree with honors in 1928. His classical languages teacher persuaded the colonial administration to grant Senghor a scholarship to do what no African had ever done before: pursue literary studies in France.

The quest for negritude

The trip to Paris made Senghor feel he had been uprooted a second time. While there, he boarded at the Parisian Lycée Louis-le-Grand, where French students prepared for the stiff entrance exams to France's most exclusive graduate schools. His closest friend was Georges Pompidou (1911-1974), who later became director of the Rothschild Bank, prime minister of France under Charles de Gaulle (1890-1970), and then president of France in 1969.

The French University completed Senghor's "Frenchification." For a time his greatest ambition was to become a "black-skinned Frenchman," but it was not long before he modified his goals. He reacted against cultural integration (blending different groups of people together as equals in one society) and began to search for his Africanness—his "negritude," as he put it. Senghor married Colette Hubert and they had three sons.

Paris was a center of artistic growth in the 1930s, and its people began a love affair with black culture and its influence—especially as captured in the rhythms of jazz music, the outrageousness of black entertainer Josephine Baker, and the beauty of African art. This trend, along with a popular colonial exhibition in the Parc de Vincennes, reawakened Senghor's long-suppressed love of Africa. He began to study the works of leading anthropologists (social scientists who study human beings in their many environments and relationships) and contemporary artists. Senghor also read works produced by black Americans of the Harlem Renaissance, a period of literary and artistic awakening among blacks in New York City in the 1920s. Artists of the Harlem Renaissance called themselves "New Negroes" and included such figures as Langston Hughes (1902-1967), Countee Cullen (1903-1946) and Jean Toomer (1894-1967), among others.

The Earth's eldest sons

Because American blacks so captivated him, Senghor at first followed their lead in flatly rejecting the integration of black and white cultures, although he advocated political integration and civil rights advancements. Relying on the work of anthropologists and prehistorians, he proclaimed that people of African descent were the "eldest sons of the Earth." He maintained that Africans had dominated the world up to and including the Neolithic Period (8000-3500 B.C. E.) and had populated the regions of the Nile and the Euphrates (rivers flowing through Egypt and Syria and Iraq, respectively). These same strong and innovative African peoples later became "the innocent victims of white barbarians," according to Senghor. He pleaded that the "protecting spirits" not let his blood "fade" like that of an "assimilated person, like that of a civilized man." (To be assimilated is to have absorbed the culture of the mainstream population.)

But the year 1936 marked a turning point in Senghor's life. The invasion of Ethiopia in 1935 by Italian Fascist leader Benito Mussolini (1883-1945) shocked him into an awareness of the perils of racial hatred. (Fascism is a highly centralized, military-based system of government characterized by rigid one-party rule and repression of all political opposition). Ethiopia was dominated by Mussolini's racist regime for six years before regaining its independence in 1941.) Senghor made a conscious decision to open his heart and broaden his views. He forgave "the white hands that fired the shots which brought the empires crumbling down, the hands that flogged the slaves." He appealed to God to forgive "those who have hunted my children like wild elephants, and broken them in with whips." Senghor forgave the Europeans because he had envisioned a new universal culture. In this culture Western civilization would recognize its debt to African music and sculpture, and black civilization would assimilate European technological tools to hasten African progress. "New York! I say New York! let the black blood flow into your blood so that it might unrust your steel joints, as a life-giving oil." It had to be a two-way street.

Eurafrica

By the late 1940s Senghor had made his mark in both the literary and political arenas. His call for the creation of a political union of blacks and whites—he called it Eurafrica—coincided with the acclaim he gained for his groundbreaking *Anthology of the New Black and Malagasy Poetry in the French Language.* The publication of this collection of poetry brought international recognition to black poets writing in the French language. It also boosted Senghor's visibility on the political front, reinforced his concept of negritude, and advanced his goal of forming a truly "united" society, free of racial distinctions.

Back in 1945, Senghor had been elected a member of the French parliament representing Senegal. Growing worldwide opinion against colonialism enabled Senghor and other Africans to push through generous reforms, including full French citizenship for all Africans in France's overseas territories. But Senghor was not a strong advocate of independence for Senegal. He was more concerned with advancing his people's civil rights. Until 1956, he advocated a new political federation linking Africa and France as equal partners. Nationalism (the push for independence) for Senghor was an "outdated weapon . . . an old hunting gun." He wanted to replace nationalism with a multiethnic, continent-wide union of equal states. Senghor became the model for Eurafrican leadership when the French invited him to assume a cabinet-level post in the government in 1955.

By the next year or so, however, Senghor's political philosophy had changed. His thinking was transformed by both the growth of independence movements in Africa and the insistent demands of the younger generation of Senegalese whom he had brought into his political party, the Bloc Populaire Sénégâlais (BPS). As the party absorbed other groups, it became known as the Union Progressiste Sénégâlaise (UPS). As a member of the committee charged with drawing up a new Senegalese constitution in 1958, Senghor advocated an independent African federation, grouping all of France's former colonies together. This would create a vast and powerful African nation linked loosely to France in a French Community of Nations.

President of an independent nation

Senghor's contemporary and rival—Félix Houphouët-Boigny (see entry), leader of the French territory of the Ivory Coast (Côte d'Ivoire) and also a member of the constitutional committee—opposed any African federation. Houphouët-Boigny exerted a strong influence on the African leaders in other French-held territories. They, in turn, adopted his point of view on independence. Sékou Touré (see entry), the leader of the French territory of Guinea, decided to withdraw from any French grouping. In September 1958 Guinea became the second European colony in sub-Saharan Africa (Ghana was the first) to achieve independence. Senghor tried to keep the rest of France's African territories in a federal union, but he failed. In September 1960 he agreed to become the first president of independent Senegal, a nation of 5 million people.

According to the independence constitution, Senghor and his prime minister, Mamaduo Dia, governed a parliamentary democracy, in which an elected assembly represents the people's interests. In 1962 Mamaduo Dia tried to overthrow Senghor. Authorities stopped the coup attempt, arrested Mamaduo Dia, and put him in prison. From this experience, Senghor realized how threatening the post of prime minister could be. (A prime minister is the head of the parliamentary assembly and the president's chief adviser.) The president pushed through a new constitution, one that eliminated the prime minister's post. In addition, all opposition parties were outlawed; existing parties could either join Senghor's party or be declared illegal. As a result, Senegal's Communist Parti

Senghor being received at the French Academy of Moral Sciences in Paris, wearing the uniform of the academicians, 1969.

Africain de l'Independence (PAI) began operating secretly. Senghor later restored the office of prime minister, but he appointed his own candidate to the post.

Senegal remained a one-party state until 1974, when Senghor allowed the formation of a multiparty system of government. Authorities released Mamaduo Dia and other political prisoners from custody. Senghor fell victim to political competition in the face of Senegal's deteriorating economic conditions. The dramatic fall in the price of groundnuts (peanuts) in the world market brought economic hardships to Senegalese farmers. Groundnuts are Senegal's chief crop. Urban workers, educators, and students were all unhappy with the country's poor economic situation. Senghor's party was able to win the 1978 elections, but the voter turnout was low. In December 1980 Senghor announced that he was retiring from office. The next month Abdou Diouf replaced him as president of Senegal.

Throughout the 1980s and 1990s Senghor continued to write. In 1984 the Académie Française, France's most honored assembly of intellectual leaders, elected him a member of a special group known as the "Immortals." Senghor sought to build a new world of interracial, intercontinental union. His poetry echoes this lifelong goal and stands as an enduring symbol for future generations to follow.

Further Reading

Contemporary Literary Criticism. Volume 54. Detroit: Gale, 1989.

Hallett, Robin. *Africa since 1875.* Ann Arbor: University of Michigan Press, 1974.

Historic World Leaders. Edited by Anne Commire. Detroit: Gale, 1994.

Hymans, Jacques Louis. *Léopold Sédar Senghor: An Intellectual Biography.* Edinburgh University Press, 1971.

Modern Twentieth-Century Writers. Detroit: Gale, 1991.

Senghor, Léopold Sédar. *Selected Poems.* Translated by John Reed and Clive Wake. New York: Atheneum, 1969.

Spleth, Janice. *Léopold Sédar Senghor.* New York: Twayne, 1985.

Vaillant, Janet. *Black, French and African.* Cambridge, MA: Harvard University Press, 1990.

Shaka

Born 1787
Zululand (now part of KwaZulu-Natal province,
South Africa)
Died September 22, 1828
Dukuzu, Zululand (now Stanger, KwaZulu-Natal province,
South Africa)

Leader of the Zulu nation

Shaka was a feared and brutal leader of his people, but he was also a military genius.

In the 1700s in southern Africa, in what is now KwaZulu-Natal province of South Africa, African people lived in small communities led by a chief. As their populations increased, the communities' grazing land for cattle became scarce, and some groups grew more prosperous than others through trade for ivory and cattle. Three powerful chiefdoms came to dominate the region. In the early 1800s the Zulu nation, led by famed chief Shaka (also spelled "Chaka"), was the most powerful and the most feared of all. For 10 years between 1818 and 1828 his highly disciplined warriors raided villages and robbed them of their crops and their cattle. They caused chaos and forced millions of people to flee. Some went as far north as Tanzania and as far south as the Cape Colony. These refugees, in turn, conquered or absorbed the peoples along their paths, changing forever the mixture of people, language, and culture throughout southern Africa and parts of central Africa. This period in African history is referred to as the *mfecane* or the "crushing."

Shaka was a feared and brutal leader of his people, but he was also a military genius. He adapted weaponry then in use and made it more accurate. He developed a military formation still in use today. And he required nearly superhuman obedience and discipline from his warriors, who feared death at his hands more than they feared death on the battlefield.

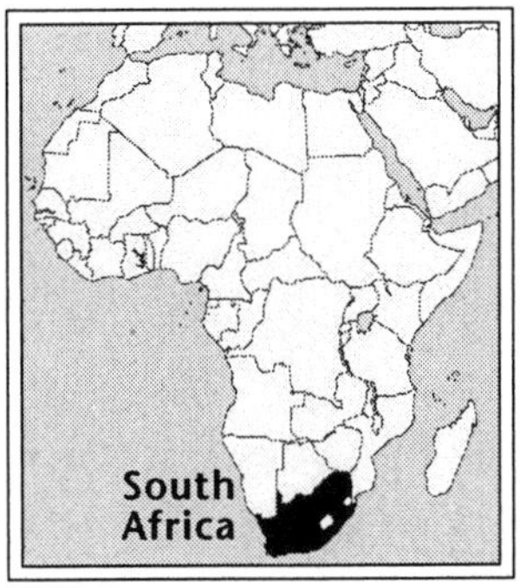

South Africa

An unhappy childhood

Shaka's mother, Nandi, was the orphaned daughter of a Langeni chief. His father, Senzangakona, was the chief of a small, neighboring Zulu clan. According to the culture, Nandi, who was pregnant, and Senzangakona could not marry because their people lived too close to one another. But, as chief, Senzangakona made the decision to defy tradition. He brought Nandi to his village. Senzangakona's other wives treated her as an unwelcome outsider and made her life miserable. (In many African societies men may marry more than one wife. This practice is called polygyny. If a man takes more than one wife, each wife and her children constitute a separate "house." These houses are considered "right-hand" or "left-hand" houses, depending on their relation to the "main" house. The house arrangement regulates inheritance.)

Shaka was born in 1787 and stayed with his mother until he was six years old. Then, according to custom, Shaka went to live in the countryside to take care of his father's sheep. The young boy inadvertently allowed a dog to kill one of the sheep. This mistake made his father extremely angry. In retaliation, the chief banished Shaka, his mother, and his baby sister from their home. They went to live in Nandi's family's village. Nandi returned to her family home at Langeni as a disgraced woman. Probably because of his mother's humiliation and his own late physical maturity, Shaka's peers bullied him and teased him. Life at Langeni was unpleasant for the lonely child and his mother.

In 1803, when Shaka was 16, a severe drought hit the Langeni people. Because they were already short of food, the village elders told Shaka and his mother they had to leave. Nandi went to live with another man, and Shaka went to live with his mother's aunt who was staying with the Mtetwa people. Shaka lived there for six years, and the Mtetwa treated him like a brother—with warmth, care, and concern. Young Shaka joined the tribal youth group and proved himself a natural leader. He killed a leopard and sent the skin to the chief of the Mtetwa, Jobe.

Proves his military ability

Jobe died in 1809. Previously, two of his sons had tried to assassinate him. One son was killed and the other fled. The latter son took the name Dingiswayo, and on his father's death he returned home to become the chief of the Mtetwa. Dingiswayo was an innovative and creative leader who strengthened the ranks of his people's military units, grouping young warriors by age instead of by village. Also, in the past, young men who had reached puberty were expected to leave the village for circumcision (the removal of the foreskin on the penis, a procedure usually performed on infant boys in the United States). Dingiswayo did away with this practice, partly because it supported local loyalties and because it required the young men to be away until the circumcision healed. These long absences deprived the military of much of its strength.

Under Dingiswayo's leadership, the Mtetwa conquered many neighboring clans. When Shaka's age group was called up for fighting, Shaka distinguished himself as a soldier. Dingiswayo made him captain of his regiment and put him on the Mtetwa Council, which determined political policy. Later, in 1814, Dingiswayo made Shaka commander in chief of all the Mtetwa forces. Shaka replaced some traditional fighting methods with new ones. He is credited with changing the use of the traditional throwing spear to that of a stabbing weapon. Shaka had the long handles cut down for use in close fighting. The new shorter spear was called an *assegai.*

In 1816 Shaka's father, Zulu chief Senzangakona, died, leaving power to Shaka's half-brother. With Dingiswayo's help and military muscle, Shaka was able to gain control himself. He then refined the already effective military formation that Dingiswayo had designed, grouping his men into distinctive regiments known as *impis,* each with its own uniforms and color-coded shields. He also created a royal guard solely for his own protection and popularized the use of the "horns movement" attack strategy:

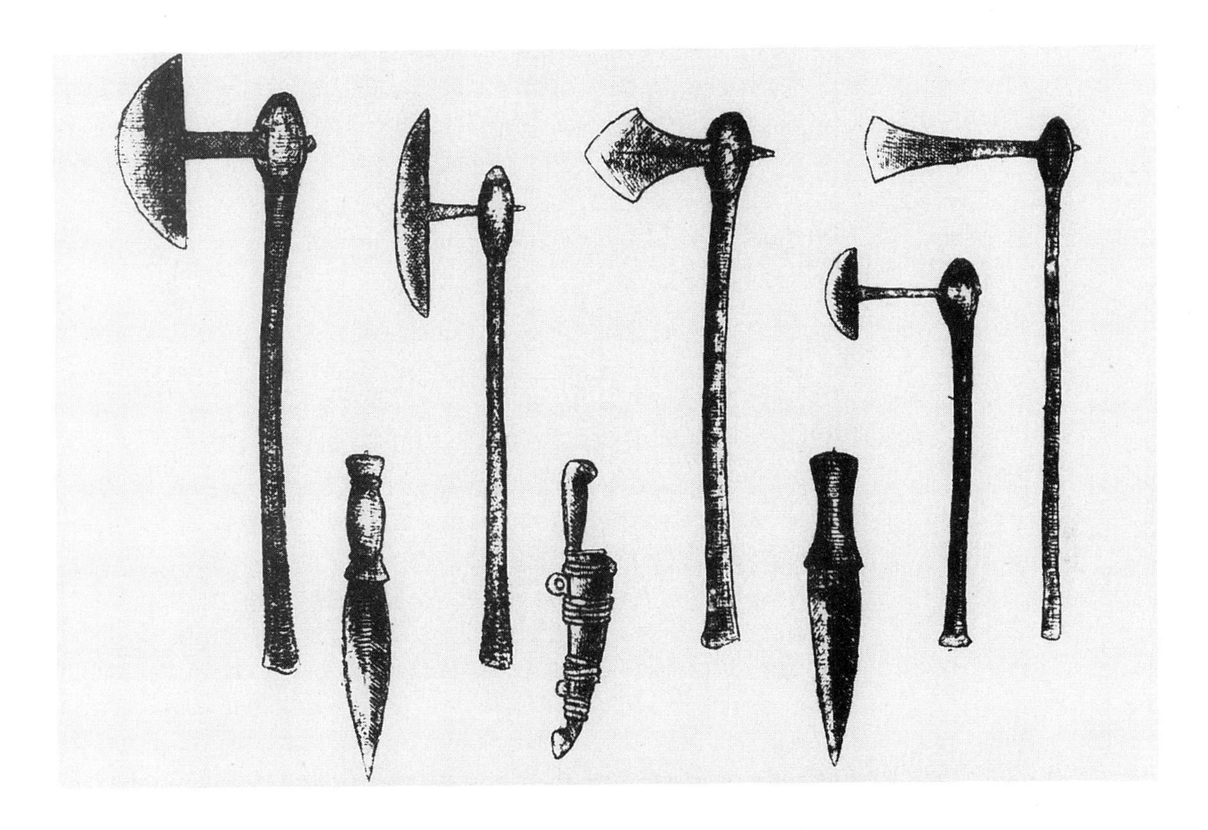

Assegai heads and axes of the type used by Shaka's warriors.

> The army was placed in the formation known as horns and the chest. The bulk of the forces composed the chest. On each side were the horns, which curved outward and forward, like a cow's horns. . . . The horns gradually enclosed the enemy, and when they met the chest would advance and annihilate the forces trapped within.

Warriors under Shaka's leadership had to prove themselves worthy of their positions and then adhere to strict and demanding codes of behavior. For instance, no warrior could have a wife or engage in any sexual relations. In addition, as a test of courage and commitment, the soldiers were forced to jog barefoot in formation on thorny ground until they could cover 50 miles a day. Anyone who failed the test risked being clubbed to death.

"The place of the one who kills"

At this point in his life, Shaka was in a position to take revenge on the Langeni people who had made life so difficult for him and his mother years before. He sent a band of men at night to surround the village. The next morning he singled out the persecutors of his youth and had them stuck onto the points of fences. The remaining Langeni were then incorporated into the Zulu clan. Shaka soon abandoned his father's village and built a new one he called Bulawayo, "the place of the one who kills." In one year alone he quadrupled the area under his control: his kingdom grew from the original 500 men that Dingiswayo had lent him to more than 2,000 men under his command.

Meanwhile, a fierce and powerful chief named Zwide was working hard to expand the territory of his Ndwandwe people. He drove the Ngwane people out of their southeast African homeland to the Lubombo Mountains where they established the foundation for the future Swaziland. Zwide then went after another Ngwane chief, Matiwane, and drove him west. Matiwane cut a path of terrible destruction, creating a domino effect on the plateau over the Drakensberg Mountains. In 1818 Zwide set a trap for Dingiswayo and killed him—probably to break Dingiswayo's hold over the trade with the Portuguese at Delagoa Bay (an inlet of the Indian Ocean on Africa's southeastern coast). When Dingiswayo died no one from the Mtetwa group was ready to take his place. Shaka stepped in and brought all the Mtetwa people into the Zulu clan. Zwide, meanwhile, continued to conquer many villages and rob the people of their cattle. Zwide's Ndwandwe kingdom continued to grow in size, and he became the Mtetwa's strongest enemy. Some people called him "The Eater-Up of Chiefs." Zwide's rampage started what is known as the *mfecane,* a time of turmoil and mass migration that changed the face of southern and central Africa.

Shaka expanded his state by conquering other chiefdoms or by intimidating them into accepting his rule. As more chiefdoms came under his authority, the size of his army increased. Shaka held a firm hand over his warriors, often using unprovoked violence to keep them obedient. On the other hand, Shaka is recognized for creating among his warriors a deep sense of belonging. Although his military was composed of people from many different areas with many different cultural traditions, Shaka introduced national ceremonies and symbols for all the people of the region. He had total and unquestionable power over the whole nation. He was the king, the courts, and the military leader. Anyone who opposed him was killed.

Zulu victory

Shaka and his Zulus were the main obstacle in Zwide's path to power. Zwide planned an attack on Shaka, but Shaka had spies who learned of the attack. The Zulu chief made all the women, children, and cattle go into hiding and had every man and boy get ready for battle. Although Zwide's warriors outnumbered the Zulus, the Zulus had the advantage with their *assegais,* the short stabbing spears, and pushed the enemy back. The Zulu warriors had some incentive for fighting hard: any man who left his spear on the battlefield was executed. Shaka defeated Zwide in 1819 and Zwide fled. The Zulu victory had a major impact on the entire region. Shaka became the supreme overlord—the absolute ruler over all other lords. No one was able to challenge him.

Some groups fled from Shaka's army. During their escape, they killed and robbed other groups in their path. Sometimes other groups joined forces with them as they fled. The leaders of two groups—the Soshangane and Zwangendabe—fled Shaka's warriors and went north, eventually establishing their own kingdoms. Soshangane settled in what is now southern Mozambique, and Zwangendabe traveled even farther north into present-day Malawi and Tanzania, nearly 2,000 miles away. In their desperate flight from the Zulu army and from those others fleeing the Zulus, nearly 3 million people were left homeless in the region, wandering in search of safety and food. Shaka had increased the size of his kingdom from 100 square miles to more than 7,000 square miles. He had brought 30 chiefs and their people into his kingdom and had a total of 20,000 men serving in his army.

Shaka's European associates

Descriptions of Shaka's rule come from several firsthand sources. From 1825 until his death Shaka received and welcomed various Europeans, some of whom had been shipwrecked off the coast. Nathaniel Isaacs was one such shipwreck survivor. He kept a diary of his life in Zululand for a period of about six years. Another three white men—Lieutenant Francis Farewell, a young man named Henry Fynn, and a Dutch merchant—had arrived at Bulawayo earlier. These men were interested in taking control of the ivory trade away from the Portuguese. (The Zulus traded elephant and hippopotamus ivory for brass and beads with the Por-

Shaka and other chiefs meet with Lieutenant Francis Farewell at Bulawayo about the ivory trade, 1824; illustration by R. Cator Woodville.

tuguese traders.) Shaka agreed to deal with the Westerners, thinking that he would be able to control them.

Shortly after their arrival the three white men gained Shaka's confidence when Fynn attended to Shaka after an assassination attempt. Fynn stayed by the wounded chief's side for five days, nursing his arm and chest wounds. The whites also pleased Shaka by bringing him an endless supply of trinkets: beads, copper, brass, oils, and even peacock feathers. In exchange, Shaka granted the whites small tracts of land near the port city of Natal.

In October 1826 Shaka received word that the Ndwandwes were approaching the Zulu frontier. Shaka gathered his army and marched with them at the head of the main division. They marched about 40 miles a day. After a decisive battle, the Zulus cornered the Ndwandwe and slaughtered all the warriors, women, and children. Upon his return to Bulawayo, Shaka decided to build a new capital 50 miles south of Bulawayo at Dukuzu (now Stanger).

A grieving son's madness

Shaka's mother, Nandi, who had been living a few miles outside Bulawayo, died in 1827. The grieving Shaka staged a massive funeral. Eyewitnesses reported that 40 oxen were slaughtered, and 7,000 people are believed to have died in a massacre at the funeral. Two young girls—both still alive—were buried along with Nandi. In addition, Shaka declared a period of mourning throughout the nation. He put a one-year ban on the growth of all crops, ordered all of his people to refrain from consuming cow's milk, and forbade all women from becoming pregnant. (The penalty for breaking the last of these three rules was death for both the woman and her husband.) After three months Shaka realized the implications of his orders and lifted the ban on crops, but his sorrow over his mother's death brought him to near-madness. Gradually, however, he recovered, though he was reportedly plagued by recurring nightmares and dreams of witches.

In the aftermath of Nandi's death, Shaka became increasingly ruthless. The people in his inner court—those who were the closest to him—began to conspire against him. As he became more and more frightened of his dreams, he pushed away all those who had once been his trusted allies and advisers. Shaka finally angered the army when he took away their bearers, the young boys who carried their baggage and supplies. Two of Shaka's half-brothers, Dingane and Mhlangana, conspired with Shaka's personal servant, Mbhopa, to kill him. They stabbed him to death on September 22, 1828. Shaka had never married. He had a harem of captured women or "sisters," but he never produced an heir. One of his half-brothers and murderers, Dingane, succeeded him.

Further Reading

Maylam, Paul. *A History of the African People of South Africa: From the Early Iron Age to the 1970s*. New York: St. Martin's, 1986.

Morris, Donald R. *The Washing of the Spears: The Rise and Fall of the Great Zulu Nation*. Abacus, 1992.

Ritter, E. A. *Shaka Zulu*. New York: Longman, 1955.

Stuart, James, and D. McK. Malcom, eds.*The Diary of Henry Francis Fynn*. Shuter & Shooter, 1986.

Taylor, Stephen. *Shaka's Children: A History of the Zulu People*. New York: HarperCollins, 1994.

Ian Douglas Smith

Born April 8, 1919
Selukwe, Southern Rhodesia (now Zimbabwe)

Prime minister of Rhodesia

In the late 1800s Great Britain had established a colony in what is now Zimbabwe and had encouraged British citizens to come to the country to farm. Later, in the 1950s, after World War II (1939-1945), African nations began freeing themselves from the control of foreign governments, and Great Britain began giving its African colonies independence based on majority rule. The white-settler government in Southern Rhodesia (now Zimbabwe), unwilling to submit to a black-led government, dug in its heels and declared itself independent from Great Britain. Under the leadership of Ian Douglas Smith, Southern Rhodesia's white government defied the rest of the world from 1965 to 1978. Rhodesia was only the second British colony in which the British settlers broke away from their mother nation (the first colony to do this was the United States in 1776). Despite the best efforts of Prime Minister

"I cannot see in my lifetime that the Africans will be sufficiently mature and reasonable to take over."

—Ian Douglas Smith, attempting to reassure whites of their continued role as leaders of Rhodesia

The Advantages of Federation for Whites

The Federation of Rhodesia and Nyasaland, a self-governing union of Southern Rhodesia, Northern Rhodesia, and Nyasaland, existed from 1953 to 1963. The English-speaking white settlers in the three south-central African territories viewed federation as the key to gaining economic and political power in the area. The whites wanted to use the profits from the rich copper deposits in Zambia to build dams and highways in all three regions. During federation, major regional improvements were indeed made, among them the construction of the Kariba Dam and electric power station, a railway line connecting Southern Rhodesia with a port in Mozambique, and a government-supported university in Salisbury (now Harare, Zimbabwe). But the white population also wanted to exercise its political muscle and form a large political unit that might later serve as the basis for a white-controlled independent state in Africa. Federation gave the whites an unfair advantage over blacks in the region's government. Thirty-five seats were set aside for whites in the legislature; only six were reserved for representatives of the black African majority population.

Ian Smith, a true believer in white supremacy (superiority based on race), the white-controlled republic of Rhodesia was short-lived. It ended in 1980 when a black majority government came to power.

Early life

Like many settlers in Rhodesia, Ian Smith's family had immigrated to the colony from Scotland. His father, John "Jock" Smith, came from Hamilton, Scotland, in 1898 at the age of 18. He married in 1911 and raised two daughters and a son, Ian, in the mining town of Selukwe (now Shurugwi). Jock Smith tried his hand at mining, farming, car repair, butchery, and other small enterprises, enjoying a mild success in business and local government. His real passion was for breeding race horses and riding them competitively. Young Ian grew up in the small town colonial atmosphere of this British outpost and enjoyed school sports. When he graduated from school, he moved on to Rhodes University in Grahamstown, South Africa, where he was elected head of the student council. He majored in business and planned to be a farmer.

When World War II started in 1939, Smith left college to volunteer for service. He trained as a fighter pilot in a Rhodesian squadron of the British Royal Air Force and was based in the Middle East. On October 4, 1943, his plane crashed on takeoff in the desert and he was badly burned. Smith underwent extensive plastic surgery on his face, half of which would be paralyzed for the rest of his life. Nevertheless, he went back into combat after his recovery. This time the air force sent him to Italy to fly missions out of Corsica. Smith parachuted to safety when German anti-aircraft fire shot down his Spitfire fighter over the Po Valley. When he finally got out of enemy territory, he went to England to recuperate. He continued flying until the end of the war. In 1945 he returned to South Africa to finish his college degree.

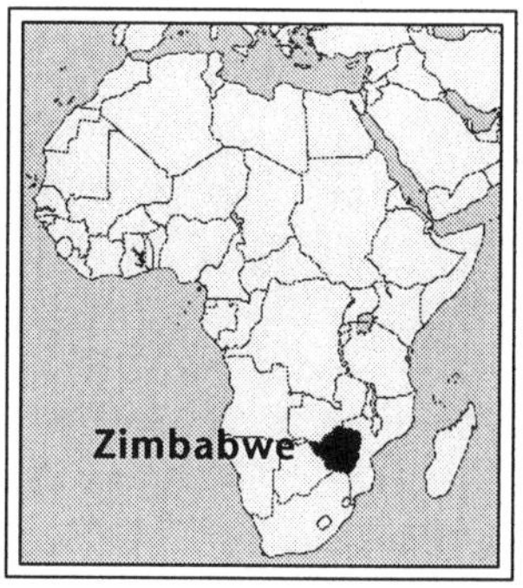

Zimbabwe

The era of federation

After graduation Smith headed back to Southern Rhodesia, where he began ranching cattle. He married Janet, a young widow with two children. An honorable war record and good relations with his farming neighbors helped get him elected to parliament in 1948. Around that time white British settlers in south-central Africa were organizing attempts to secure their own political power in the region. In 1953—following pressure from the settler groups in Southern Rhodesia, Northern Rhodesia (now Zambia), and Nyasaland (now Malawi)—Great Britain allowed the three territories to unite as the self-governing Federation of Rhodesia and Nyasaland. Black Africans strongly opposed the formation of the white-run federation, but it lasted for 10 years, from 1953 to 1963.

Although Smith initially opposed federation, he was elected to the Rhodesian parliament in 1953 as a member of the United Federal party, the party of Sir Godfrey Huggins and his pro-federation government. Smith also became a delegate to the Commonwealth Parliamentary Association, traveling widely to India, Pakistan, and other former British colonies.

The economies of Northern and Southern Rhodesia, like those of other southern African territories, were based on the mining of copper, chrome, gold, coal, iron, and tin. Some white settlers believed that these resources, along with tobacco and sugar exports, made the colonies wealthy enough to break free from British control. Southern Rhodesia had the strongest economy of the three federated regions, the largest white population, and the strongest will to deny blacks their own government. Over the years the white-run government of Southern Rhodesia had earned a notorious reputation for its deeply entrenched racism.

Black political groups in Southern Rhodesia were becoming increasingly impatient with the lack of action being taken to advance black rights. The African National Congress (ANC) under Joshua Nkomo (see entry) was urging armed resistance to white rule. Moreover, Africans opposed to federation favored the creation of two independent black states, Zambia and Malawi. (This movement was led by Kenneth Kaunda [see entry] in Northern Rhodesia and Hastings Banda [see entry] in Nyasaland.) Smith's racial views, like those of other white Southern Rhodesians, grew more and more conservative (rigid, traditional) as the call for black rights resonated throughout central Africa.

In the face of strong African opposition to federation, a royal commission from Britain toured the three territories. In its 1960 report, the commission recommended that the territories be allowed to withdraw from the federation under black majority governments. But white British settlers—especially those in Southern Rhodesia—were terrified of the prospect of domination by a black-run government. Unforeseen events in the Belgian Congo, another colonial nation gaining its independence at the time, horrified Southern Rhodesia's white population. The Belgian colonial government had left the Congo abruptly, without naming any Africans to take over. In the ensuing fight for power in the Congo, a bloody civil war erupted. The Belgian whites who stayed behind were finally forced to flee the nation. Southern Rhodesia's whites feared the same fate.

Smith founds Rhodesia Front party

Northern Rhodesia and Nyasaland withdrew from federation in 1963 and became the independent countries of Zambia and Malawi within a year. But the Southern Rhodesian whites refused to accept a multiracial government in their country. They tried to persuade Britain to accept a constitution with token African representation instead. Britain refused.

Meanwhile, the conservative whites turned to a political party more to their own liking. Smith had helped set up the Rhodesia Front (RF) party in 1962. The RF wanted independence and white supremacy, and it won the general election in 1962. Two years later Smith launched a palace coup—a coup, or government overthrow, from within the party. He removed the party leader and became Rhodesia's prime minister.

Smith signs proclamation of independence for Rhodesia, November 11, 1965.

Smith took a hard line in discussions with British authorities. The British wanted all the people of Southern Rhodesia to be consulted about the formation of a new government. Smith, however, proposed to consult only the tribal chiefs and headmen because he knew they depended on him for their jobs and salaries. In a five-day *indaba* (council meeting), the chiefs ended up supporting his independence proposal.

Declares Rhodesia independent

The British government rejected this council decision and informed Smith that a declaration of independence to create a racist white regime would be an act of treason (betrayal of the British government). Unmoved, Smith called an election at the beginning of 1965. The Rhodesian Front won another large majority in parliament. On November 11, 1965, Smith made his party's Unilateral Declaration of Independence (UDI), claiming that, apart from a moment of shock, the rest of the world would treat it as a "nine-day wonder" and soon lose interest. He had miscalculated. Britain at once retaliated by declaring trade sanctions (refusal to carry on trade with the new Rhodesian government). A long stalemate began. At the end of 1966 the United Nations (an international organization promoting world peace) joined Britain in enforcing the sanctions. The Organization of African Unity (OAU) made threats against any African nation that violated them.

The state struggles to survive

Smith—a tall, lanky, plainspoken Scotsman—was popular with most whites. He was one of them and they trusted him. They referred to him with affection as "good old Smithy," a man of unshakable determination and self-confidence. He was always clear about what he wanted. He reassured whites: "I cannot see in my lifetime that the Africans will be sufficiently mature and reasonable to take over." The slogan for the Rhodesia Front became "Never in a thousand years."

Although no governments except for those of South Africa, Portugal, and Malawi would recognize Smith's regime or trade openly with it, independent Rhodesia survived. The expected early collapse never happened. The government stepped in and bought the tobacco harvest from the white farmers because sanctions prohibited tobacco sales to foreign buyers. And the discovery of nickel deposits in 1968 helped the economy. Rhodesia continued to export chrome despite the sanctions, which were more widely violated with each passing year. White-run South Africa, first under Hendrik Verwoerd (see entry) and then, after his assassination in 1966, under Johannes Balthazar Vorster, remained loyal supporters. South Africa's wealth and physical closeness helped Rhodesia survive.

Like his South African allies, Smith believed all the opponents of his government were communists. (Communism is a system of government in which the state controls the means of production and the distribution of goods. It clashes with the American ideal of capitalism, which is based on private ownership and a free market system.) His accusation was believable because the main opposition groups were getting military supplies from the Soviet Union and China. This was at the height of the Cold War, when the nations of the West were trying to limit the influence of Communist China and the Soviet bloc countries.

Smith saw himself as a hero of the "Free World" and "Christian Civilization." Although the United States openly opposed communism, it opposed Smith's racist philosophy as well. America was involved with its own civil rights movement in the 1960s and could not afford to associate itself with Rhodesia's racist regime. Regardless of Western opposition, Smith stood firm. In economic terms, he knew he had the upper hand: many British firms had invested large sums of money in Rhodesia, and Britain did not want to risk financial upheaval by bringing in British troops against whites.

Smith drove hard bargains in his talks with British officials. He made matters worse when he declared Rhodesia an independent republic in 1970. The RF also enacted more race laws and restrictions in the cities. The Land Tenure Act of 1969 divided Rhodesia's land along racial lines, designating 44 million acres to blacks and 44 million to the far smaller white population.

The conflict intensifies

Smith faced severe problems along with his short-term advantages. In particular, the white population of Rhodesia had always been small by comparison with that of South Africa. From about 1961 on, despite frantic efforts to attract new white settlers with the promise of almost cost-free farmland, more whites were leaving Rhodesia than arriving. By the mid-1960s, four and a half million blacks and only one-quarter of a million whites lived in the country. The whites had the best farmland, but they could not run the farms, or mines, or factories without African laborers.

The Africans in Southern Rhodesia were united by the goal of ridding their country of the white government, but they were also divided by deep-rooted personal rivalries. The two leading African opposition groups were the Zimbabwe African National Union (ZANU) and the Zimbabwe African People's Union (ZAPU). Their membership generally fell along regional and cultural lines—ZANU was predominantly Shona, and ZAPU was predominantly Ndebele. The Shona and Ndebele peoples argued throughout the 1960s, allowing internal fighting to interrupt their joint struggle against the white regime. Nevertheless, time and world opinion were on the side of the black African fighters. Their situation improved markedly after 1974, when the Portuguese military overthrew Portugal's military dictator. The new government in Portugal rapidly withdrew from its African colonies, which included neighboring Mozambique and Angola. With a black majority government installed in Mozambique by 1975 under Samora Machel, ZANU freedom fighters gained access to a strategically located base outside Rhodesia. As fighting expanded in the countryside, blacks began moving into the cities. Soon the cities became centers of political activity.

With an independent black government in Mozambique, South Africa put pressure on Smith to end the conflict in Rhodesia. A 1975 meeting of Zimbabwean independence groups ended with no concessions and no agreement on anything. Smith won Rhodesia's 1977 elections, but he could not disguise the fact that he was standing on the edge of a volcano. The whites who stayed in Rhodesia were depressed and exhausted. All able white men had to serve in the military for nine months and be on call for three years. Many left the country rather than fight. Smith finally realized that he would have to yield ground to black (and world) pressure. In March 1978 he reached a compromise settlement with Bishop Abel Muzorewa, a man he believed he could control. Under the terms of their agreement, Muzorewa assumed a position of leadership in the government, but whites still outnumbered blacks in his cabinet (body of advisers). The leader of ZANU, Robert Mugabe (see entry), refused to recognize this so-called "internal settlement."

Losing power

Britain had never accepted UDI and never acknowledged Smith as a head of state. Now it sought to reach a permanent settlement in its former colony. The British foreign secretary called all the major figures to attend a conference to work out a temporary constitution. They finally agreed on black majority rule in Zimbabwe but reserved 20 seats for whites in the 100-seat parliament for at least the first seven years. Elections were held in 1980. Even though widespread terrorism clouded the election, the people voted overwhelmingly for Robert Mugabe.

Smith remained the leader of the Rhodesian Front party, which won all 20 seats reserved for whites. Mugabe and Smith were constantly at odds, but Smith maintained high visibility in the government. In the 1985 election the RF won 15 of the 20 seats for whites. Later, Smith took an extremely unpopular stand by speaking out against the international pressure on South Africa to dismantle apartheid, its system of racial segregation that favored the nation's white minority. Smith never apologized for his faith in white supremacy, and he never accepted the new state of affairs in Zimbabwe. In 1997 he toured the major cities in South Africa and Zimbabwe promoting his new book, *The Great Betrayal.*

Further Reading

Blake, Robert. *A History of Rhodesia.* Eyre Methuen, 1977.

The Cambridge History of Africa. Vol. 8. Edited by Michael Crowder. New York/UK: Cambridge University Press, 1984.

Davis, Dorothy K. *Race Relations in Rhodesia.* Rex Collings, 1975.

Historic World Leaders. Edited by Anne Commire. Detroit: Gale, 1994.

Wills, A. J. *An Introduction to the History of Central Africa: Zambia, Malawi, and Zimbabwe.* New York/UK: Oxford University Press, 1985.

Windrich, Elaine. *Britain and the Politics of Rhodesian Independence.* Africana Publishing, 1978.

Young, Kenneth. *Rhodesia and Independence.* Eyre & Spottiswoode, 1967.

Sobhuza II

Born July 22, 1899
Zombodze, Swaziland
Died August 23, 1982
Mbabane, Swaziland

King of Swaziland

"As one of the last countries to achieve independence, we have had the opportunity of learning from nations which have won their independence before us."

—Sobhuza II, commenting on Swaziland's freedom from British domination in 1968

At his death in 1982 at the age of 83, King Sobhuza II (*so-BOO-zuh*) of Swaziland was the world's longest reigning monarch. Having ruled for 60 years, he was the only leader most of his people ever knew. Swaziland is a mountainous landlocked region of southern Africa, surrounded by South Africa and Mozambique. During Sobhuza II's reign he successfully restored to the kingdom some of the land taken by Europeans under the rule of his grandfather, Mbandzeni.

Sobhuza II was the great-great grandson of Sobhuza I (1785-1836), the founder of the Swazi nation. In the early 1800s, after the Ndwande chief Zwide attacked them, Sobhuza I led the remnants of his Ngwane people into the mountains for safety. His son Mswati (or Mswazi; c. 1820-68) shaped these refugees into a nation state (later called Swazi after him) that endures today. During Mswati's reign, the Swazis became one of the most powerful groups in southern Africa. But when he died, the authoritative structure he had devised collapsed. For the next 10 years the Swazis fought each other over his successor. Finally in 1875 the fighting that set brother against brother ended in compromise when Mbandzeni became king.

A "frenzied scramble" for land

When gold was discovered in 1873 in the eastern Transvaal, South Africa, prospectors flocked into Swaziland. They overwhelmed Mbandzeni with their demands for land. In 1876 he granted 36,000 acres in southern Swaziland to two speculators. His policy was highly profitable but short-sighted. Over the next decade the kingdom received as much as 20,000 British pounds per year. But as Mbandzeni grew old and his health declined toward 1889, "the concessionaires [those who received the land grants] entered into a final frenzied scramble to secure what resources were left," noted Paul Maylam in *A History of the African People of South Africa.* "The economic assets of the kingdom [were] progressively stripped."

With the king weakened by ill health, the members of the court fought each other for control. The contest resulted in the execution of several elder councillors accused of plotting to overthrow Mbandzeni. Mbandzeni died in 1889 and his son, Bhunu or Ngwane V, succeeded him. Bhunu was only 14 years old at the time, and his mother acted as regent (meaning she governed the kingdom until her son became old enough to rule himself).

Until 1890 Swaziland had remained fairly independent, although the policies of Mbandzeni brought it considerable dependence later. In 1894 Britain and the Transvaal Republic agreed between themselves that Swaziland would come under the control of the Transvaal. With the British annexation of the Transvaal at the end of the Boer War (1899-1902), however, the supervision of Swaziland fell to the British governor of the Transvaal. (The Boers, or Afrikaners, were Afrikaans-speaking European farmers from the Cape Colony. The Boer Wars were fought by the British and the Boers for control over two of South African's provinces.) Then, in 1906, the governor's powers were transferred to the office of the British High Commissioner.

Bhunu died in 1899 at the age of 24. Traditionally, Swazis do not choose a crown prince because they want to prevent a designated successor from becoming a rival to the father. When Bhunu died, a council of elders selected Nkhotfotjeni, a son of Bhunu and one of his wives, Queen Lomawa Nxumalo, to become the next king. He was given the name Sobhuza II and was only a year old when he became king. Because of his age he did not take the throne until about 20 years later. Sobhuza's grandmother Ndlovukazi ("the She-Elephant") Labotsibeni Mdluli acted as queen regent. Well aware of the weaknesses of her husband, King Mbandzeni, Labotsibeni was determined that the new king would be well educated in both traditional and Western ways. In her grandson she placed her hopes for the restoration of the Swazi lands that her husband had foolishly granted to Europeans.

During Labotsibeni's regency, however, the Swazi people effectively lost control of their state. In 1903 Swaziland came under British authority, and four years later a resident commissioner representing the British government arrived. Previously, the British government had appointed a commission to investigate and make recommendations on ways to settle the conflicting claims over land and concessions granted by Mbandzeni. But the Swazis maintained that the land ultimately belonged to the nation and was only temporarily assigned to the concessionaires. In 1907 the commission recommended partitioning, or dividing, the land among the claimants. As a result, the Swazis lost about 63 percent of their land area, and nearly half the Swazi population suddenly found themselves living outside the area designated as Swaziland. Those living on land outside the reserved areas could safely remain for only five years before facing the prospect of eviction (being forced out of their homes).

Becomes "the Lion"

Given Swaziland's history of land loss, the queen regent was determined to win back her people's land. She sent the young Sobhuza to primary and secondary schools in Swaziland that had been created especially for him, with teachers brought in from South Africa. Then, from 1916 to 1918, he attended Lovedale College in Cape Province, South Africa.

Sobhuza was installed as Ngwenyama, "the Lion," in December 1921. His grandmother had instilled in him the unwavering desire to restore Swazi land. This became the focus of his reign. In 1922, the year after his enthronement, Sobhuza challenged the

1907 British High Commissioner's partition of the Swazi people's lands. Sobhuza and a Swazi delegation traveled to London to petition King George V to restore the lands. The king and his secretary of state for the colonies, however, turned down his appeal. The determined Sobhuza pursued the case for 15 years. Finally, King George VI agreed to help acquire land from white owners for Swazi occupation. Because of Sobhuza's efforts, the land area held by the Swazis increased from 37 percent at the time of partition to a little more than 50 percent in 1960, an increase of 13 percent.

Avoiding crocodiles

Sobhuza was equally at home in the traditional and Western worlds. He was a tall lanky man who appeared before his subjects as a bare-chested warrior might or in fancy military dress. He led the Swazis' many traditional ceremonies and rituals and was popularly referred to as "the Great Mountain," "the Bull," "the Son of the She-Elephant" and "the Inexplicable." (Inexplicable means incapable of being explained.)

In an effort to keep Swazi traditions alive, Sobhuza held fast to his royal powers. He kept the right to name and dismiss chiefs, to establish courts, to regulate the constitution, and to control the newly established Swazi treasury. But he was also an advocate of modern technology and adopted Western ways that were advantageous to him and his people. Dickie quotes him as saying:

> As one of the last countries to achieve independence, we have had the opportunity of learning from nations which have won their independence before us. We have watched them crossing rivers [and] have seen [them] being swallowed by crocodiles. Now that we have seen the crocodile-infested drifts, we shall try to cross through crocodile-free drifts to a peaceful independent Swaziland.

In the pre-independence days of the early 1960s, Sobhuza aligned royal interests with those of the white electorate. Together, they won control of all but one seat in the 1964 legislative elections. In 1968, when Britain granted Swaziland independence, Sobhuza became head of state with wide-ranging powers.

Rules absolutely

When his political opponents challenged him in the legislative elections of 1973, Sobhuza suspended (or set aside the rules of)

Sobhuza II dressed in traditional Swazi attire, 1973.

the constitution, dissolved parliament, and banned all political parties and trade unions. He became an absolute ruler, making all judicial, executive, and legislative decisions in a traditional tribal government.

Sobhuza ruled as an absolute monarch until his death in 1982. Throughout his 60-year rule he held the Swazi kingdom firmly together, maintaining its traditional rights but negotiating as nec-

Although Swaziland was economically dependent on South Africa, for years it served as an important transit route for the African National Congress (ANC), the leading black organization working to overthrow white rule in South Africa. The ANC had been getting both guerrillas (independent fighting units) and arms into South Africa—through Swaziland— from Mozambique.

The ANC Connection

essary with the race-based South African government. To show mourning for their king's death, everyone in the Swazi kingdom—men and women alike—shaved their heads. Sobhuza left behind a family conservatively estimated at 70 wives and 150 children. Because no crown prince had been designated, it took a considerable amount of time and negotiating to determine which of his wives would rule as queen regent and which of his 67 sons would take the throne. In 1986 Crown Prince Makhosetive (1968-) was installed as Mswati III.

Further Reading

Dickie, John, and Alan Rake. *Who's Who in Africa.* Africa Buyer and Trader, 1973.

Kuper, Hilda. *Sobhuza II: Ngwenyama and King of Swaziland.* London: Duckworth, 1978.

Lipschutz, Mark, and R. Kent Rasmussen. *Dictionary of African Historical Biography.* Aldine Publishing, 1978.

Maylam, Paul. *A History of the African People of South Africa: From the Early Iron Age to the 1970s.* New York: St. Martin's Press, 1986.

Wole Soyinka

Born July 13, 1934
Abeokuta, Nigeria

Nigerian author, actor, and political activist

"[A writer is] the voice of vision in his own time."

—Soyinka, commenting on the function of an artist in society

In 1986 Wole Soyinka (*WOH-leh Shaw-YIN-ka*) won the Nobel Prize for literature, thereby becoming the first black writer and the first African to win the award. When the Swedish Academy presented him with the prestigious prize, its members praised his ability to describe the complex nature of his African culture. Soyinka and other African intellectuals have written that Westerners (meaning Europeans and Americans) have a distorted perception of Africa and its people—an inaccurate perception of Africa as a primitive land. In his desire to celebrate Africa, though, Soyinka does not romanticize his native land; he is as willing to charge Nigerian politicians with barbarity and corruption as he is to condemn the greed and materialism of the West.

Soyinka's Nigeria is a society in transition. Nigerians are attempting to mold a new nation out of a variety of rich, tribal cultures and a turbulent legacy of European colonization. (Colonization is the control by one power—in this case, control by various European countries—of a territory that lies beyond its own borders—in this case, land in western Africa.) Soyinka maintains that an artist is "the record[er] of the . . . experience of his society and . . . the voice of vision in his own time." As a playwright, he combines aspects of European and African culture, integrating Western dramatic forms with elements of traditional Yoruba performance, such as masks, dance, and drums.

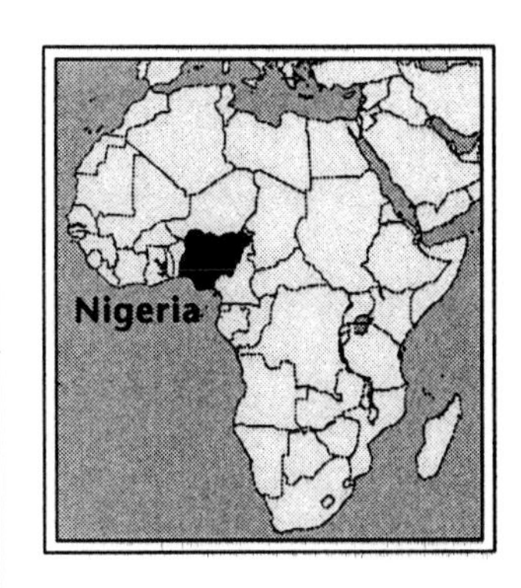

Soyinka was born July 13, 1934, in Abeokuta, a village on the rocky banks of the Ogun River in western Nigeria. His given name was Akinwande Oluwole Soyinka. About 10 million Yoruba people inhabit southwestern Nigeria and the nearby country of Benin. Although many people have adopted Christianity and Islam, about 2 million still practice the rituals of the traditional ancestral spirit cults. Soyinka's mother, Eniola Soyinka, became a Christian convert so devout that he nicknamed her "Wild Christian." His father, Soditan Akinyode, was the scholarly headmaster of a Christian primary school established in their village by the British. (Soyinka nicknamed his father "Essay" for his occupation and for his initials—S. A. Although he worked in a Christian school, S. A. was an agnostic, meaning he felt that humans can never really know if God exists.) In contrast with these European influences, Soyinka was also schooled in the spiritual history of his people. His paternal grandfather and the village *ogboni,* or tribal elders, saw to it that young Wole was exposed to the teachings of Yoruba mythology.

Christian saints and Yoruba spirits

Soyinka wrote the story of the first 11 years of his life in a book called *Ake: The Years of Childhood.* In *Ake* the Christian saints and the Yoruba ancestral spirits, or *egungun,* comfortably coexist. The egungun return to Yorubaland whenever someone puts on one of their masks and dances with it at village festivals. They call this "dancing the mask." In his memoir Soyinka remembers that as a child he thought St. Peter was an egungun. In the stained glass window of the Christian church in the author's village, St. Peter was depicted wearing robes similar to the robes the egungun wear. Later, as Soyinka's father encouraged him to apply for a scholarship to the colonial government school in Ibadan, his paternal grandfather secretly made him take part in an initiation rite into Yoruba manhood. He consecrated the young child to the Yoruba god Ogun, although Soyinka's Christian mother had entrusted him to Christ. But these contradictions did not trouble young Soyinka; rather, he gained a sense of security from the fact that he was cared for by his entire extended family of living relatives and ancestral spirits, along with the *ogboni.*

Soyinka spent his early years living on the grounds of the Christian school his father headed. He was an active and curious child; the adults in his life reportedly warned each other: "He will kill you with his questions." By the time Soyinka was just four years old, the rich variety of life beyond the school's walls already fascinated him. One day, as he writes in *Ake,* he wandered off the grounds of the compound, following a police band all the way to the colorful, noisy, village market. Hours later a policeman brought him home on the crossbar of his bicycle. The memoir records Soyinka's realization of the pull of tradition and modernization straining in opposite directions.

Drama inspired by Yoruba and Greek mythology

Soyinka went to the University College at Ibadan as his father had hoped. Among his classmates was Chinua Achebe (see entry), who later became an internationally known writer. Soyinka studied literature at the college, with an emphasis on drama, from 1952 to 1954. During this time he explored Yoruba and Greek mythology, laying the groundwork for the imaginative combination of tribal and Western sources he would use in his plays. While at Ibadan, Soyinka published several poems and short stories in the literary magazine *Black Orpheus.* His first published poem, "Telephone Conversation," shows his flair for satire (poking fun at a serious situation); he treated with great humor the difficult subject of a racial confrontation between an African student and his English landlady.

The author then left Africa to study drama at Leeds University in England. While in London he also worked as a reader at the Royal Court Theater, where his first play, *The Invention,* was staged in 1957.

A new Nigerian drama

Three years later Soyinka triumphantly returned to the University of Ibadan as a Rockefeller research fellow in drama, and he

Selected Productions of Wole Soyinka's plays

- *The Swamp Dwellers,* produced in London, England, 1958.
- *The Invention,* first produced in London at Royal Court Theatre, 1959.
- *The Lion and the Jewel,* first produced at Royal Court Theatre, 1966.
- *A Dance of the Forests,* produced in London, 1960.
- *Camwood on the Leaves,* broadcast by Nigerian Broadcasting Corporation, 1960; produced in Lagos, 1982.
- *The Republican,* produced in Ibadan, Nigeria, 1963.
- *The Road,* produced in Stratford, England, at Theatre Royal, 1965.
- *Before the Blackout* (revue sketches), produced in Ibadan, 1965.
- *Kongi's Harvest,* produced in Lagos, Nigeria, 1965; produced Off-Broadway, 1968.
- *The Strong Breed,* produced in Ibadan, 1966; produced Off-Broadway, 1967.
- *The Trials of Brother Jero* (one-act), produced Off-Broadway, 1967.
- *The Bacchae of Euripides: A Communion Rite,* (adapter), first produced in London, 1973.
- *Jero's Metamorphosis,* produced in Bristol, England, 1974.
- *Death and the King's Horseman,* first produced in Ife, Nigeria, 1976.
- *Before the Blow-Out,* produced in Ife, 1978.
- *Opera Wonyosi* (light opera), produced in Ife, 1977.
- *Rice or Rice Scene,* produced in Lagos, 1981.
- *Priority Projects,* produced in Ife, 1982.
- *A Play of Giants,* produced in New Haven, Connecticut, 1984.
- *Requiem for a Futurolgist,* produced in Ife, 1983.
- *Before the Deluge,* produced in Lagos, 1991.
- *A Scourge of Hyacinths,* broadcast by BBC Radio 4, 1991.
- *From Zia, with Love,* produced in Siena, Italy, 1992.

began a serious study of Nigerian folklore. It was at this time that he founded his influential amateur theater group, Masks, dedicated to forging a new Nigerian drama. The Masks' first major production was Soyinka's *Dance of the Forests,* which had been commissioned for the Nigerian independence celebrations of October 1960. Despite the festive occasion, Soyinka transmitted a powerful message through *Dance of the Forests,* effectively warning his fellow Nigerians to avoid the violence and pettiness of their past.

Soyinka went on from Ibadan to lecture in English literature at the University of Ife, which he left in 1963 for what he termed "political reasons." He spent the next two years traveling, writing, and directing plays. In 1964 he disbanded the Masks to assemble a professional theater troupe called the Orisun Repertory. The following year he returned to England for the Commonwealth Festival production of what some have called his most beautiful tragedy, *The Road.* Soyinka named the Yoruba god Ogun, to whom his grandfather consecrated (devoted) him in childhood, as his muse. His play is set in modern Nigeria, where Ogun—the god of iron and the forge, of creation and destruction—has become the god of electricity and the guardian of highways. In *The Road,* car accidents symbolize Ogun's destructive power over the careless traveler. His high priest, called the Professor, is a madman who deliberately rearranges crucial road signs, hoping to discover the meaning of life amid the bloodshed he causes.

Politics and war

In 1964 the Nigerian government arrested Soyinka and accused him of forcing a radio announcer at gunpoint to broadcast incorrect results in the federal election. His arrest sparked a protest campaign by PEN, the international writers' organization. Such influential American authors as Norman Mailer and William Styron called for his release. The police never produced any evidence to prove the charges against the author. After three months they released Soyinka. It is now known that the election was rigged (fixed in advance for a desired result), and it led to a breakdown in law and order in the region.

In 1967 Soyinka became the chair of the Department of Theater Arts at the University of Ibadan. In August of that year, however, authorities arrested him again. At the time Nigeria's civil war (1967-70)—a war Soyinka opposed—was raging. The conflict stemmed from a clash in beliefs between the nation's varied peoples. Nigeria, which is roughly twice the size of the state of California, is occupied by people speaking hundreds of different languages. Divisiveness among the populace peaked when Christians in the southeastern section broke away from Nigeria and formed a separate nation called Biafra. In 1967, after a military coup (the overturning of an existing government) by Ibo officers had been put down, tens of thousands of Ibos living in the North were killed. The Ibos homeland is in the southeastern region of Nigeria, and the Hausa-Fulani, who are Muslims, dominate the North. More than one million Ibos fled the North, returned to the southeastern region, and declared themselves an independent country. The discovery of oil in the delta region of Biafra compounded the issue. The federal Nigerian government then sent troops to Biafra to put down the rebellion. Soyinka lived on the federal side of Nigeria, and his own Yoruba tribe supported the federal cause. He defied those loyalties and set about organizing Nigerian intellectuals to lobby for a ban on arms sales to both sides.

Soyinka's peaceful initiative failed, however, and the federal government immediately arrested him. In October 1967 authorities released a faked confession, in which Soyinka supposedly admitted to helping the Biafrans overthrow the government. Ironically, the government specifically accused Soyinka—a champion of nonviolence—of supplying weapons to the rebels.

Soyinka spent two years as a political prisoner at the Kaduna Prison facility, mainly in solitary confinement. When his jailers vaccinated most of the prisoners against the deadly disease meningitis (inflammation of the membranes surrounding the brain and spinal cord), they bypassed Soyinka. In addition, he was denied medical attention when he developed eye problems. When prison officials refused to give him reading and writing materials, he made his own ink, composed a prison diary, and wrote poetry on cigarette packages and toilet paper. Every time he miraculously smuggled a letter or poem from prison, the international press seized upon it both as an important literary event and as welcome evidence that he was still alive. Soyinka was released from prison in 1969 and left Nigeria. He did not return until after a change of government in 1975.

Post-prison writings

Many critics have remarked on a distinct darkening of tone in Soyinka's writing after his second imprisonment. His prison diary, published in 1972 as *The Man Died: Prison Notes of Wole Soyinka,* is a fragmented account of his agonizing experience. Two poems smuggled from Soyinka's cell were published in 1969 in a pamphlet entitled *Poems from Prison*; these were republished later in a larger volume called *A Shuttle in the Crypt.*

Late in 1971 Soyinka accepted a fellowship at Churchill College, Cambridge, England. His reception at Cambridge was rather awkward. In 1973 the university's English Department withdrew its support of a lecture series he had proposed to give on the subject of African literature and society. Soyinka went ahead with the series with the backing of the Department of Social Anthropology instead. After his stay at Cambridge, Soyinka settled briefly in Ghana to edit the African cultural magazine *Transition.* Then, in 1975, he accepted a position as professor of comparative literature at the University of Ife in southwestern Nigeria.

Soyinka published the novel *Season of Anomy* several years after his release from prison. Some critics found the book horrifying in its detailed descriptions of torture and murder but compelling in its message that those who hope for peace must first confront such horrible realities.

Not all of Soyinka's post-prison writings strike the same despairing note, however. The beautiful memoir *Ake,* for instance, was written after his imprisonment. And in 1988 Soyinka published *Isara: A Voyage around Essay.* The book is a tribute to Soyinka's father, who died while the author was in political exile (forced exit from his home country) after his imprisonment. In 1983 Soyinka had discovered a box containing a collection of Essay's papers, and these papers gave him the idea to reconstruct the lives of his father's generation of Nigerians. Essay, one of many children sent away from their native village to be educated in a teacher's training seminary, found himself caught between two conflicting cultures. Each of the book's six chapters centers on Essay or one of his friends grappling with this cultural strife during the years leading up to World War II (1939-45). Soyinka's father comes to represent the entire generation of Nigerian people forced to resolve the gaping differences between the traditions of Africa and the philosophy of the West.

Living in exile

In 1991 Soyinka returned to magazine editing, reclaiming his post as editor of *Transition* (renamed *Ch'Idaba*). Throughout 1992

Soyinka poses with fellow Nobel prize-winning American writer Toni Morrison in Paris after eluding Nigeria's repressive military government by leaving the country, 1994.

and early 1993 the military government of General Ibrahim Babangida was preparing for nationwide presidential elections. The voters went to the polls in June 1993 and elected Mashood Abiola, a Muslim from the southwest of the country. The government immediately canceled the election results because it favored the other candidate. Rioting erupted throughout the country. Babangida could not sustain the pressure and stepped down in favor of an appointed interim president. In November 1993 General Sani Abacha took over the presidency. On the first anniversary of the election, Abiola declared himself the nation's legitimate president. Abacha launched a quick response, ordering Abiola's arrest and imprisonment. Soyinka and other democrats were outraged and criticized the government's actions in the international media. The author's reputation brought more attention to the opposition viewpoint than the press might otherwise have given.

In 1994 Soyinka and other opposition leaders formed a new prodemocracy group called the National Democratic Coalition. (NADECO). As their criticism of the government grew stronger, federal authorities detained many of its members; others fled the country. In late 1994 the government seized Soyinka's passport. Soon after, the author left the country. (He claimed he had gone on a partridge hunt through the forest and disappeared across the border.) Charged with treason after he left the country, Soyinka has been in exile since then, although he says he has snuck in and out of Nigeria on occasion. Sani Abacha died in June 1998, and his successor was Abdulsalam Abubakar, another member of the same military government that had exiled Soyinka. Demands from various Nigerian groups arose for the release and reinstatement of the democratically elected Abiola as president. In July 1998, however, Abiola died suddenly while still in custody.

Further Reading

Contemporary Black Biography. Volume 4. Detroit: Gale, 1993.

Contemporary Literary Criticism. Detroit: Gale, Volume 3, 1975; Volume 5, 1976; Volume 14, 1980; Volume 36, 1986; Volume 44, 1987.

Dictionary of Literary Biography Yearbook: 1986. Detroit: Gale, 1987.

Gibbs, James, ed. *Critical Perspectives on Wole Soyinka.* Washington, DC: Three Continents, 1980.

Jones, Eldred. *Wole Soyinka.* New York: Twayne, 1973.

Katrak, Ketu. *Wole Soyinka and Modern Tragedy: A Study of Dramatic Theory and Practice.* Westport, CT: Greenwood Press, 1986.

King, Bruce, ed. *Introduction to Nigerian Literature.* New York: Africana Publishing, 1972.

Larson, Charles R. *The Emergence of African Fiction.* Rev. ed. Bloomington: Indiana University Press, 1972.

Laurence, Margaret. *Long Drums and Cannons: Nigerian Dramatists and Novelists.* New York: Praeger, 1968.

Moore, Gerald. *Wole Soyinka.* New York: Africana Publishing, 1971.

Pieterse, Cosmo, and Dennis Dueren, eds. *African Writers Talking: A Collection of Radio Interviews.* New York: Africana Publishing, 1972.

Roscoe, Adrian A. *Mother Is Gold: A Study in West African Literature.* New York/UK: Cambridge University Press, 1971.

Schmemann, Serge, "Foe of Nigeria's Military Fears It Will Rule On," *New York Times,* June 12, 1998.

Soyinka, Wole. *The Man Died: Prison Notes of Wole Soyinka.* New York: Harper, 1972.

Soyinka, Wole. *Myth, Literature, and the African World.* New York/UK: Cambridge University Press, 1976.

Soyinka, Wole. *Ake: The Years of Childhood.* New York: Random House, 1981.

Tippu Tib

Born c. 1837
Zanzibar
Died 1905
Zanzibar

Central African ivory and slave trader

Tippu Tib was "a pirate of considerable charm and delicacy."

—A nineteenth-century historian, commenting on the trader-ruler of Zanzibar

In the 1850s and 1860s European explorers unintentionally opened the interior regions of central Africa to traders dealing in ivory and slaves. Tippu Tib (also known as Tippu Tip; pronounced *TEE-poo tib*), a trader of mixed descent from Zanzibar, became one of the wealthiest and most powerful slave and ivory traders in central Africa. A tall and striking dark-skinned man known for his thick black beard and incredible wardrobe, he also possessed a magnetic personality—and used it to acquire enormous wealth and power. He was authoritative, intelligent to talk to, and, as one historian called him, "a pirate of considerable charm and delicacy." In his memoirs Tippu Tib admitted that he liked to play the *grand seigneur,* the "lord of the manor." He was capable of atrocious acts of cruelty, yet he was considered by many to be an engaging and worldly gentleman. His power as a trader-ruler rivaled that of the sultan (the title given to the king of a Muslim state) of Zanzibar.

Tippu Tib was the nickname given to Hamed Bin Muhammed el Murjebi because of a tick or nervous twitch he had in one eye. He was born in the 1830s on the island of Zanzibar off the East Coast of Africa. Tippu Tib was of mixed racial heritage. His mother was an Arab woman whose family came from Muscat; his father and grandfather were Swahili traders from the African coast, and his father's mother was the daughter of an African chief of the Nyamwezi.

Learns the trade

As a young man Tippu Tib represented his father's business interests in the interior of the continent. He traveled with Nyamwezi trading caravans around the southern end of Lake Tanganyika, south to Katanga in what is today the Democratic Republic of the Congo (called Zaire from 1971 to 1997). Tippu Tib stayed in Katanga for about two years. The chief power broker there at that time was M'Siri (see entry), a Nyamwezi who had built up a vast political and commercial empire with slaves, ivory, and copper that he traded for guns.

Nyamwezi were African traders who lived between Lake Tanganyika and the coast, about 600 miles inland. They were exceptionally good porters or bearers, and by the early 1800s they had developed a trading network across the region. The Nyamwezi traders dealt in ivory, slaves, and copper well before Arab traders ventured into Africa's interior. By 1840, however, the price of ivory had increased dramatically, and its rising value made the long trek to the interior profitable for coastal traders. A core of Arab traders went to the Nyamwezi area and formed a partnership with the Nyamwezi traders and porters. The Arabs founded a town called Tabora in western-central Tanzania. This town became the center for the ivory and slave trade, rivaling Zanzibar in its activity. Traders kept storehouses full of merchandise that they could sell to the caravans from the coast. Increasingly, the caravans went to Tabora to begin their more difficult trips farther into the interior.

Caravans might have as many as 1,000 porters or bearers. Sometimes traders' caravans would travel in convoys (large organized groups) because they could protect themselves better—and bargain better. Local chiefs imposed tolls on the caravans going through their territories. Traders were particularly vulnerable if a chief controlled a river crossing or water supply in a dry area.

Warfare and slave raiding moved into the interior with the caravans. When guns became widely available in the 1870s and 1880s, the raiding and slaving become more violent.

Amasses a fortune

Tippu Tib was a product of this time. He was a shrewd businessman, cut off from his traditional roots and moral code. He had a charismatic personality and was dependent on no one—only his gun and his wits. To be sure, Tippu Tib was not the only man of this type; there were others like him, but because of his relations with European explorers he gained the most notoriety.

Tippu Tib traveled throughout the African interior, amassing a fortune in ivory and gaining valuable experience in the business of commerce. Around 1869 he went northwest looking for ivory. In a daring raid against Nsama, a chief reputed to have killed Arabs, Tippu Tib captured his capital and took his ivory. Tippu Tib's victory over this much-feared chief gained him the reputation of a powerful and dangerous man. Other chiefs paid him tribute in elephant tusks. So great was his store of ivory that he had special storage places built to house it.

About the time Tippu Tib was establishing himself in trade, several Arab merchants from Zanzibar reached the Lualaba River and founded a settlement called Nyangwe. A major market center grew up there. In 1874 the Arabs recognized Tippu Tib as the overlord of the area. He had a large and impressive base of operation, controlling vast amounts of territory. His personal empire was huge: it stretched west from Lake Tanganyika as far as the Lomami River and north to the Congo forest. Although Tippu Tib held this territory in the name of the sultan of Zanzibar, he actually served as an independent ruler. Tippu Tib established himself as the "Big Man of Nyangwe" and made his capital, Kasonga, into a showpiece on the Lualaba River. European visitors were shocked by the richness and extravagance of his interior settlement: "Even the common soldiers slept on silk and satin mattresses, in carved beds with silk mosquito curtains," one observer was quoted as saying in Robin Hallett's *Africa since 1875.* The visitors reported that the roads in the capital surrounded large plantations that had been cleared of virgin forests, yielding "splendid crops of sugar cane, rice, maize, and a variety of fruits, including oranges, guavas, pineapples, and pomegranates."

Though not officially a sultan, Tippu Tib ruled like one. With his monopoly on the sale of ivory, he controlled the political structure of his kingdom. He selected local leaders as chiefs and appointed his own officials to supervise the chiefs, to collect tribute, to enforce the laws, and to recruit soldiers.

Runs the caravans

From his base west of Lake Tanganyika, Tippu Tib maintained good relations with the Nyamwezi to the east of the lake. These relations were important because the Nyamwezi lay between Tippu Tib and his outlet to the Indian Ocean coast.

In usual practice, African or Arab traders would hire a band of slavers (known as *ruga ruga*) or send their own men out on so-called commercial ventures. The traders would pay a casual visit to a village to see if the chief had hidden away any ivory. If so, they would return later with sufficient men and fire power to take the ivory from the chief. Or, when they raided the villages, they would take captives, usually women and children, and then ransom them to the village chief for his ivory. If the village did not have sufficient ivory, they would take the remaining captives along with them as they continued their travels, then trade them in another place.

Sometimes Tippu Tib's men would form an alliance with a local chief, and together they would raid a neighboring village. The raiders would set fire to the huts, wait for the villagers to run out, and then capture the women and children. Later they would take them to market and either trade them locally for food and supplies or take them to the coast for sale at the slave market in Zanzibar. Westerners frequented the markets at Zanzibar because they could fill the cargo space in their ships with slaves *and* ivory at one place.

On Zanzibar the slaves would be used as house servants for local Zanzibaris. They might be shipped to the clove plantations on Pemba Island or sent to Muscat for re-export to Arabia, Persia (Iran), Syria, or Turkey. African slaves were important to the Muslim nations because Muhammad the Prophet said Muslims could not be enslaved. Slave trade along the Indian Ocean coast also grew in response to restrictions placed on slave trade along the Atlantic Coast. (Great Britain had ships patrolling the Atlantic waters to prevent slave export.) The major Western powers—the

United States, France, Britain, and Germany—had all sent representatives to Zanzibar to protect their commercial interests. The United States even established a consulate there in 1836. (Consuls are officials appointed by a government to represent that government's commercial, or business, interests in a foreign land.)

By the late 1890s the United States was importing 80 percent of the ivory exported from Zanzibar. Western demand for ivory reflected the affluence of the societies. Ivory from East and Central Africa was soft and ideal for carving. It was used for such household items as knife handles, piano keys, billiard balls, umbrella handles, snuff boxes, and ladies' fans. Religious statues and crucifixes were often made of ivory as well.

Encounters Stanley

In 1876 Tippu Tib met with Henry Morton Stanley (1841-1904), Britain's famous explorer. Historians disagree about where they met, but the reason for the encounter was that Stanley wanted Tippu Tib's help in exploring the upper reaches of the Congo River (called the Lualaba River). Several years before, Stanley had gained notoriety in the West by finding the Scottish missionary and explorer David Livingstone near Lake Tanganyika. Now Stanley was trying to pick up where Livingstone had left off in his quest to find the source of the Nile River. Stanley wanted Tippu Tib to accompany him along the Lualaba River for 300 miles.

Tippu Tib apparently enjoyed entertaining whites, and he welcomed Stanley to his capital. Stanley was actually the third European explorer Tippu Tib had assisted. In 1867, when he was working for his father, he guided Dr. Livingstone's caravan south toward Lake Mweru. From 1872 to 1874 he escorted Verney Lovett Cameron part of the way on his trek to the Atlantic Coast from Lualaba. The explorers and slave traders needed each other: European explorers needed the help of men like Tippu Tib because of their intimate knowledge of the African terrain. The slavers and ivory hunters benefitted from the explorers because they helped open new paths to Africa's interior.

Stanley is said to have given $5,000 to Tippu Tib for his guidance. Tippu Tib also supplied 140 men with guns, another 140 men with spears and traditional weapons, and about 20 women from his harem. The trader-ruler could not understand what motivated

Meeting between explorers Henry Morton Stanley and David Livingstone on Lake Tanganyika (in present-day Tanzania), 1871. Tippu Tib accompanied both men in some of their explorations.

Stanley and the other white explorers he had met. For Tippu Tib, these travels were strictly business. In *The Scramble for Africa,* Thomas Pakenham quoted him as having said:

> You Wasungu [white men] are desirous of throwing away your lives, it is no reason we Arabs should. We travel little by little to get ivory and slaves, and are years about it—it is now nine years since I left Zanzibar—but you white men only look for rivers and lakes and mountains, and you spend your lives for no reason, and to no purpose. . . . For what?

Later, Tippu Tib agreed to accompany Stanley for 60 days beyond Nyangwe and then return. The two men left with a caravan of 700 people. The caravan paralleled (ran next to) the river until it came upon the dark and curving rain forest. The overgrowth was so thick that the men had to crawl along the damp and smelly ground on their hands and knees. When the caravan first encountered the rain forest, Tippu Tib predicted they would not get through it and announced that he was returning to his base. Stanley offered him $2,600 more if he would continue the journey. Tippu Tib eventually did turn back, but Stanley continued to travel along the river. Two months after Tippu Tib left him, Stanley came out onto a lake 15 miles across surrounded by white cliffs. He named the lake Stanley Pool after himself. (It is now known as Malebo Pool.) From there, Stanley and his men followed the raging river 220 miles to Matadi, where the river became navigable again, and they went the final 100 miles to the river's mouth. In all it had taken him 999 days to cross the African continent from the Indian Ocean to the Atlantic Ocean.

Opens up river areas

Stanley's successful trip down the Lualaba encouraged travel by the once-skeptical traders. In fact, Tippu Tib was one of the first of the traders to follow. The traders created chaos along the river. They burned and looted entire villages and took people captive. According to Peter Forbath in *The River Congo,* Stanley was shocked at what he saw six years later when he revisited the area:

> On my old map, it is marked Mawembe, and was strongly palisaded; but now . . . I could detect no sign of palisade or hut. . . . Not a house or living thing could be seen anywhere. . . . All had vanished. . . . Surely there had been a great change! . . . A few miles higher up on the same bank we came abreast of another scene of desolation, where a whole town had been burnt, the palms cut down, bananas scorched, many acres laid level with the ground.

As they traveled on down the river, Stanley described another village where the slave traders had come in and taken their captives:

> There rows upon rows of dark nakedness, relieved here and there by the white dresses of the captors. . . . I observe that mostly all are fettered [chained]; youths with iron rings around their necks, through which a chain . . . is drove [driven], securing the captives by twenties. The children over ten are secured by three copper rings. . . . The mothers are secured by shorter chains. . . . My nerves are offended with the rancid effluvium [offensive smell] of the unwashed herds within this human kennel. The smell of other abominations annoy me. . . . For how could poor people, bound and rivetted together by twenties, do otherwise than wallow in filth!

Later Stanley learned that this camp held 2,300 captives taken in raids on 118 villages. The slavers had killed at least another 4,000 Africans.

Although the situation shocked Stanley, he realized he had to deal peaceably with the Arabs. They had benefited from modern technology and now had superior firepower. Arms and ammunition had flooded the African interior. European merchants traded guns with the region's merchants for slaves and ivory. Tippu Tib reportedly had acquired some 50,000 guns by the mid-1880s.

In 1885 Stanley returned to the Congo to head a relief expedition. He went to Zanzibar in 1887 to ask Tippu Tib to help him. In exchange, Stanley appointed Tippu Tib the Belgian governor of Stanley Falls (Kisangani), an area he already controlled. This was Stanley's solution to curbing the Arab aggressiveness around Stanley Falls. One condition of the arrangement was that Tippu Tib had to agree to try and stop the slave trading. Although he could not succeed in doing this, he was able to stop the Arabs from coming into contact with the Europeans.

Tippu Tib, Stanley, and their expedition force of 700 men sailed south from Zanzibar, rounded the Cape of Good Hope, and sailed up the south Atlantic Coast to the mouth of the Congo River. From there they went to Stanley Pool. Stanley went on into the interior, and Tippu Tib remained behind to organize replacements. Tippu Tib and Stanley had a falling out and Stanley accused him of not honoring his promise to send up extra men for the expedition. When Stanley returned he sued in a Zanzibar court, but Tippu Tib won the case.

Tippu Tib left the interior in 1890 and retired to Zanzibar. He died there in 1905. His son, Sef, represented his interests at Stanley Pool. When the Belgians settled in the area and tried to restrict the Arabs by force from trading in slaves, the Arabs rose against them. Sef was killed in 1892, and within 18 months the Belgians had completely crushed the Arabs.

Further Reading

Farrant, Leda. *Tippu Tip and the East African Slave Trade.* London: Hamish Hamilton, 1975

Forbath, Peter. *The River Congo.* New York: Harper, 1977.

Hallett, Robin. *Africa since 1875.* Ann Arbor: University of Michigan Press, 1974.

Hibbert, Christopher. *Africa Explored: Europeans in the Dark Continent, 1769-1889.* New York: Norton, 1982.

McLynn, Frank. *Hearts of Darkness: The European Explorations of Africa.* Pimlico, 1992.

Moorehead, Alan. *The White Nile.* New York: Harper, 1971.

Oliver, Roland, and Anthony Atmore. *Africa since 1800.* New York/UK: Cambridge University Press, 1972.

Pakenham, Thomas. *The Scramble for Africa.* Jonathan Ball, 1991.

Sékou Touré

Born January 9, 1922
Faranah, Guinea
Died March 26, 1984
Cleveland, Ohio, USA

President of Guinea

"We prefer to live in poverty in liberty than to riches in slavery."

—Touré, on French withdrawal from Guinea

Sékou Touré was the absolute ruler of Guinea from 1958, the year of its independence, until the day of his death 26 years later. Located along the Atlantic Coast of West Africa, Guinea had become part of French West Africa back in 1904. Independence came to Guinea rather suddenly when the country voted in 1958 not to accept French president Charles de Gaulle's offer of membership in a community of French overseas territories. It was the only French colony to refuse the offer. At the time Touré was secretary-general of the dominant political party, Parti Démocratique de Guinée (Democratic Party of Guinea; PDG). Earlier that year the PDG had won 57 of the 60 representative seats in elections held under French colonial supervision.

Touré refused to join the French community because he believed that black equality and colonialism could not exist together. (Colonialism is the extension of a nation's power beyond its own borders, usually for economic gain. During the 1800s, France and other European powers established colonies in Africa.) He championed freedom for African nations—no matter what the cost—and looked to the groundbreaking example of Kwame Nkrumah (see entry), the leader of Ghana, as his model. (Ghana was the first African nation to achieve independence.) Unfortunately, Touré's idealistic aspirations led to economic chaos in Guinea.

Experience as a trade unionist

Touré was born in the small village of Faranah. His parents, Alpha and Aminata Touré, were small-scale Malinké farmers. Touré attended French Guinean primary schools and later went to the Ecole Professionnelle Georges Poiret in the capital city of Conakry. He also studied abroad at the Institute of Economic Science in Prague, Czechoslovakia. Touré's parents raised him as a Muslim. In his older years he proclaimed himself a member of "All Faiths."

Touré was active in labor unions and held several government positions in his early years. During the 1940s he was secretary-general of the Post and Telecommunications Workers' Union and helped found another, the Federation of Workers' Unions of Guinea. In 1946 he became involved in African politics when Félix Houphouët-Boigny (see entry) formed the Rassemblement Démocratique Africaine (African Democratic Rally; RDA), a territory-wide political party in the Ivory Coast (Côte d'Ivoire). After holding several positions in Guinea, Touré was elected mayor of Conakry in 1955. The next year, he won a seat in the National Assembly in Paris, where he impressed delegates with his public speaking ability.

Touré continued his labor union activity while performing his legislative role. In 1957 he was named vice president of the Governmental Council of Guinea, a post equivalent to that of prime minister under the French governor. As council vice president, he moved to restructure and democratize the traditional chieftaincy system. He took traditional powers away from the chiefs and instead empowered more than 4,000 village councils elected by the people.

French Politics

During the Fourth Republic in France (1946-58), the French government declared its African colonies to be overseas territories of France. Under the Union structure, France permitted African territories to elect the members of their own assemblies as well as to send representatives to the French National Assembly in Paris.

Develops policy of "positive neutrality"

Immediately after the 1958 referendum on joining the French Union, Guinea gained its independence from France. Having followed Ghana's lead, it become the second African nation to achieve independence. Within a few days Touré became president of the new republic. With the PDG as the nation's only legal political party, Guinea emerged as a one-party, totalitarian (dictatorial) state. France and all its allies quickly withdrew support and would not give the country any aid. The French were particularly nasty in their break with the country, destroying valuable equipment and files, suspending all aid and technical assistance, and stopping almost all investment in Guinea's mining operations. In response Touré is reported to have said: "We prefer to live in poverty in liberty than to riches in slavery."

French withdrawal created great bitterness in Guinea. With the newly independent country desperate for outside aid to replace what France had been providing, Touré turned to his friend and ally Nkrumah. The two leaders shared the ideals of Pan-Africanism, a doctrine that stressed the unity and mutual support of all African nations. Ghana quickly lent Guinea some $28 million.

Touré also appealed to the Eastern bloc countries—the communist states of East Europe—for assistance. (Communism is a system of government in which the state controls the means of production and the distribution of goods. It clashes with the American ideal of capitalism, which is based on private ownership and a free market system.) In 1960 he traveled first to China, then to the Soviet Union, where he was honored with the Lenin Peace Prize. The Soviets were willing to provide aid, thereby establishing a bond that damaged relations with the United States and other countries in the West, but Touré's exclusive association with the Communists was short-lived. In 1961 he expelled the Russian

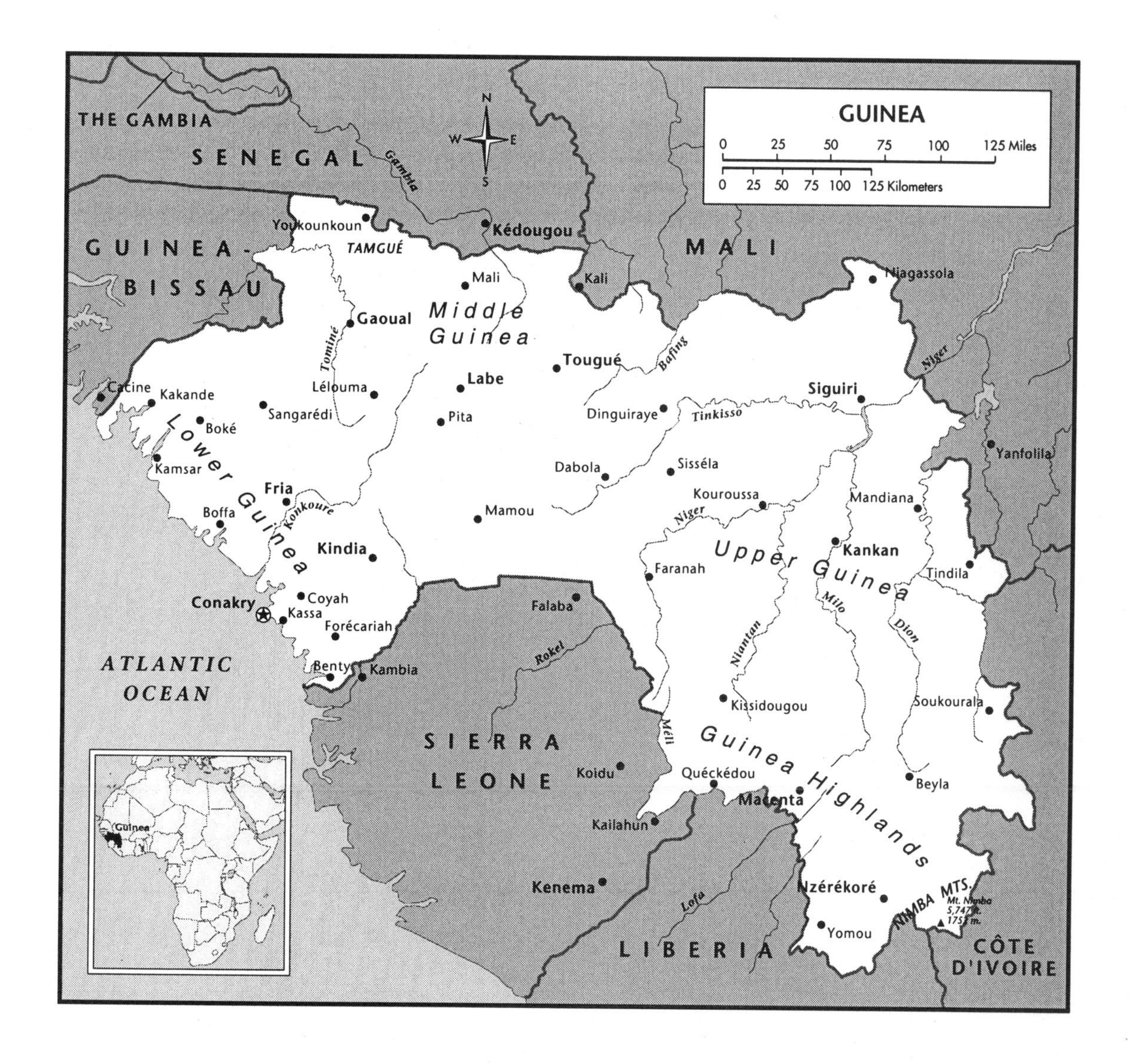

ambassador for interfering in the internal affairs of his country, accusing the Soviets of plotting a revolution.

Following this episode, the United States became a significant source of aid to Guinea. In 1963 Touré met with U.S. president John F. Kennedy, and the United States subsequently lent Guinea $400 million to develop its bauxite (a source of aluminum) industry. Throughout the 1960s Touré maintained a stance of "positive neutrality" with respect to the political tension that existed between the superpowers, accepting aid from both the United States and the Soviet Union.

Downward turn

Following the break with France, Touré stopped traditional trade and ended private ownership of industry. Consequently, many Guineans migrated to neighboring countries, such as Senegal and the Côte d'Ivoire, which had less centralized (government controlled) economies. For 20 years these neighboring countries were home to hundreds of thousands of Guineans who opposed Touré. Touré later accused both nations of training mercenaries (soldiers for hire) to invade Guinea.

Throughout the 1960s Guineans continued to leave their homeland because of insecurity and poor economic conditions. Touré remained in power, though, for three main reasons: first, he dominated all of the central government's activities; second, he relied on a close group of trusted collaborators; and third, he balanced the authority of the Guinean army against the PDG's people's army. Touré used his party's militia, which grew to some 30,000 in the mid-1960s, to enforce new modes of justice and production throughout the country.

The discovery of plots against the government caused tension between Guinea and its neighbors in the early 1960s. In 1965 an opposition group called the Front pour la libération nationale de Guinée (Front for the National Liberation of Guinea; FLNG), began organizing under the leadership of disgruntled Guineans living in Abidjan, Côte d'Ivoire; Dakar, Senegal; and Paris, France. By the late 1960s, Touré was preoccupied with FLNG activity and feared an invasion. Army unrest seemed to point to a plot to separate Guinea's Labé region, located in the western central part of the nation, from the rest of the country. In June 1970, Radio Conakry reported on an impending invasion of Guinea by forces that were being trained in Portuguese Guinea, now known as Guinea-Bissau. A few months later a group of mercenaries was arrested in Labé.

Touré supported the long anticolonial struggle being waged in Guinea-Bissau. For generations the Portuguese government had held the tiny African province in its grip. Touré sent freedom fighters to Guinea-Bissau and provided both base facilities and diplomatic support for the revolutionary effort. But Portugal's hard-hitting counterattack convinced Touré that the conspiracy against his government was universal.

Crackdown follows 1970 invasion

The Portuguese invasion of Guinea took place on November 22, 1970. At least 350 troops, consisting mainly of Guinean exiles (Guineans forced to leave their homeland) in the Portuguese-led army, landed from the sea off Conakry. As destructive as it was, the invasion failed to unseat Touré; instead, it led to a reign of fear, suspicion, and violence in Guinea. Public figures suspected of holding opinions critical to Touré and his government were arrested. Secret mass trials and executions followed. The bodies of the condemned were displayed in public places.

Many political prisoners were held in Boiro camp near Conakry. The camp became notorious for the torture and inhumane treatment of its prisoners. The repression grew as more plots against the Guinean government, real and imaginary, were discovered and announced. More people fled and settled in other West African countries and in Europe, especially in Paris. According to French estimates, 2 million out of a population of 5.5 million chose to live in exile.

Among those affected by purges (moves by the government to eliminate "unwanted" elements in Guinea) were such groups as intellectuals, traders, state employees, civil servants, the military, and members of the Fulani ethnic group. (The Fulani people of northern Guinea felt that their traditional, nomadic way of life was threatened by Touré's fierce grip on the nation.) These practices resulted in a loss of talented individuals from Guinea and crippled the administration of the country. Many exiles and relatives of the victims of Touré's purges responded by establishing powerful anti-Touré pressure groups.

The terror brought on by the Guinean government alternated with periods of relative calm, as suspicion of further attacks against the government subsided briefly in 1972. Nevertheless, by the next year, the assassination in Conakry of a leader of the Portuguese-Guinea liberation struggle prompted renewed fears. Relations with neighboring countries crumbled once more due to exile activities there.

Repression and povery lead to riots

Repression in Guinea had reached such proportions that a 1977 report was submitted to the United Nations (UN; an international organization promoting world peace) detailing the mistreatment of Guinean political prisoners. The next year, Amnesty International, a worldwide human rights group, cited cases of imprisonment without trial and examples of torture and execution. Subsequently, the Guinean government claimed the abuse had ended, and authorities released many political prisoners.

By the mid-1970s Guinea had clearly been left behind economically. Guineans were accustomed to scarcity, yet neighboring countries had bountiful markets, luxury shops, and factories that were fully operative. The growing popular discontent hit a fever pitch in 1977 over the country's economic policy and shortage of food. Workers with low incomes were facing starvation, and foreign debt was crippling the economy.

These conditions led to mass protests in many regions of the nation. One held by the market women of Conakry in August 1977 touched off riots in nearby towns and led to the murder of three territorial governors. Such events shook the government because the women had been instrumental in the success of the ruling PDG over the years. Touré conceded (gave in) to many of their demands and instituted a more liberal internal economic policy, allowing new freedom to small-scale private traders and disbanding the country's "economic police."

Greater economic freedom in Guinea coincided with diplomatic efforts that Touré had been undertaking since 1975. That year he was actively involved in a regional peace effort involving a border dispute between Mali and Upper Volta (now Burkino Faso). It was the first time he had traveled outside Guinea since the 1970 invasion, and it gave him a sense of how the world was changing.

In 1976 Guinea, West Germany (now Germany), and France reestablished diplomatic and trade relations under the guidance of the United Nations. Touré later reconciled with the leaders of Senegal and the Côte d'Ivoire, two consistently pro-French neighbors, and traveled to 16 countries in Africa and the Middle East, including several rich, oil-producing states. In addition, he attended his first Organization of African Unity (OAU) summit in 11 years. Economic development became Touré's principal goal. He looked specifically to the United States, Canada, and Great Britain for support, using his country's rich mineral resources as his main incentive for foreign investment.

Touré speaks at a meeting of the Special Committee of 24 on decolonization in Conakry, Guinea, 1972.

In the aftermath

In the early 1980s Touré was actively engaged in African and international affairs. Before his death from a heart attack during heart surgery in March 1984, Touré had been actively pursuing the chairmanship of the OAU. But the OAU summit, originally scheduled to be held in Conakry in 1983, was delayed until 1984 because of expected Libyan opposition. Despite his efforts to attract foreign investment, Touré died leaving Guinea in a state of economic collapse; he had ruled the nation for 26 years. At his death some 1.5 million people had fled the country, more than 20 percent of the country's population. In April 1984, the army staged a coup and took over the country, filling the political void left by his death.

Further Reading

Adamolekun, Ladipo. *Sékou Touré's Guinea: An Experiment in Nation Building.* New York: Methuen, 1976.

Africa Report, May-June 1981; November-December 1993.

Contemporary Black Biography. Volume 6. Detroit: Gale, 1994.

Moïse Tshombe

Born November 19, 1917
Musumba, Belgian Congo (known as Zaire from 1971 to 1997; renamed Democratic Republic of the Congo, May 17, 1997)
Died June 30, 1969
Algiers, Algeria

President of the secessionist state of Katanga, Congo Republic; prime minister of Congo Republic

Tshombe proved much more successful in politics than in business.

Moïse Kapenda Tshombe (*CHOM-bay*) was a Congolese businessman turned politician from Katanga province (later Shaba province, Zaire) in the former Belgian Congo. The Katanga region of the Democratic Republic of the Congo (Zaire's name was changed in 1997) is three times the size of Great Britain and the richest of the five provinces of the vast Congo colony. Often called a geological miracle, the province holds vast fields of copper, gold, diamonds, and uranium. In the past it supplied the colony with 40 percent of its revenue. Katanga was also the heartland of the Lunda people, 4 million strong, stretching to Angola and Zambia from southeastern Congo. Between the fourteenth and nineteenth centuries, the Lunda controlled one of the largest empires in all of Africa.

Tshombe's father, Joseph Kapenda Tshombe, was a Katanga trader who became one of the most successful Congolese merchants in the colony. He brought his children up in an atmosphere of wealth and privilege, and they married into the ruling Lunda royal family. Moïse Tshombe was born on November 19, 1917, at Musumba, capital of the old Lunda empire of the great chief Mwant Yav in Katanga province. He was the oldest son of 11 children. His father began as a village blacksmith and earned his fortune by buying the produce of small-scale farmers of the Sandoa and Katanga districts and reselling it in the Katanga copper mining area. On return from the copperbelt, he—and later his seven sons—brought back general goods to sell in his more than 16 village stores. As his wealth increased, his daughters and sons married into the royal family of the Mwant Yav.

Joseph was a member of Provincial Council of Katanga that advised the Belgian governor in the Congo, and in 1947 he became the first Congolese to pay for his own trip to Belgium. In the late 1800s Belgian king Leopold II had taken over the rich Congo land and eventually made it into a colony of the Belgian government.

An early start

As the eldest son in his family, Moïse was to inherit his father's business. His parents sent him to a local school run by U.S. Methodist missionaries in Sandoa and then to a Methodist teachers' training institute in Kanene, about 120 miles south of Musumba. After four years' study, Tshombe entered business as bookkeeper and produce-carrier for his father's firm. He also organized a boy scout troop run by the Methodist Youth Association. In the early 1940s his father sent him to Elisabethville (now Lubumbashi), the capital of Katanga province, to expand the family's business interests. In the much more cultured and sophisticated capital, Tshombe soon involved himself with the *évolué* (Western-educated African) community. But when he started to show more interest in the urban nightclubs and cafes than in business, his father brought him home to work in the Sandoa "bush stores." Tshombe was not interested in business, and his father had to bail him out of bankruptcy three times. Recalling these years, Tshombe noted that "in some transactions with Belgium traders I just miscalculated, in others [I was] over trustful." In 1951 Tshombe married Ruth Matschik, the daughter of Chief Mbaku

Ditend, who became Mwanta Yav Ditend Yavu a Nawej III (king of the Lunda who reigned from 1951 to 1963).

Becomes involved in politics

Tshombe proved much more successful in politics than in business. Following his father's death in 1951, he took over as director of the family businesses in Elisabethville. The Congolese chamber of commerce elected him president, and he took his father's seat on the Provincial Council. But Tshombe ran into business difficulties largely because Belgian colonial law did not permit Africans to obtain credit from banks—even when they owned land and real estate.

As a member of the royal family Tshombe became deeply involved in Lunda ethnic politics. In 1956 he founded a Lunda tribal association approved by the colonial administration as a nonpolitical club and was elected president of the Association of African Middle Classes (ACAMAF) and president of the Grouping of Mutual [Ethnic] Associations of the Lunda Empire (GASSOMEL).

The next year was the very first year that the colonial administration permitted Africans to stand as candidates for local councils. The Lunda in Elisabethville received a shock when Luba mine workers (members of another ethnic group) from Kasai province won three out of four seats on the council. In response to the victory of "foreigners" over "native Katangans," Tshombe and his supporters organized the Confédération des associations tribales du Katanga (Confederation of Tribal Associations of Katanga; CONAKAT) with the goal of sending 160,000 Luba back to Kasai. The next year a sharp recession (economic slowdown) led to widespread layoffs in the mining centers of Katanga, increasing the competition between native Katangans and Luba immigrants.

Elsewhere in Africa, African colonies were beginning to win their independence from the European powers that held them. In 1957 Ghana—led by Kwame Nkrumah (see entry)—had just won its independence from Great Britain. In October 1958 Charles de Gaulle (1890-1970), then president of France, made a trip to Brazzaville in the neighboring French Congo and offered all French African colonies their independence. In Leopoldville (present-day Kinshasa), capital of the Belgian Congo, Patrice Lumumba (see entry) organized the Mouvement National Congolais (the National Congolese Movement; MNC) to press for independence.

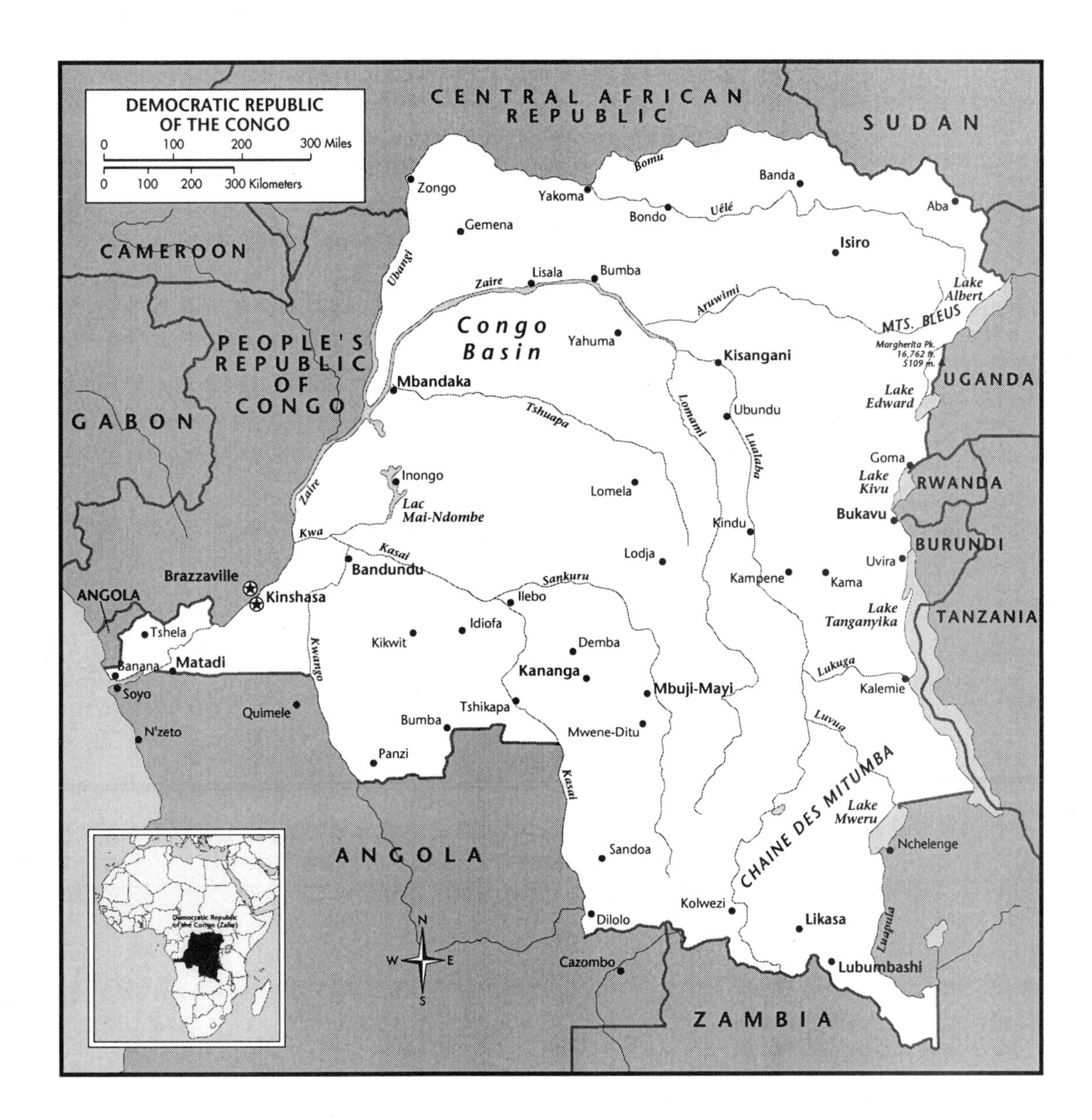

Branches of the MNC supported by the Kasai Luba appeared in Elisabethville to challenge CONAKAT.

The importance of heritage

Lumumba felt that the future Congo should be a unitary state—one in which the central power would rest with a national assembly based in Leopoldville. Tshombe supported Lumumba's major rival, Joseph Kasavubu of the ABAKO (Association des Ba-Kongo) party, who argued for a federal-type government that would allow each province to have its own powers. Tshombe preferred this structure because he wanted the mining wealth to stay in Katanga rather than flow to Leopoldville, more than a thousand miles away. The Belgian business elite—especially leaders of the mining companies that had once been his competitors and enemies—quickly became Tshombe's supporters.

Political turmoil spread throughout the Congo in 1959. Rioting flared in the lower Congo when ABAKO petitioned to become a separate state. In Katanga, the Kasai Luba and several smaller ethnic groups joined the MNC or organized their own political parties. Violence between them and the Lunda often erupted. By the end of the year growing disorder in the Congo had produced alarm in Belgium. The government reluctantly convened a conference of Congolese leaders in Brussels on January 20, 1960. While Tshombe and Kasavubu pressed for a federal constitution, Lumumba's MNC won the day when the conference agreed to a unity government with a national assembly in Leopoldville. Much to Tshombe's dismay, they scheduled elections for a new government for May and independence for June. Thus, with only 16 Congolese college graduates, the Africans had six months to organize a nation as large as West Europe and just as ethnically diverse.

In the May elections, CONAKAT won only eight out of the 137 seats in the National Assembly. This placed Tshombe's party far behind Lumumba's MNC (33 seats) and Kasavubu's ABAKO (12), and just ahead of a dozen other smaller parties and individuals throughout the country. Though Lumumba tried to form a coalition government with CONAKAT, the negotiations broke down. When Lumumba formed a parliamentary majority with Kasavubu, Lumumba became prime minister and Kasavubu became president. This situation left CONAKAT and the Katangan mining interests with no significant influence in the national government.

Declares Katanga independent

Tshombe wanted to proclaim Katanga independent of the central government, but his Belgian advisers told him to wait. Violence again broke out soon after Lumumba delivered a highly critical independence day speech on June 13. On July 5, the national army—still under the command of Belgian officers—mutinied (rebelled) against their white officers. Insurrection spread throughout the country as undisciplined troops attacked white and black citizens. In Katanga, Tshombe hired European mercenaries (soldiers for hire) to crush the mutiny and then, on July 11, 1960, declared Katanga an independent country. He now ruled a secessionist state.

Convinced that Belgium was trying to reestablish colonial rule, Lumumba demanded that Belgium remove its troops from their bases. He also severed diplomatic relations with Brussels and turned to the United Nations (UN) for assistance. On July 15, the UN agreed to send peacekeeping troops and asked Belgium to remove its army. By the end of July, the UN had stationed troops in all the provinces except Katanga. When the UN refused to use its troops to restore Katanga to the Congo, Lumumba—without consulting his cabinet—asked the Soviet Union for help. Infuriated, Kasavubu fired Lumumba as prime minister; Lumumba in turn fired Kasavubu as president. Finally, in September 1960, Joseph Mobutu (see entry), a 29-year-old commander of Congolese troops stationed in Leopoldville, seized supreme power. Lumumba was placed under house arrest. When he tried to escape to his stronghold in Stanleyville, Mobutu's soldiers captured him and secretly put him on a plane to Elisabethville. In January 1961 he was beaten to death by Tshombe's Katanga troops.

Shocked at the murder of Lumumba, the UN decided to expand its military operations and demanded that all foreign troops leave the country. Tshombe refused the order, denouncing it as a declaration of war by the UN against the Congo. Early in 1961 most of the leaders of the Congo factions (various political groups) agreed to meet in Tananarive in the Malagasy Republic (now Madagascar). There, they agreed on proposals for a united Congo and on a resolution to demand the removal of UN troops. Three months later, however, when Tshombe went to Coquilhatville (now Mbandaka) for a conference to implement the proposals, police arrested him and charged him with treason against the central government. Later released, Tshombe returned to Katanga.

Forced to give in

The Congolese central parliament finally met in August, without representatives from Katanga, and elected Cyrille Adoula as prime minister. The following month UN troops attempted to seize control of Katanga, but the Katangan forces—including white mercenaries and Belgian settlers (32,000 lived in Katanga)—showed more resistance than the UN anticipated. All attempts at negotiations failed, and the secretary-general of the UN, Dag Hammarskjöld (1905-1961), was killed in a plane crash en route to negotiations. In November, Congo's central government army, under the command of Mobutu, attempted to invade Katanga and was forced to retreat with heavy losses. On December 5, 1961, another offensive was launched. This time the UN was prepared and managed to surround Elisabethville, forcing Tshombe to negotiate with Adoula.

Two days later, the central government announced that Tshombe recognized the "indivisible unity of the Congo" and acknowledged Kasavubu as head of state and the supreme authority of the central government over all the republic. Tshombe agreed to send Katangan representatives to Leopoldville, to place his army under the authority of the central government, and to respect the resolutions of the UN security council. But even after cutting this deal, Tshombe did all he could to delay taking any real action. He claimed that the Katangan assembly still had to endorse the agreement. Negotiations between Leopoldville and Elisabethville, with constant interruptions and occasional armed clashes, continued throughout the spring, summer, and fall. By stalling, Tshombe hoped that either the central government would collapse or the UN would go bankrupt, forcing a withdrawal of its forces. Neither happened. To break the deadlock, the UN threatened to impose economic sanctions (measures taken to force a nation to obey international law). Fearing that the Adoula government might fall, giving way to a pro-Soviet government, the administration of U.S. president John F. Kennedy decided to provide the UN with whatever military equipment was necessary to bring down Tshombe's government.

Katanga secession ends

In late December, the UN Emergency Force (the Blue Helmets) took control of Elisabethville and cautiously moved against other towns, forcing Tshombe to flee to Northern Rhodesia (now Zambia). Despite Tshombe's threats that the people of Katanga would defend their independence at any cost, the UN forces met little resistance and the Katanga army fled to the bush, leaving their arms and equipment behind. Eight tribal chiefs, including Tshombe's father-in-law, jointly pledged their support to Adoula's government.

Tshombe returned to Elisabethville in early January and informed the UN he was ready to end the Katanga secession. In return, the UN and Adoula promised him amnesty (meaning they would pardon him rather than try him) for political offenses. On January 23, 1962, the two-and-a-half-year long Katangan revolt officially ended. Several weeks later, Tshombe went into self-imposed exile in Spain.

Turmoil continues

The settlement of the Katanga crisis did not end the Congo's political troubles. The central government under Adoula was corrupt and nearly bankrupt. Financially drained, the UN quickly pulled out its troops, leaving the country in the hands of the ill-disciplined Congolese army. A full-scale rebellion engulfed most of the country. By mid-1964 political leaders in Leopoldville were seeking Tshombe's help in forming a new central government. The rebels refused to disarm, so Tshombe again turned to European mercenaries to support the Congolese army. Together they recaptured the territories held by the rebels. Other African countries severely criticized Tshombe, and the Organization of African Unity (OAU) demanded that he stop hiring mercenaries. His popularity in the Congo, however, was higher than ever before.

In the June 1965 elections, Tshombe's new political party, the National Congolese Convention (CONACO), won parliamentary control of the national assembly. President Kasavubu, fearing that Tshombe might dismiss him in the transition to a new government, asked for Tshombe's resignation. When Tshombe refused, Kasavubu dismissed him, but Tshombe declined to step down. With the country again in a constitutional crisis, Mobutu dismissed both Kasavubu and Tshombe and proclaimed himself president and chief executive of the Congo for five years.

Tshombe again left the country for Spain. In July 1967, while traveling from Madrid to the Balearic Islands, an ex-convict hijacked his plane and forced it to land in Algeria. Algerian authorities put Tshombe under house arrest while the Congo held an inquiry into his involvement in Lumumba's death. Tshombe remained in Algeria until June 30, 1969, when he died of a sudden heart attack.

Further Reading

Bouscaren, A. E. *Tshombe.* 1967.

Dictionary of African Biography. Algonac, MI: Reference Publications, 1976.

Gérard-Libois, J. *Sécession au Katanga.* 1963.

Hempstone, Smith. *Katanga Report.* Winchester, MA: Faber, 1962.

Hunter, Gary. "Moise Tshome." In *Historic World Leaders.* Edited by Anne Commire. Volume 1. Detroit: Gale, 1994.

William V. S. Tubman

Born November 29, 1895
Harper, Maryland County, Liberia
Died July 23, 1971
London, England

President of Liberia

When William V. S. Tubman became its president in 1944, Liberia had been an independent country for nearly 100 years. Free blacks—former slaves in the United States who had gained their freedom—established Liberia as a place where they could resettle in Africa. (Liberia takes its name from the Latin word for "free.") From the beginning the founding families and their descendants, known as Americo-Liberians, set themselves above the local people, excluding them from the economic or political life of the country.

"He is certainly the hardest-working man in Liberia, and, I heard it said, the only man with the real interests of the country at heart."

—John Gunther, author of *Inside Africa*, commenting on Tubman

In retrospect it was too little too late, but Tubman tried to break down the barriers separating the indigenous (African-born) people from the opportunities secured by the elite (Americo-Liberians). A socially and professionally prominent figure in Liberia, he made revolutionary changes in the legal structure of the country. In his 27 years as president he expanded the vote to all property-owning men

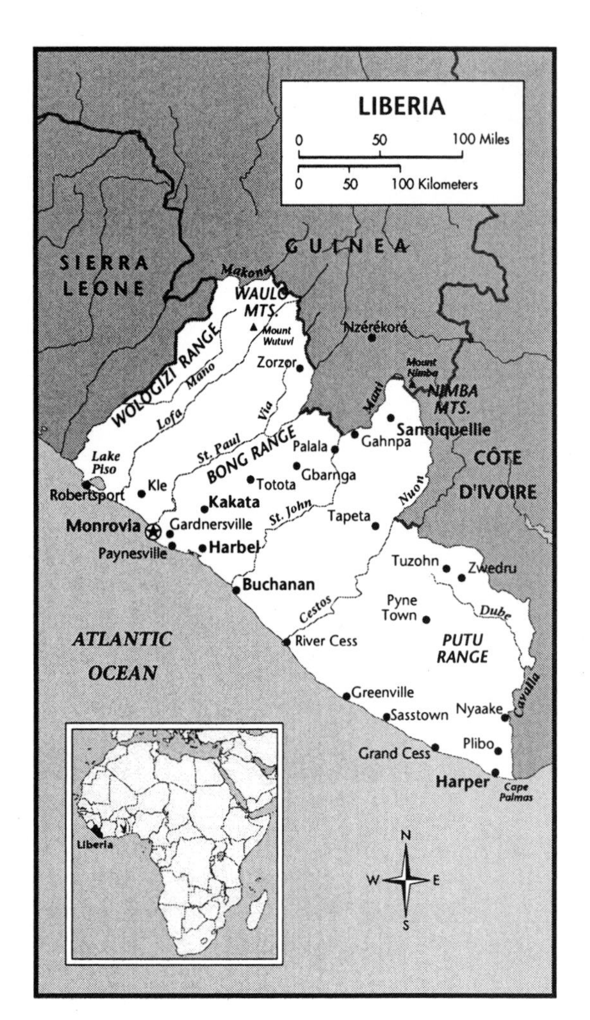

and women, created an investment climate that brought in jobs and funding, and gave the people from Liberia's interior a role in the economic and political development of the country.

Slaves find a home

By 1790 in the United States about 80,000 African slaves had been emancipated or given their freedom. They had gained their status as free men and women in a variety of ways, possibly by serving in the military, by being willed free at their owners' death, by being purchased and set free, or by escaping. In 1808 a successful ex-slave, a shipper named Paul Cuffe from Rhode Island, heard about the colony for former slaves in Sierra Leone that had been started by the British Church Missionary Society. He investigated the colony and organized societies in the United States to raise money to send freed U.S. slaves back to their homeland. The idea was quite popular with American whites, who were beginning to fear a large population of freed blacks. And while slavery was still being practiced in the United States, plantation owners in the South worried that free blacks might give their slaves ideas of freedom. The planters were particularly disturbed by news of a slave revolt in Haiti, where slaves had killed their masters and won their independence in 1804. Liberal whites also supported the "back to Africa" idea because they thought blacks would not be treated fairly in the States and that their only opportunities for social and economic advancement lay in their homeland.

The American Colonization Society and other private organizations raised enough money to send black families back to the West Coast of Africa. The first group left the United States in 1821. By 1867 approximately 20,000 people had settled in Liberia, mostly on land that had been purchased from local tribes. Of the settlers, the majority were from the United States; another large group were Africans who had been seized from slave ships by U.S. naval patrol boats and taken to Liberia; still others were from Barbados, an island in the Caribbean.

The settlers tended to splinter off into isolated groups of their own, forming settlements along the Liberian coast such as "Mississippi in Africa" at Greenville, or "Maryland in Liberia" at Harper. The original settlement at Cape Mesurado grew into the present-day capital of Monrovia, named after U.S. president James Monroe, whose administration aided the settlement. The settlers built houses reminiscent of the large brick Georgian colonial buildings they knew in the U.S. South. In 1847 the settlers declared the colony independent of the American Colonization Society.

Problems for the future

An enduring problem for Liberia is the basis on which it was founded. Sierra Leone—the other colony for former African slaves—differed from Liberia in one key way: the African settlers there had never been enslaved in the United States, the Caribbean, or South America. Although they were from different parts of Africa, these people maintained connections with their traditional ways. The settlers in Liberia, on the other hand, were several generations removed from their African traditions, and they tended to look down on the Africans who had remained in Africa. The returned Africans created a class system and closed political networks that prevented most of the native Africans from sharing in the benefits of the new society. Not only did they keep them out of the system, they took their lands and destroyed their traditional authorities. Americo-Liberians seemed to believe that their role was to civilize a "vast population of degraded subjects." They apparently saw themselves as the "civilized vanguard" (leaders at the forefront of an action or movement) whose task it was to dominate the "natives" or "aborigines" and spread Christianity.

The hostility and resentment of the Africans toward the Americo-Liberians finally exploded in the early 1980s with the brutal executions of Tubman's successor, President William R. Tolbert, Jr., and high-ranking government officials.

A distinguished background

Tubman belonged to an old and prominent Americo-Liberian family. His mother, Elizabeth Rebecca Barnes, came from Sparta, Georgia. His father, the Reverend Alexander Tubman, was from Atlanta, Georgia. The senior Tubman was a Methodist minister, a general in the Liberian army, a former speaker of the Liberian House of Representatives, and a former senator.

William V. S. Tubman was born on November 29, 1895, in Harper, Maryland County, Liberia. He went to primary school in Harper, then to the Methodist Cape Palmas Seminary, and finally to Harper County High School. Between 1910 and 1917 he served part time in the Liberian army in expeditions settling boundary disputes with people in the interior. Tubman studied law under private tutors, then worked as a recorder in the Maryland County Monthly and Probate Court, and later as a collector of internal revenue. In 1917 the county appointed him its legal representative.

Rubber trees in Liberia

From the beginning the country of Liberia had few resources. Its major trade was in palm oil, coffee, sugar, and molasses. Through some ill-advised financial schemes, the government found itself in serious debt by 1871. The country's financial problems continued until the 1920s, when the Firestone Rubber Company developed rubber tree plantations.

The *Hevea brasiliensis* of the Spurge family is a tree from South America that produces latex, from which rubber is made. In 1906 British planter Sir Harry Johnson imported 35,000 *Hevea* trees from Brazil and developed his Mount Barclay Rubber Plantation. Twenty years later U.S. industrialist Harvey Samuel Firestone, a rubber tire manufacturer from Ohio and a U.S. senator, set out to lower the high price of rubber. He bought the Mount Barclay company in 1926 and then brought in more trees. Firestone developed a new site, Harbel, near Monrovia. In 1980 the Harbel estate had 72,000 acres planted in *Hevea,* making it the largest continuous *Hevea* plantation in the world. The Firestone company was the principal employer in Liberia for 50 years, employing between five and ten percent of the population.

To raise additional money, the Liberian government engaged in several questionable enterprises. One included allowing ship owners to register ships under the Liberian flag. The exchange was profitable to both parties. The Liberians did not inspect the ships and charged relatively low fees, attracting considerable business. The foreign owners got freedom of movement without having to wrestle with the politics of their home countries.

Another moneymaking enterprise—a much more serious one—was undertaken by the Liberian government around 1930. It revealed the total disregard that Liberia's ruling elite had toward the long-established people of the country's interior. In 1931 a League of Nations report revealed that the Liberian government was trading slaves. (The League of Nations, an international peace organization formed after World War I [1914-18], was the model for its successor, the United Nations.) The League's report accused Liberian president Charles Dunbar Burgess King and his vice president, Allen Yancy, of buying young black men from local chiefs and selling them as laborers to cacao growers on the Spanish island of Fernando Po, off the Atlantic coast. When the League revealed the extent of the trade, President King was forced to resign and the legislature impeached Yancy (removed him from office). Tubman, a senator at the time, was connected with the controversial slaving venture because he served as one of Yancy's lawyers. Because of the League's report, the United States broke off diplomatic relations with Liberia for four years, until 1935.

The politics of the Americo-Liberian elite

Tubman entered national politics when he was 28 years old. In 1923 he was elected senator from Maryland County to the national legislature. The Liberian governmental system was modeled after the U.S. system, with a House of Representatives and a Senate. In 1937 President Edwin Barclay appointed Tubman associate justice of the Liberian Supreme Court. Although removed from daily politics, Tubman remained active in the True Whig party, Liberia's only political party. Since 1883 the country's leaders had justified creation of a one-party state because, they said, it would unify the region's people. Controlled by prominent settler families, the True Whig party became the vehicle for amassing wealth and power. The Americo-Liberians made up only about two percent of the entire population, yet they controlled the country through the party. Opposition groups found it difficult to be critical because the elite regulated the police, the army, and the job market.

In 1943 President Barclay named Tubman as his successor. U.S. president Franklin D. Roosevelt invited them both to the States. Roosevelt was courting the Liberians because he was anxious to secure the black American vote. Also, in 1942, the U.S. had signed a defense agreement with Liberia to build the Robertsfield airbase there.

A new path

In his inauguration speech in 1944, the new president outlined his plans to change the structure of Liberian society. Tubman announced new legislation to achieve two main goals: the unification of the region's various groups and the attraction of new investment. From the start he addressed the problems of Liberia's disfranchised people (deprived of a legal right, especially the right to vote), particularly those living in the interior. Previously, the government had closed the interior to foreign traders so as to favor the coastal people. As a result, virtually no inland development had taken place; the interior had no paved roads, hospitals, or schools. The seventh amendment to the Liberian constitution gave representation in the House and Senate to the provinces in the interior. The eighth amendment gave people of both sexes the right to vote—but only if they owned property or paid taxes on their property or hut. Tubman's government also created unification councils to give inland chiefs a chance to voice their concerns and complaints.

The "open door"

President Tubman called his program of addressing the country's investment needs "The Open Door." Tubman wanted to attract new investment, companies with capital (money), to develop Liberia. By 1950 only two foreign investors had come in: the Liberia Mining Company and the Liberia Company, which established cacao plantations. (Cacao trees produce beans used to make cocoa.) After 1950, however, Tubman's incentives brought in more than 50 companies, with a total investment of $800 million. The largest of these was the Liberian-American-Swedish Minerals Company (LAMCO), which was interested in mining the recently discovered iron ore deposits at Mt. Nimba. German investors developed the Bong and Wologosi ranges. On the labor front, Tubman raised the minimum wage for an agricultural worker to 8 cents an hour and for an industrial worker to 15 cents an hour. In 1961 he introduced pension rights and two years later adopted a modern labor code.

Before Tubman's administration, the country was almost solely dependent on the Firestone Rubber plantations. The Open Door policy diversified the economy and increased the revenues

John Gunther, author of *Inside Africa,* characterized Tubman this way:

> [President Tubman is a] bon vivant, [who] likes to sit around with the boys. He is of medium height; he looks tough, clever and supple. He likes the company of women, and has been married several times. . . . One of his sons went to a Massachusetts preparatory school and entered Harvard in 1954. . . . Mr. Tubman is a staunch Methodist—in fact he is a lay preacher and likes to be called 'Doctor.'. . .
>
> Of course the President has defects, but he is sharply intelligent, alert and accessible; that he keeps his fingers on everything is his chief source of power. He is certainly the hardest-working man in Liberia, and, I heard it said, the only man with the real interests of the country at heart. He has done more to stamp out petty corruption among officials than any President in Liberian history. No government payment over British pounds 100 may be made without his personal approval, and together with the Secretary of the Treasury, he signs all government requisitions.

brought into the government. In 1945 the government raised $1 million; in 1968 it raised $55 million.

Alters the constitution

Initially Tubman was elected for an eight-year term. Under the constitution he could not run for reelection after that. To remedy this situation, the government amended the constitution so that he could run in 1951 for a four-year term. Then in 1953 the House and Senate passed a resolution asking him to run again in 1955. He agreed. Tubman was eventually elected seven times, his final election being just a few months before his death in 1971.

In the election of 1951 women and indigenous (African-born) property owners voted for the first time. In the interior two political parties—the Reformation and the United Peoples' parties—won enough votes to threaten the True Whig party. (Following their loss in the election, though, these parties arrested or exiled their leaders.) In the 1955 election voters returned Tubman to office, but someone tried to assassinate him during his victory party. The courts charged 30 people with treason (betrayal of one's

President Tubman stands in his car as he is welcomed by the people of Monrovia, Liberia, 1963.

country); they convicted two former ministers and five others of trying to kill the president.

High expectations

The programs put in place by the Tubman administration did not reach the source of Liberia's problems. Until the 1950s only Americo-Liberian children went to school. When Tubman's programs brought schools to the interior, they raised the hopes and desires of the people. His policies brought the people in the interior more access to information, and groups like the U.S. Peace Corps brought them new knowledge. As they became increasingly exposed to outside ways, they began to want more—a chance to work and improve their lives. Unfortunately, the growth in revenues to the government did not translate into new job opportunities. Other than jobs in rubber tapping and mining, the nature of the investment did not create jobs for the students graduating from the schools. In the years to come the failure of the economy to provide jobs and the long simmering resentment caused by the elite structure of the society would have tragic consequences.

Shortly after Tubman was elected for a seventh term in 1971, he was taken ill and traveled to London, England, for surgery. He did not survive the surgery and died on July 23, 1971. He left a widow, Antoinette Padmore Tubman, and six children, one of whom, William V. S. Tubman, Jr., was president of the Congress of Industrial Organization, Liberia's principal trade union federation. In a peaceful transfer of power, Vice President William R. Tolbert succeeded Tubman as president.

Tolbert was an ordained Baptist minister, the grandson of freed South Carolina slaves. Although he continued the policies started by Tubman, Tolbert could not control the Liberian people's expectations, the high cost of living, and the lack of job creation. Following riots over the high price of rice (Liberia's staple food) and the nationwide strike for extending the vote to non-property owners, Master Sergeant Samuel K. Doe led the army against Tolbert on April 12, 1980. In a bloody coup, they killed Tolbert and took leading members of his administration to the beach and shot them. In 1990 Doe himself was killed in another coup. The civil war that followed his death had a devastating effect on the country of Liberia.

Further Reading

Curtin, Philip, and others, eds. *African History: From Earliest Times to Independence.* 2nd. ed. New York: Longman, 1995.

Davidson, Basil. *The Black Man's Burden: Africa and the Curse of the Nation-State.* James Curry, 1992.

Gunther, John. *Inside Africa.* North Pomfret, VT: Hamish Hamilton, 1955.

Hallet, Robin. *Africa since 1875.* Ann Arbor: University of Michigan Press, 1974.

Harden, Blaine. *Africa: Dispatches from a Fragile Continent.* New York: HarperCollins, 1990.

Harris, Joseph E. *Africans and Their History.* New York: New American Library, 1972.

Oliver, Roland, and Anthony Atmore. *Africa since 1800.* 2nd ed. New York/UK: Cambridge University Press, 1972.

Pedler, F.J. *West Africa.* New York: Methuen, 1951.

Weh, Tuan. *The Love of Liberty: The Rule of President William V. S. Tubman in Liberia, 1944-1971.* New York: C. Hurst/Universe Books, 1976.

Desmond Tutu

Born October 7, 1931
Klerksdorp, South Africa

South African religious leader, Nobel Peace Prize winner, and activist

"Here was a man who had inspired an entire nation with his words and his courage, who had revived the people's hope during the darkest of times . . . who selflessly fought the evils of racism during the most terrible days of apartheid."

—Nelson Mandela, commenting on Tutu's relentless campaign against racial division in South Africa

With most of the anti-government leaders in South Africa in jail or living outside the country in the 1980s, Desmond Mpilo Tutu rose from obscurity (being unknown) to spearhead the global campaign that brought an end to the country's racist policies and police state in 1994. As the representative of Christian churches in South Africa, he openly challenged the country's white supremacist rulers (believers in superiority based on race). They were not Christians as they claimed to be, Tutu lectured them to their faces. Like an Old Testament prophet, he warned the rulers they were destined to wind up the "flotsam and jetsam [the scum] of history."

Tutu even risked imprisonment—or worse, assassination—for advocating international economic sanctions against South Africa. A global agreement to cut trade with South Africa, he reasoned, would shatter the wealth of South African whites and thereby pressure them into giving up their hold on the country's power and profits.

Above all, Tutu instilled a sense of worth and pride in South Africa's black majority. He filled black Africans with faith that they were ascending from the lowest depths of injustice—injustice that had condemned them to a status lower than human beings. "We will be free, we will be free!" was his battle cry in the worst, most chaotic of times. Nobel judges awarded Tutu the Peace Prize in 1984 in recognition of his nonviolent crusade to change the white minority government kept in power by its military forces. The Nobel committee also succeeding in bolstering his standing in the international campaign against apartheid.

Nelson Mandela (see entry), who came out of prison to be chosen South Africa's first black president in 1994 democratic elections, paid tribute to Tutu, calling him "a man who had inspired an entire nation with his words and his courage, who had revived the people's hope during the darkest of times . . . who selflessly fought the evils of racism during the most terrible days of apartheid."

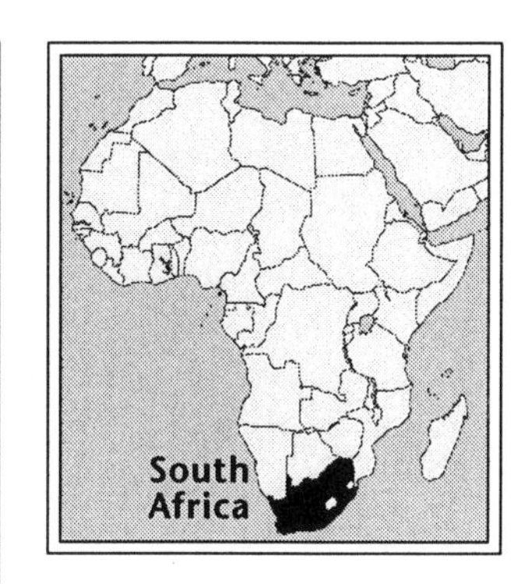

Quite a character

A short, small man with a large nose, the energetic Tutu brings an array of talents to a task. Blessed with a knack for humor, his sense of timing would have insured him success as a stand-up nightclub comedian had he not answered a loftier calling. Tutu has often employed humor to drive home a large and serious point to his audiences. His abilities include being able "to handle tricky situations in a way that is little short of miraculous." One observer noted that "when uncertain what to do he simply plays the clown, frequently diffusing tense situations by scrapping his prepared text and amusing his audience until they are ready to hear what he has to say. . . ."

Tutu has often used earthy images to poke into pretentious piousness. In one of his sermons he said, "Many religious people think long sulky faces somehow are related to holiness—they often look like they have taken an unexpected dose of castor oil and find it hard to laugh in church, being somewhat sheepish when they do. And yet Jesus was funny when He described the chap who is concerned to remove a speck of dust from his brother's eye while a huge beam was sticking out of his own. Jesus was poking fun at this chap and His audience would roar with laughter. . . . Our God does not reign over puny guilt-ridden obsequious [fawning or subservient] creatures. . ."

As a preacher of the Christian gospel, Tutu was anything but flippant. "He is a man of God," said Helen Joseph, a white opponent of the apartheid government who was prevented from speaking publicly for years. Tutu could also be temperamental. When the United States and European countries dragged their feet on imposing sanctions against South Africa, he exploded: "America and the West can go to hell."

Tutu likes to tell stories in which he stars as a fall guy, but that make a point. One story he tells goes like this: When Tutu was Anglican bishop of Johannesburg, he and South African President P. W. Botha, who always wore a hat, met privately in a small boat on Zoo Lake in the northern part of the city. But the privacy didn't last. The press heard about the meeting and gathered around the lake armed with binoculars and telephoto lenses. As the two men talked, a puff of wind blew the president's hat off his head, across the water. The confident bishop told the president to sit tight, not to worry, jumped out of the boat, and walked on the surface of the water to pick up the hat and return it to Botha. The next day newspaper headlines read: "Tutu can't swim." The point: Tutu couldn't do anything right in the eyes of his critics.

Elected the first black archbishop of Cape Town in 1986, a delighted Tutu told news reporters: "I'm tongue-tied, and some people hope it's permanent."

His early childhood

Tutu was born October 7, 1931, in Klerksdorp, a small mining town in an agricultural region west of Johannesburg, the middle child of Zachariah and Aletha Tutu. Educated at Christian mission schools, Zachariah was headmaster of the Methodist Primary School in Klerksdorp. He was a tall, proud man who wanted his children to grow up strong, healthy, and well educated. At times, however, he drank too much, and during some of his binges he abused his wife. Tutu's mother, Aletha, had little education and worked as a domestic servant. She was a gentle woman who exerted a profound influence on Tutu.

While Tutu was young, the family lived in black townships near Ventersdorp, Roodepoort, Krugersdorp, and other small towns west of Johannesburg, due to Zachariah's job. Although black South Africans did suffer varying degrees of discrimination back then, racial division was less extreme in the 1930s—when Tutu was growing up—than after 1948. That was the year the white National party imposed its policy of apartheid, a program intended to separate all races and restrict blacks to inferior education.

In the mid-1940s Tutu met British-born bishop Trevor Huddleston, then a parish priest in the mostly black township of Sophiatown. In this lively and historic township on the western edge of Johannesburg, people of all races and classes mixed, carried on business, and socialized together. Huddleston turned out to be Tutu's greatest role model.

When he was 14 years old, Tutu lived for a time at a hostel supported by the Fathers of the Community of the Resurrection in Sophiatown, near where he attended Madibane High School (named for a famous black headmaster celebrated as an educator and Anglican churchman.) He got to know Father Huddleston before being stricken with tuberculosis and confined for treatment at a state sanatorium for 20 months. Each week Huddleston visited young Tutu in the hospital, bringing books and encouragement. "He was full of laughter and caring," Tutu recalled, as quoted by Du Boulay. "He made you feel special. He was a wonderful man . . . a white man who made you feel you mattered." During his illness Tutu made the decision to become an Anglican priest.

Gifted with a photographic memory, Tutu excelled as a student despite missing months of school. He recovered from his illness and graduated from Madibane High in 1950, then obtained a teacher's certificate from Pretoria Bantu Normal College in 1953 and a bachelor's degree from the University of South Africa in 1954.

An Anglican priest

From 1955 to 1958 Tutu taught at Munsieville High School. He studied for the priesthood at St. Peter's Theological College in Rosettenville near Johannesburg from 1958 to 1960. After being ordained a deacon in 1960, he worked as an assistant at St. Alban's Church in Benoni township, east of Johannesburg. The church's rector set up Tutu, his wife, Leah, and their first two children in

Tutu's Family

On July 2, 1955, Tutu married a woman named Leah Shenxane in Munsieville, the black township in Krugersdorp. Leah had been a student of Tutu's father, who was headmaster of an Anglican primary school in Munsieville. She was also a close friend of Tutu's younger sister, Gloria. When she was attending school in Munsieville, Leah lived with one of her elder brothers in a shack in a rented backyard. Her mother worked as a domestic servant in a town on the other side of Johannesburg. By the time Tutu asked her to marry him, Leah was studying at a teacher training college. The Tutus have a son (Trevor, named for Tutu's mentor, Father Trevor Huddleston) and three daughters (Theresa, Naomi, and Mpho).

horrible housing—a Benoni garage next to a fly-infested stable. In 1961 Tutu was ordained an Anglican priest and assigned to a church in Thokoza, a black township southeast of Johannesburg.

Tutu and his family would never have to sleep in a garage again. In 1962 Tutu was awarded a scholarship for study abroad. Church officials arranged for Tutu to study for a degree in theology at King's College at the University of London. London was "paradise" for the family. Tutu didn't have to carry a pass as he did in South Africa. His family could walk or travel where they wished in England. They could enter front doors or any public entrances or exits they pleased. Porters addressed him as "sir." He preached in the affluent white village of Bletchingley, won wide acceptance, and was invited to local Gin and God parties—occasions in lush gardens where guests were given a dry Martini upon arrival and treated to a gourmet meal before getting down to prayer and worship. Tutu's time in London helped him to reject the conditioning imposed by apartheid:

> You didn't know that gnawing away at you was this worm which was sowing a horrible kind of self-doubt in you. . . . The most horrible aspect of apartheid, a blasphemous aspect, is it can make a child of God doubt that they are a child of God, when you ask yourself in the middle of the night, "God, am I your step-child?"

Similarly, in his 1986 Martin Luther King Peace Prize address, Tutu described the self doubt resulting from the state system of racial discrimination:

> You are brainwashed into an acquiescence in your oppression and exploitation. You come to believe what others have determined about you, filling you with self-disgust, self-contempt and self-hatred, accepting a negative self-image . . . and you need a lot of grace to have

> that demon of self-hatred exorcised. . . . You accept that only white races really matter and you allow the white person to set your standards and provide your role models.

Tutu obtained his bachelor's degree in theology in 1965 and his master's degree the following year. He then returned to South Africa to study for his doctorate and teach at the Federal Theological Seminary in Alice, a town in southeastern South Africa. At this point he began to sense serious discontent rising among young black South Africans. Tutu lectured in Lesotho for a couple of years before returning to England in 1972 as associate director for Africa of the Theological Education Fund, an organization founded to help free churches in Africa, Asia, and Latin America. In 1974, however, Tutu was called home to become Johannesburg's first black bishop.

Thrown into the fight

Tutu found himself in the spotlight during the next decade. On March 1, 1978, he became general secretary of the South African Council of Churches—a position that catapulted him to the forefront of the fight against apartheid just as black rebellion was reaching fever pitch. Three years later the white government held hearings to investigate the Council of Churches, drawing worldwide attention to Tutu and the black majority cause. After the hearings he embarked on a tour of Europe and the United States. Tutu returned to Johannesburg a hero to black South Africans. Peter Storey, Methodist bishop of Johannesburg, was at the airport to welcome Tutu home. According to Du Boulay, Storey "sensed on that return that here was someone who knew—perhaps had always known—that he came back as someone with destiny on his shoulders. A sense of having to be the instrument of his people's liberation, to be their spokesman."

Tutu tried to warn South African leaders—Prime Minister John Vorster (prime minister from 1966 to 1978) and later President P. W. Botha (president until 1989)—of the swelling tide of violence among blacks. The heads of state ignored his warnings. Risking a charge of treason (betrayal of one's country), Tutu called for the world to shut off trade with South Africa and for foreign businesses to withdraw investments. No legal action was taken against him, however, because arresting Tutu would have caused worldwide backlash against the white government. He had won

Tutu's View

In the introduction to his *African Prayer Book*, Tutu sums up his outlook on human relationships. He retells the Christian creation story—of Adam's feeling of incompleteness before God created Eve, the first woman:

> **And so God asked Adam to choose a mate for himself from among the animals which paraded before him in procession. God would ask his human friend, "What about this one?" Adam would reply, "Not on your life! No, thank you!" And so God decided to put Adam to sleep and produced from his rib [a woman named] Eve; and when Adam awoke he exclaimed: "Wow! This is just what the doctor ordered!"**
>
> **This beautiful story tells a fundamental truth about us—that we are made to live in a delicate network of interdependence with one another, with God, and with the rest of God's creation. We say in our African idiom: "A person is a person through other persons." A solitary human being is a contradiction in terms. A totally self-sufficient human being is ultimately subhuman. . . . I have gifts that you do not; and you have gifts that I do not. Voila! So we need each other to become fully human.**

the 1984 Nobel Peace Prize and this international acclaim made him virtually arrest-proof.

On February 11, 1990, black activist Nelson Mandela was released after more than 27 years in prison. He and his wife, Winnie, spent his first night of freedom with Archbishop Tutu and Leah at their church residence, Bishopscourt, in a wealthy—and mostly white—Cape Town suburb. Proclaiming he was "over the moon," Tutu said he was turning the political fight against apartheid back to Mandela, and he would return to preaching.

Heads the Truth and Reconciliation Commission

After retiring in 1995 as Anglican archbishop of Cape Town, the church's most influential position in South Africa, Tutu was back in the political limelight in 1996 as chairman of South Africa's Truth and Reconciliation Commission, which investigated the crimes of South Africa's apartheid government. Criticized for heading a commission that granted amnesty if full confessions were submitted, Tutu retorted: "Victims and survivors who bore the brunt of the apartheid system need healing. Perpe-

Tutu at the Nigerian consulate, expressing outrage on behalf of South African organizations over the execution of nine political activists in 1995.

trators [those who carried out the racist policies] are, in their own way, victims of the apartheid system and they, too, need healing."

As commission chairman Tutu gained the satisfaction of hearing five white South African security police officers plead for forgiveness of their crimes and admit the inherent worth of *all* "children of God," no matter what their color. In their amnesty petition, the security officers stated:

> We were brought up to believe in apartheid. We were made to believe that apartheid was sanctioned by God, through the church. We were made to believe that our participation in the Security Forces was justified to uphold apartheid. We were made to believe that black people were inferior, and the needs, emotions and aspirations of black people differed from ours. We were made to believe that we were superior, and that these differences justified apartheid. We have come to realize that these beliefs were wrong, morally and in reality.

Though being treated for prostate cancer, Tutu continued to guide the commission from 1996 to 1998 through particularly difficult times. "Nobody but Tutu could have headed that commission," said Father Michael Lapsley, a chaplain at the Cape Town

Trauma Centre who lost both hands and an eye to a letter bomb sent to him in 1990 by agents of the former white government.

Further Reading

Botman, H. R., and Robin M. Petersen, eds. *To Remember and to Heal: Theological and Psychological Reflections on Truth and Reconciliation.* Human & Rousseau, 1996.

Du Boulay, Shirley. *Tutu: Voice of the Voiceless.* North Pomfret, VT: Hodder & Stoughton, 1988.

King's College Newsletter, December 1984.

Mandela, Nelson. *Long Walk to Freedom.* New York: Abacus, 1995.

Sparks, Allister. *The Mind of South Africa.* North Pomfret, VT: Heinemann, 1990.

Tutu, Desmond. *An African Prayer Book.* North Pomfret, VT: Hodder & Stoughton, 1995.

Tutu, Desmond. *Hope and Suffering: Sermons and Speeches.* Skotaville Publishers, 1983.

Tutu, Desmond. *The Rainbow People of God: South Africa's Victory over Apartheid.* New York: Bantam Books, 1995.

Hendrik Verwoerd

Born 1901
Holland
Died September 6, 1966
Cape Town, South Africa

South African politician

Hendrik Frensch Verwoerd (*fer-VURT*) designed and implemented the apartheid system in South Africa, one of the largest schemes of social engineering of the twentieth century. Apartheid, which means "apartness," divided the population into separate systems whose degree of privilege was measured solely by race. As minister of native affairs (1950-58) and later as prime minister (1958-66) of the South African government, he constructed the laws that elevated whites to positions of privilege at the expense of black laborers. An extraordinarily repressive police force controlled black efforts to resist the system.

"If we do not take this one step now, we . . . will . . . experience all the suffering of the whites who are being attacked in and driven out of one African territory after the other."

—Verwoerd, in a 1960 speech, pushing voters to approve the formation of the Republic of South Africa

In 1948 the National party of conservative Afrikaners won control of the South African government, defeating the moderate English-Afrikaner coalition government. (Afrikaners are descendants of Dutch, French, and German immigrants who fled Europe primarily to avoid religious persecution in the 1600s and 1700s.

They speak a language called Afrikaans.) On taking power, the National party needed to unify and strengthen its electoral base and improve economic conditions for Afrikaners. As church-going, God-fearing Calvinists (members of a strict Christian religious sect), the Afrikaners needed a philosophy or a concept to justify establishing a society based on racial discrimination. They found it in Verwoerd's program of separate development.

Separate development called for the creation of nine territories, so-called Bantustans or homelands, to which the government assigned blacks citizenship and voting rights. Generally, these areas were poor in land quality and rainfall, and they could not support the millions of people assigned to them. The land reserved for blacks equaled about 14 percent of the total land, whereas the blacks made up about 85 percent of the population. Denied political rights in white South Africa and unable to support themselves and their families in the homelands, blacks became a ready source of cheap labor, with no rights of residence or ownership in white areas.

Always an outsider

Hendrik Verwoerd was born in Holland, but his family migrated to South Africa when he was two years old. His father, Wilhelm J. Verwoerd, was a building contractor who wanted to be a missionary. He saw an opportunity to do so among the "coloured" people of South Africa. The family settled in Cape Town's predominantly English suburb of Wynberg, and young Hendrik went to an English boys' school.

When the Dutch Reformed Church in Rhodesia called his father to do missionary work in Bulawayo, Rhodesia (now Zimbabwe), the family moved north. As a teenager Verwoerd attended another British school. At home, however, his family raised him as an Afrikaner. They proudly retold the stories of the Afrikaners who left Cape Colony more than 100 years before to find new lands in the interior of South Africa, beyond the grasp of the British. As an Afrikaner in a British school, Verwoerd was something of an outcast among his schoolmates. Finally, when Verwoerd was 16 years old, the family returned to South Africa and set up house in a small settlement in the Orange Free State. This was the first time he had actually lived in an Afrikaner community.

Verwoerd went to the Afrikaans university, Stellenbosch, in the Cape Colony. Like many other Afrikaans nationalists (people who held a deep pride in their heritage and sought self government) he studied theology as an undergraduate. For his advanced courses he switched to psychology and earned a doctoral degree. Just as the anti-Jewish Nazi party was rising, Verwoerd traveled to Germany to study at the universities of Hamburg, Leipzig, and Berlin. Already engaged to an undergraduate friend, Betsie Schoombie, herself an Afrikaans lecturer, he married her in Hamburg in 1927. They toured the United States on a working honeymoon, each of them teaching and lecturing. Returning to South Africa with an already well-respected academic reputation, Verwoerd took up the position of professor of applied psychology at Stellenbosch. He soon established himself as a fluent speaker, a prolific writer, and an outspoken defender of Afrikaner nationalism and white supremacy (the notion of superiority based on race).

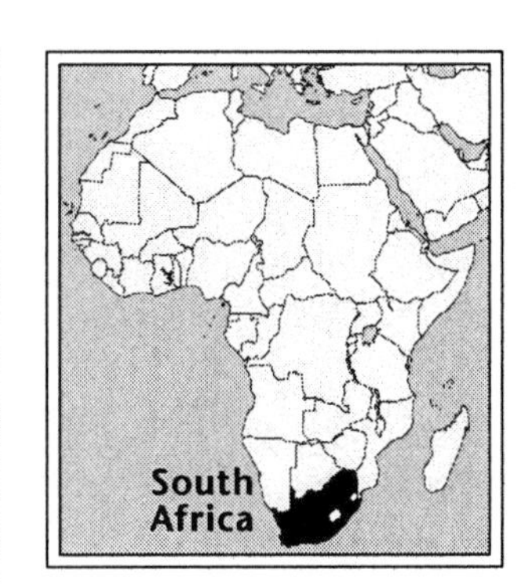

Edits nationalist newspaper

In 1937 Verwoerd resigned from his teaching post and moved to the Transvaal to become the editor of *The Transvaaler,* a newspaper that would become the mouthpiece of the National party. He edited the paper throughout World War II (1939-45), advocating Afrikaner nationalism and white supremacy and taking a definite pro-Nazi stand. During the war some Afrikaners favored the Nazis and sympathized with their racial policy of promoting "Aryan purity" (white—especially German—purity). Others believed that German leader Adolf Hitler (1889-1945) was likely to win the war and that cooperation with him might end British control of South Africa. In 1943 the *Johannesburg Star* accused Verwoerd and *The Transvaaler* of spreading pro-Nazi opinions. Verwoerd responded by suing for libel but lost his case; the jury was unconvinced that the *Star* had portrayed him inaccurately. *The Transvaaler* also supported the *Broederbond,* initially a sort of service organization founded in 1918 that championed the poor white Afrikaners in the cities and on farms. Over the years it became a semi-secret society whose membership was composed exclusively of white Afrikaner men; it developed enormous political and economic influence.

South Africa held national elections in 1948. The then-ruling United party had the support of most English speakers and many

Slums in the squatter camp of Cross Roads, South Africa.

moderate Afrikaners. It expected to hold its majority in parliament. But in the greatest electoral upset in the history of the country, the United party lost 36 seats to the Afrikaner nationalist coalition (union) of the National party (NP) and the Afrikaner party (AP). This stunning turnaround is usually attributed to the rural voters (who were over-represented in proportion to urban voters), the NP's promise to look after white voters, and the NP's appeal to Afrikaner nationalism. In the 1953 election the NP increased its majority in parliament.

The new South African prime minister was Daniel Francois Malan. He purged (or rid) the army, police, and civil service of high-level British-origin officers, so that by 1951 all the top officeholders and most of the leading non-elected officials were Afrikaners. Malan once explained to an American clergyman how he saw the fundamental differences between white and black groups. He stated, as quoted by Dan O'Meara in *Forty Lost Years: The Apartheid State and the Politics of the National Party, 1948-1994,* that the "difference in colour" was "merely the physical manifestation of the contrast between two irreconcilable ways of life, between barbarism and civilisation, between overwhelming numerical odds on the one hand and insignificant numbers on the other."

The institution of apartheid

In 1950 Malan appointed Verwoerd minister of native affairs. Verwoerd vigorously began to implement the National party's policy of apartheid. He saw apartheid and racial distinctiveness as religious issues that were divinely approved (the will of God). Within five years the department of native affairs had affected every aspect of government policy and South African life. The 1950 Population Registration Act, the backbone of the apartheid legislation, assigned every person in South Africa to one of four racial categories: whites, Bantus (blacks), coloreds (people of mixed race), and Asiatic. Once the bureaucrats had classified people by race, the state set about enforcing the separation of the races. It designated where people could live, what land they could own, and which jobs they could hold. It determined where they went to school and what public facilities—toilets, bus stops, hospitals, and the like—they could use. It even denied marriage to people in different racial categories. The Group Areas Act of 1951 assigned blacks citizenship to homelands (also called Bantustans), an imaginative creation of whites based on their ill-conceived concept of tribal affiliations. The government had the authority to force blacks to move to the homelands. Legislation in 1952 required blacks to meet certain requirements in order to live in the cities; it required all Africans over the age of 16 to carry a pass at all times.

African National Congress (ANC) leaders voiced opposition to Verwoerd's policies and to Africans who accepted it. The ANC wanted South Africa to become a color-blind society—one free of racial strife and divisions—clearly the opposite of Malan and Verwoerd's plans. Although they faced severe persecution and mass arrests for their acts of civil disobedience, ANC activists created international awareness of their cause and won the support of the United Nations. Young, well-educated members of the ANC, including Nelson Mandela (see entry) and Oliver Tambo, sought a more aggressive policy against the whites than the old guard leadership under such activists as Albert Lutuli (see entry).

Verwoerd leads National party

Prime Minister Malan retired in 1954 at the age of 80, and Johanes Strijdom replaced him. Strijdom, a Transvaaler who shared a fervent faith in apartheid, died in 1958, shortly after winning re-election. In a secret ballot the National party elected Verwoerd to succeed Strijdom. Verwoerd wanted to speed up the actual separation of black and white races, and he outlined his plan in a 1959 speech to parliament. He proposed creating within South Africa separate, self-governing, cooperating nations—black and white—a sort of South African Commonwealth of nations.

The Promotion of Bantu Self-Government Act of 1959 and the Native Laws Amendment Bill of 1960 prevented black Africans from moving to cities unless they had employment there. The laws also regulated the labor market more closely, while encouraging permanent black settlement in homelands away from the cities. But because the white minority government controlled foreign policy, currency, transport, and internal security in the homelands, the black populations were unable to generate sufficient income for themselves. Instead, most black Africans had to continue their migration to the cities, where they were at a disadvantage both economically and legally.

Becomes an independent republic

Verwoerd had his eye on another sovereignty question, however. Ever since the Boer War (1899-1902; wars fought by the British and the Boers [Afrikaners] to gain control of two provinces of South Africa), South Africa had been a self-governing British colony. In January 1960 Verwoerd announced in parliament that there would be a referendum asking all white voters whether South Africa should become a republic. He warned voters, all of them white:

> Should South Africa remain a monarchy, it will have to suffer, time and again, from instigated racial clashes and economic setbacks. . . . If we do not take this one step now, we ourselves may possibly, but our children certainly will, experience all the suffering of the whites who are being attacked in and driven out of one African territory after the other.

Out of 1.5 million votes cast, the voters accepted the status of a republic by a majority of a hundred thousand. Verwoerd told Harold Macmillan, Britain's prime minister, that the Republic of South Africa would remain part of the British Commonwealth so long as they granted it complete internal autonomy (self-rule). He could not get any such assurances and so, in October 1961, South Africa severed all its ties with Britain. In a famous speech delivered to the South African Parliament, Macmillan said that "the wind of change" was blowing through Africa, a wind of black self-government. Verwoerd answered firmly and politely that it was not going to blow in South Africa. The new republic's president, C. R. Swart, became a national figurehead, but real power stayed in Prime Minister Verwoerd's hands.

Demonstrations at Sharpeville

Meanwhile, confronted with Verwoerd's acceleration of the separate development policy in 1959, the ANC had split into several factions or groups. Robert Sobukwe formed a more radical (forceful and revolutionary) splinter group called the Pan-African Congress (PAC). Sobukwe favored direct action rather than negotiation. A period of mass demonstrations followed, with Pan-African Congress supporters pushing for an end to pass laws for blacks. On March 21, 1960, in Sharpeville (on the border of the Transvaal and the Orange Free State) policemen fired into a crowd of 5,000 unarmed demonstrators who had surrounded their barracks. The police killed 69 demonstrators and wounded 300. The black leaders and their white sympathizers responded to the Sharpeville massacre by calling for a general strike.

Declaring a state of emergency, Verwoerd called out the army to keep the peace. His regime seemed vulnerable for a moment, especially when he was shot in the head by an angry farmer of British descent named David Pratt a few weeks later. But, undeterred by opponents or even by this severe injury, Verwoerd responded aggressively. His Unlawful Organizations Bill, passed in the wake of Sharpeville, outlawed the ANC and the PAC. In the years that followed, he gave increasing power to the police, army, and the Justice Department. People in South Africa could be imprisoned without trial for up to 90 days, and the press was subject to severe censorship.

As the opposition split, Verwoerd's hold on power increased. White voters returned him to office with a huge majority in the election of 1961. Most ominous of all for anti-apartheid South Africans was that Verwoerd was by this time attracting whites of British descent, not just Afrikaners.

Verwoerd arriving at Meyerton, a suburb of Johannesburg, responding to the violence at Sharpeville, 1960.

By 1966 Verwoerd appeared to have weathered the storms of Sharpeville and hostile world opinion. Bitterly unpopular throughout Africa and the West, South Africa was nevertheless richer and more powerful than any other nation on the continent, and those who denounced it most loudly could do the least to change it. In order to make good on his claims that the homelands policy would result in real independent states, Verwoerd willingly negotiated with black African leaders in a way that no predecessor had done. Some of the former British colonies in the area, including Bechuanaland (Botswana), Basutoland (Lesotho), and Swaziland, hoped to live at peace with South Africa and so followed a policy of cooperation with the government.

As Verwoerd prepared to address parliament on September 6, 1966, a man named Demetrio Tsafendas fatally stabbed him. Tsafendas was part Greek and part Mozambican, and he had a history of mental illness. One of Verwoerd's most ardent supporters, Minister of Justice Balthazar J. Vorster (in office 1966-79), succeeded him as prime minister.

Further Reading

Davenport, T. H. R. *South Africa: A Modern History.* Toronto, Ontario: University of Toronto Press, 1987.

Fisher, John. *The Afrikaners.* New York: Cassell, 1969.

Historic World Leaders. Edited by Anne Commire. Volume 1. Detroit: Gale, 1994.

LeMay, G. H. L. *Black and White in South Africa: The Politics of Survival.* American Heritage Press, 1971.

O'Meara, Dan. *Forty Lost Years: The Apartheid State and the Politics of the National Party, 1948-1994.* Athens: Ohio University Press, 1996.

Sampson, Anthony. *Black and Gold.* North Pomfret, VT: Hodder & Stoughton, 1987.

Sparks, Allister. *The Mind of South Africa.* North Pomfret, VT: Heinemann, 1990.

Wilson, Monica, and Leonard Thompson, eds. *The Oxford History of South Africa: 1870-1966.* New York: Clarendon Press, 1975.

Yaa Asantewa

Born c. mid-1800s
Ejisu, Ashante (formerly Gold Coast; now Ghana)
Died c. 1921
Seychelles

Ashanti war leader

Yaa Asantewa infused Ashanti warriors with extraordinary courage in their fight against the British in 1900.

Yaa Asantewa (*ah-sahn-TEE-wah*) is the best-known female hero of the Ashanti nation. The Ashanti empire—located in the southern portion of what is now the West African nation of Ghana—had been established early in the 1700s. A fierce and defiant leader, Yaa Asantewa rallied her people in the last of a series of wars against their British colonizers. (Colonialism is a nation's control of a territory that lies beyond its own borders—in this case, Britain's control over the Ashanti people's kingdom.) She infused Ashanti warriors with extraordinary courage in a futile fight against the enemy in 1900.

As David Sweetman noted in *Women Leaders in African History,* an Ashanti ballad still praises Yaa Asantewa as "the warrior woman who carries a gun and a sword of state in battle." Though photographed wearing a warrior's battle dress and holding a rifle, it is doubtful that the aging Yaa Asantewa led troops in combat. But no doubt exists that she provided the inspiration for determined Ashanti warriors in the six-month war of 1900. The British army defeated the Ashanti, colonized them, and sent Yaa Asantewa into exile. But the European intruders failed to capture the golden stool, which had represented the "soul" of the Ashanti nation for 200 years. According to centuries-old legend, the stool had descended from the clouds and settled on the lap of Osei Tutu, a divine sign that he be named the first Ashanti king or *asantehene* (see box on p. 482). The stool is still believed to hold the power and the spirit of the Ashanti nation.

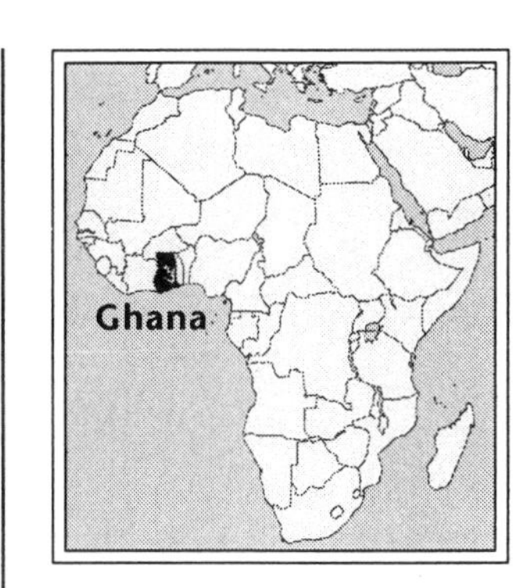

Stool triggered war

The Yaa Asantewa War was triggered by a British governor's demand that the Ashanti bring forth the mythical golden stool for *him* to sit on—something not even an *asantehene* was allowed to do. This arrogant demand—a demand that clearly demonstrated Britain's lack of regard for African traditions—was made to a proud Ashanti nation already raging over a military defeat by the British in 1874. The British had humiliated and imprisoned their king, Asantehene Prempeh I (see entry), and declared their control over Ashanti territory.

In 1896, when the British insisted on sending a resident to rule at Kumasi (the Ashanti capital in the central area of today's Ghana), Ashanti warriors wanted to resist. But Prempeh I (see entry) knew of Britain's destructive firepower. He sought to preserve the Ashanti nation and to avoid the inevitable slaughter of his people. Only by invoking his royal position was the asantehene able to convince the warriors to yield to British demands. Prempeh I even endured the humiliation of submitting to British rule by lying face down on the ground before British officials as his people watched.

Major Robert Baden-Powell (founder of the Boy Scouts) had led the British force to occupy Kumasi in 1896. He had observed the ceremony during which Prempeh was forced to submit. Yaa Asantewa's presence obviously impressed him. "The only 'man' among them was the Queen," he later wrote, as quoted by Sweetman.

Rebellious queen mother

Yaa Asantewa was born in Ejisu, an Ashanti clan state about 10 miles east of Kumasi. Her son, Nana Afrane Kuma, eventually became Ejisu's ruler. He supported Prempeh I in a civil war fought among Ashanti clans in the 1880s to decide who would be the asantehene. The British imprisoned Prempeh I, other family members, and top Ashanti chiefs in 1896, then exiled them to the Seychelles (an island group in the Indian Ocean) in 1899. Yaa Asantewa's son was among those chiefs exiled. With the key Ashanti leaders gone, the position of Ashanti queen mother fell to Yaa Asantewa. (In Ashanti culture, the queen mother exercises unusual powers. She plays a key role in designating a new asantehene if the position comes open. Many of her functions in the kingdom are second only to those of the king.) Immediately she sought support from Ashanti chiefs to organize a rebellion against the British.

Yaa Asantewa's anger over her son's exile and the loss of Ashanti independence still boiled when Frederick Hodgson, the British governor from 1898 to 1900, arrived in Kumasi on his first official visit on March 25, 1900. Three days later, at a Kumasi ceremony where he received the Ashanti nobility, Hodgson issued his demand. "Where is the Golden Stool?" he is said to have asked the Ashanti chiefs. "Why am I not sitting on the Golden Stool at this moment?. . . Why did you not take the opportunity of my coming to Kumasi to bring the Golden Stool, give it to me to sit upon. . .?" The Ashanti rulers were stunned by the demand. No one, not even the king, was allowed to sit on the sacred stool. "This was the last straw; all the pent-up resentment of the humiliated Ashanti burst out in the popular revolt known as the Yaa Asantewa War, after the Queen Mother of Ejisu," noted Albert van Dantzig in *Forts and Castles of Ghana.*

At Yaa Asantewa's urgings, war soon broke out. With British troops in Kumasi vastly outnumbered, Hodgson tried to negotiate a peace agreement. The Ashanti demanded return of their asantehene. It was a demand Hodgson had no authority to grant. He tried to telegraph to the coast, where British troops were stationed, for help. But the Ashanti had cut the telegraph wires. Hodgson and other British officials and soldiers sought refuge in a fort the British had built in Kumasi. From April 25 until June 23, 1900, the Ashanti surrounded and attacked the fort. Hundreds of people died before Hodgson and a small group of the British escaped and made their way to the coast to sound an alarm.

Historical descriptions of Yaa Asantewa conflict sharply. For instance, the *Dictionary of African Biography* describes her as "short, stout, and very dark, with small eyes." Another source, *Women Leaders in African History,* portrays her as "a thin, brown, leathery old lady, with fierce blazing eyes." All sources seem to agree on one thing, though—that she made a striking and impressive appearance.

What Did She Look Like?

No match for Maxims

The British assembled a force of 1,400 soldiers from other parts of Africa to send to Kumasi. The British force was confronted by between 40,000 and 50,000 Ashanti warriors, but the warriors could not match the power of the Maxim machine guns used by the British. The Kumasi fort was taken by the British on July 15, 1900. Yaa Asantewa and 3,000 warriors retreated to a stockade (an enclosure surrounded by posts) in Ejisu. A British force of 350 men, armed with Maxim guns, destroyed the stockade at the end of August. The Ashanti survivors, Yaa Asantewa among them, retreated into the forest. She sent representatives to the British to negotiate terms of surrender. In the meantime, though, the dwindling Ashanti warriors fought on. Then, on September 30, 1900, they were surrounded by the British and forced to accept defeat. It is said the last Ashanti to be captured was Yaa Asantewa.

The British officer who apprehended Yaa Asantewa "claimed that she spat in his face," reported Sweetman. The British executed a few of the chiefs and jailed others as prisoners of war. Yaa Asantewa was sent to the Seychelles, where she joined her son in exile. She died on the Indian Ocean islands around 1921 but lives on in Ashanti legend as a symbol of fierce resistance to outside oppression.

Further Reading

Dantzig, Albert van. *Forts and Castles of Ghana.* Sedco Publishing Ltd., 1980.

Dictionary of African Biography. Algonac, MI: Reference Publications, 1977.

Obeng, Ernest E. *Ancient Ashanti Chieftaincy.* Ghana Publishing Corporation, 1988.

Sarpong, Peter. *The Sacred Stools of the Akan.* Ghana Publishing Corporation, 1971.

Sweetman, David. *Women Leaders in African History.* Portsmouth, NH: Heinemann Educational, 1984.

Tufuo, J. W., and C. E. Donkor. *Ashantis of Ghana: People with a Soul.* Anowou Educational Publications, 1989.

Warren, Dennis M. *The Akan of Ghana.* Rev. ed. Pointer Limited, 1986.

Bibliography

Wole Soyinka.

Books

Adam, H., and K. Moodley. *The Negotiated Revolution.* Jonathan Ball, 1993.

Adamolekun, Ladipo. *Sékou Touré's Guinea: An Experiment in Nation Building.* New York: Methuen, 1976.

Africa Watch staff. *Conspicuous Destruction: War, Famine, and the Reform Process in Mozambique.* New York: Africa Watch/Human Rights Watch, 1992.

Africa Watch staff. *Kenya: Taking Liberties.* New York: Africa Watch/Human Rights Watch, 1991.

al-'Umari, Shihab al-Din Ibn Fadi and el Amsar. *Masalik el Absar fi Mamalik.* Traduit par Gaudefroy-Demombynes, Librarie Orientaliste Paul Geuthner, 1927.

Anglin, Douglas G., and Timothy M. Shaw. *Zambia's Foreign Policy: Studies in Diplomacy and Dependence.* Boulder, CO: Westview Press, 1979.

Arhin, Kwame. *Traditional Rule in Ghana, Past and Present.* Sedco Publishing Ltd., 1985.

Arnold, Millard. *Steve Biko: Black Consciousness in South Africa.* New York: Random House, 1978.

Ayittey, George B. *Africa Betrayed.* New York: St. Martin's Press, 1992.

Azikiwe, Nnamdi. *My Odyssey.* Hurst, 1970.

Beach, D. N. *The Shona and Zimbabwe: 900-1850.* Mambo Press, 1980.

Beach, D. N. *Zimbabwe before 1900.* Mambo Press, 1984.

Bender, Gerald J. *Angola under the Portuguese: The Myth and the Reality.* Berkeley: University of California Press, 1978.

Benson, Mary. *African Patriots: The Story of the African National Congress.* 1963.

Benson, M. *Chief Albert Luthuli of South Africa.* 1963.

Benson, M. *South Africa: The Struggle for a Birthright, International Defence, and Aid Fund for Southern Africa.* 1966.

Bermann, Richard A. *The Mahdi of Allah.* 1931.

Biko, Steve. *I Write What I Like: A Selection of His Writings.* South Africa: Ravan Press, 1996.

Binsbergen, W. M. J. van. "Religious Innovation and Political Conflict in Zambia: A Contribution to the Interpretation of the Lumpa Rising." In *African Perspectives: Religious Innovation in Modern African Society.* Volume 2. Leiden: Afrika-Studiecentrum, 1976.

Black Literature Criticism. Detroit: Gale, 1992.

Black Writers. Detroit: Gale, 1989.

Blake, Robert. *A History of Rhodesia.* Eyre Methuen, 1977.

Blakely, Thomas D., Walter E. A. van Beek, and Dennis L. Thomson. *Religion in Africa.* Provo, UT: David M. Kennedy Center, 1994.

Boahen, Adu. *Topics in West African History.* New York: Longman, 1966.

Bond, George C. "A Prophecy That Failed: The Lumpa Church of Uyombe, Zambia." In *African Christianity: Patterns of Religious Continuity.* Academic Press, 1979.

Botman, H. R., and Robin M. Petersen, eds. *To Remember and to Heal: Theological and Psychological Reflections on Truth and Reconciliation.* Human & Rousseau, 1996.

Bourdillon, Michael, *The Shona Peoples,* revised edition. Mambo Press, 1982.

Bouscaren, A. E. *Tshombe.* 1967.

Bradt, Hilary. *Guide to Madagascar.* Bradt Publications, 1988.

Bretton, Henry. *The Rise and Fall of Kwame Nkrumah.* New York: Praeger, 1966.

The Cambridge History of Africa. Vol. 8. Edited by Michael Crowder. New York/UK: Cambridge University Press, 1984.

Cary, Robert, and Diana Mitchell. *African Nationalist Leaders in Rhodesia: Who's Who 1980.* Books of Rhodesia, 1980.

Cary, Robert. *A Time to Die.* 1969.

Churchill, Lord Randolph. *Men, Mines, and Animals in South Africa.* Originally published in 1892. Reprinted. Books of Rhodesia, 1975.

Contemporary Authors. Detroit: Gale, 1990.

Contemporary Black Biography. Detroit: Gale, 1994.

Contemporary Literary Criticism. Detroit: Gale, 1983.

Contemporary Musicians. Detroit: Gale, 1992.

Contemporary Newsmakers. Detroit: Gale, 1989.

Contemporary Novelists. Detroit: St. James Press, 1991.

Cooper-Chadwick, J. *Three Years with Lobengula.* Books of Rhodesia, 1975.

Cromwell, Adelaide M. *An African Victorian Feminist: The Life and Times of Adelaide Smith Casely Hayford, 1868-1960.* Washington, DC: Howard University Press, 1992.

Crosby, Cynthia. *Historical Dictionary of Malawi.* Metuchen, NJ: Scarecrow Press, 1980.

Crowder, Michael. "History of French West Africa until Independence." In *Africa South of the Sahara: 1982-83.* London: Europa Publications, 1982.

Crowder, Michael. *The Story of Nigeria.* Winchester, MA: Faber, 1978.

Curtin, Philip, ed. *Africa Remembered: Narratives by West Africans from the Era of the Slave Trade.* Madison: University of Wisconsin Press, 1967.

Curtin, Philip, and others, eds. *African History: From Earliest Times to Independence.* 2nd ed. New York: Longman, 1995.

Dantzig, Albert van. *Forts and Castles of Ghana.* Sedco Publishing Ltd., 1980.

Davenport, T. R. H. *South Africa: A Modern History.* Toronto, Ontario, Canada: University of Toronto Press, 1987.

Davidson, Basil. *Africa in History.* New York: Macmillan, 1974.

Davidson, Basil. *Africa History, Themes and Outlines.* New rev. ed. New York: Collier Books, 1974.

Davidson, Basil, *The Black Man's Burden: Africa and the Curse of the Nation-State.* James Curry, 1992.

Davidson, Basil. *The Growth of African Civilisation: History of West Africa, 1000-1800.* New York: Longman, 1965.

Davis, Dorothy K. *Race Relations in Rhodesia.* Rex Collings, 1975.

Days, Drew S., et al. *Justice Enjoined: The State of the Judiciary in Kenya.* Robert F. Kennedy Memorial Center for Human Rights, 1992

Decalo, Samuel. *Psychoses of Power: African Personal Dictatorships.* Boulder, CO: Westview Press.

DeKlerk, W. A. *The Puritans in Africa.* Rex Collings, 1975.

De Klerk, Willem. *The Man in His Time: F. W. De Klerk.* Jonathan Ball, 1991.

Delf, George. *Jomo Kenyatta: Towards Truth about "The Light of Kenya."* New York: Doubleday, 1961.

Depelchin, H., and C. Croonenberghs. *Letters of Journey to Gubuluwayo.* Books of Rhodesia, 1979.

Dickie, John, and Alan Rake. *Who's Who in Africa.* Africa Buyer and Trader, 1973.

Dictionary of African Biography. Algonac, MI: Reference Publications, 1977.

Drechsler, Horst. *Let Us Die Fighting.* Akademie-Verlag, 1966.

Du Boulay, Shirley. *Tutu: Voice of the Voiceless.* North Pomfret, VT: Hodder & Stoughton, 1988.

Duerden, Dennis, and Cosmo Pieterse, eds. *African Writers Talking: A Collection of Radio Interviews.* Africana Publishing, 1972.

Duggan, William Redman, and John R. Civille. *Tanzania and Nyerere: A Study of Ujamaa and Nationhood.* London: Orbis Books, 1976.

Eilersen, Gillian Stead. *Bessie Head: Thunder Behind Her Ears.* North Pomfret, VT: Heinemann, 1996.

Ellert H. *Rivers of Gold.* Mambo Press, 1993.

Ellert, H. *The Rhodesian Front War.* Mambo, 1989.

Encyclopaedia Africana, Dictionary of African Biography. Vol. 2. Sierra Leone-Zaire: Reference Publications, 1977.

Equiano's Travels: His Autobiography: The Interesting Narrative of the Life of Olaudah Equiano or Gustavus Vassa the African Life. Paul Edwards, editor. London: Heinemann, 1967.

Farrant, Leda. *Tippu Tip and the East African Slave Trade.* London: Hamish Hamilton, 1975

Farwell, Byron. *Prisoners of the Mahdi: The Story of the Mahdist Revolt Which Frustrated Queen Victoria's Designs on the Sudan.* New York: Norton, 1989.

Fisher, John. *The Afrikaners.* Cassell, 1969.

Forbath, Peter. *The River Congo.* New York: Harper & Row, 1977.

Forrest, Ronald. *An African Reader.* New York: Longman, 1965.

Forster, E. M. *Alexandria: A History and a Guide.* Bath Press, 1922.

Froehlich, Manuel. "The Old and the New UN Secretary-General." In *Aussen Politik,* 48:3, 1997, pp. 301-9.

Gérard-Libois, J. *Sécession au Katanga.* 1963

Gertzel, Cherry. *The Politics of Independent Kenya: 1963-1968.* Northwestern, 1970.

Gertzel, Cherry. "Uganda's Continuing Search for Peace." In *Current History,* May 1990.

Gibbs, James, ed. *Critical Perspectives on Wole Soyinka.* Washington, DC: Three Continents, 1980.

Gossler, Horst. *Portfolio Lalibela.* Africa Environment and Wildlife, 1996.

Graham, Shirley. *Julius K. Nyerere: Teacher of Africa.* New York: Messner, 1975.

Gray, Stephen. *Southern African Literature: An Introduction.* 1979.

Greschat, Hans-Jurgen. "Legends? Frauds? Reality? Alice Lenshina's Prophetic Experience." In *Africana Marburgensia.* Edited by Hans-Jurgen Greschat and Hermann Jungraithmayr. Volume 1. 1968.

Gunther, John. *Inside Africa.* North Pomfret, VT: Hamish Hamilton, 1955.

Guy, Jeff. *The Destruction of the Zulu Kingdom: The Civil War in Zululand, 1879-1884.* University of Natal Press, 1994.

Hallet, Robin. *Africa since 1895.* Ann Arbor: University of Michigan Press, 1974.

Halpern, Jack. "Botswana: Recent History." In *Africa South of the Sahara, 1981-1982.* London: Europa, 1981.

Harden, Blaine. *Africa: Dispatches from a Fragile Continent.* New York: HarperCollins, 1990.

Harris, Joseph E. *Africans and Their History.* New York: New American Library, 1974.

Hatch, John. *Tanzania: A Profile.* New York: Praeger, 1972.

Hatch, John. *Two African Statesmen.* Regnery, 1975.

Helbig, Ludwig, and Werner Hillebrecht. *The Witbooi.* Longman Namibia, 1992.

Hempstone, Smith. *Katanga Report.* Winchester, MA: Faber, 1962.

Hibbert, Christopher. *Africa Explored: Europeans in the Dark Continent, 1769-1889.* New York: Norton, 1982.

Hiskett, Mervyn. *The Sword of Truth: The Life and Times of the Shehu Usuman dan Fodio.* New York/UK: Oxford University Press, 1973.

Historic World Leaders. Edited by Anne Commire. Detroit: Gale, 1994.

Hoile, David. *Mozambique: A Nation in Crisis.* Claridge Press, 1989.

Holt, P. M. *The Mahdist State in the Sudan: 1881-1898.* 1958.

Holt, P. M. *A Modern History of the Sudan.* 1966.

Hymans, Jacques Louis. *Léopold Sédar Senghor: An Intellectual Biography.* Edinburgh University Press, 1971.

James, Lawrence. *The Rise and Fall of the British Empire.* Boston: Little, Brown, 1994.

Jenny, Hans. *South West Africa: Land of Extremes.* Southwest Africa Scientific Society, 1976.

Johnson-Odin, Cheryl. *For Women and the Nation: Funmilayo Ransome-Kuti of Nigeria.* University of Illinois Press, 1997.

Jones, Eldred. *Wole Soyinka.* New York: Twayne, 1973.

Jones, G.I. "Olaudah Equiano of the Niger Ibo," *Africa Remembered: Narratives by West Africans from the Era of the Slave Trade.* Philip D.Curtin, ed. Madison: University of Wisconsin Press, 1977.

Kaplan, Irving, Howard Blutstein, Peter Just, and others. *Area Handbook for Mozambique.* American University Press, 1977.

Katrak, Ketu. *Wole Soyinka and Modern Tragedy: A Study of Dramatic Theory and Practice.* Westport, CT: Greenwood Press, 1986.

Kaunda, Kenneth D. *The Riddle of Violence.* New York: Harper, 1980.

Kaunda, Kenneth D. *Zambia Shall Be Free: An Autobiography.* New York: Praeger, 1963.

Kenney, Henry. *Power, Pride & Prejudice.* Jonathan Ball, 1991.

Kenyatta, Jomo. *Facing Mount Kenya.* North Pomfret, VT: Secker & Warburg, 1938.

Kenyatta, Jomo. *Harambee! The Prime Minister of Kenya's Speeches, 1963-1964.* New York/UK: Oxford University Press, 1964.

Kenyatta, Jomo. *Kenya: The Land of Conflict.* International African Service Bureau, 1945.

Killam, G. D. *The Novels of Chinua Achebe.* Africana Publishing, 1969.

King, Bruce. *Introduction to Nigerian Literature.* Africana Publishing, 1972.

Kuper, Hilda. *Sobhuza II: Ngwenyama and King of Swaziland.* London: Duckworth, 1978.

Lamb, David. *The Africans.* New York: Random House, 1984.

Landeg, White, and Tim Couzens, eds. *Literature and Society in South Africa.* 1984.

Larson, Charles R. *The Emergence of African Fiction.* Bloomington: Indiana University Press, 1972.

Lau, Brigitte. *Namibia in Jonker Afrikaner's Time.* Namibia Archives, 1987.

Laurence, Margaret. *Long Drums and Cannons: Nigerian Dramatists and Novelists.* New York: Praeger, 1968.

Leakey, Louis. *White African: An Early Autobiography.* Originally published in 1937. Reprinted. New York: Ballantine Books, 1973.

Leakey, Louis. *By the Evidence: Memoirs, 1932-1951.* Orlando, FL: Harcourt, 1974.

Leakey, Mary. *Disclosing the Past.* New York: Doubleday, 1984.

Leakey, Richard. *One Life: An Autobiography.* Salem House, 1984.

LeMay, G. H. L. *Black and White in South Africa: The Politics of Survival.* American Heritage Press, 1971.

Levtzion, Nehemia. *Muslims and Chiefs in West Africa.* New York/UK: Oxford University Press, 1968.

Lipschutz, Mark, and R. Kent Rasmussen. *Dictionary of African Historical Biography.* Aldine Publishing, 1978.

Lodge, Tom. *Black Politics in South Africa since 1945.* Ravan Press, 1990.

Lunn, John, and Christopher Saunders. "Recent History of Namibia." In *Africa South of the Sahara: 1994.* 23rd ed. London: Europa, 1994.

Luthuli, Albert. *Let My People Go.* Collins, 1962.

Mack, John. *Madagascar: Island of the Ancestors.* British Museums Publications, 1986.

MacPherson, Fergus. *Kenneth Kaunda of Zambia: The Times and the Man.* New York/UK: Oxford University Press, 1974.

Maier, Karl. *Into the House of the Ancestors.* Chichester, W. Sussex, U.K.: John Wiley, 1998.

Major Twentieth-Century Writers. Detroit: Gale, 1991.

Makeba, Miriam, and James Hall. *Makeba: My Story.* New York: New American Library, 1987.

Makers of Modern Africa: Profiles in History. 3rd. ed. Africa Books, 1996.

Mandela, Nelson. *Long Walk to Freedom.* Boston: Little, Brown, 1994.

Mandela, Winnie. *Part of My Soul Went with Him.* Edited by Anne Benjamin. New York: Norton, 1985.

Marquard, Leo. *The Peoples and Policies of South Africa.* 4th ed. New York/UK: Oxford University Press, 1969.

Maylam, Paul. *A History of the African People of South Africa: From the Early Iron Age to the 1970s.* New York: St. Martin's, 1986.

Mboya, Tom. *Freedom and After.* Boston: Little, Brown, 1963.

McLynn, Frank. *Hearts of Darkness: The European Explorations of Africa.* Pimlico, 1992.

Meintjes, Johannes. *President Paul Kruger.* Cassell, 1974.

Meltzer, Milton. *Winnie Mandela: The Soul of South Africa.* New York: Viking Kestrel, 1986.

Meredith, Martin. *First Dance of Freedom.* New York: Harper, 1984.

Meredith, Martin. *The Past Is Another Country: Rhodesia UDI to Zimbabwe.* London: Pan Books, 1980.

Modern Twentieth-Century Writers. Detroit: Gale, 1991.

Mondlane, Eduardo. *The Struggle for Mozambique.* Zed Press, 1969.

Moore, Gerald. *Wole Soyinka.* New York: Africana Publishing, 1971.

Moorehead, Alan. *The White Nile.* New York: Harper, 1971.

Morell, Virginia. *Ancestral Passions: The Leakey Family and the Quest for Humankind's Beginnings.* New York: Simon & Schuster, 1995.

Morris, Donald R. *The Washing of the Spears: The Rise and Fall of the Great Zulu Nation.* Abacus, 1992.

Mosely, Nicholas. *African Switchback.* Travel Book Club, 1958

Mosley, Leonard. *Haile Selassie I: The Conquering Lion.* Englewood Cliffs, NJ: Prentice Hall, 1965.

Mostert, Noël. *Frontiers: The Epic of South Africa's Creation and the Tragedy of the Xhosa People.* North Pomfret, VT: J. Cape, 1992.

Mudenge, S. I. G. *A Political History of Munhumutapa: c. 1400-1902.* Zimbabwe Publishing House, 1988.

Murray-Brown, Jeremy. *Kenyatta.* Allen & Unwin, 1979.

Murphy, E. Jefferson. *History of African Civilization.* New York: Dell, 1972.

Murphy, E. Jefferson. *The Bantu Civilization of Southern Africa.* New York: Thomas Crowell, 1974.

Niane, D.T. *General History of Africa.* Volume 4. UNESCO, 1984.

Niane, D.T. *Sundiata: An Epic in African History.* New York: Longman, 1965.

Nichols, Lee, ed. *Conversations with African Writers.* Washington, DC: Voice of America, 1981.

Nkomo, Joshua. *Nkomo: The Story of My Life.* New York: Methuen, 1984.

Nkrumah, Kwame. *Autobiography.* Sunbury-on-Thames, Middx., U.K.: Thomas Nelson, 1957.

Nyagumbo, Maurice. *With the People.* Akron, OH: Graham Publishing, 1980.

Nyerere, Julius K. *Freedom and Development.* New York/UK: Oxford University Press, 1974.

Obeng, Ernest E. *Ancient Ashanti Chieftaincy.* Ghana Publishing Corporation, 1988.

Odinga, Oginga. *Not Yet Uhuru: An Autobiography.* Heineman, 1967.

Oliver, Roland. *The African Experience.* Pimlico, 1994.

Oliver, Roland, and Atmore, Anthony. *Africa since 1800.* 2nd ed. New York/UK: Cambridge University Press, 1972.

Oloka-Onyango, J. "Uganda's 'Benevolent' Dictatorship." In *Current History,* May 1997.

Omara-Otunnu, Amii. *Politics and the Military in Uganda: 1890-1985.* New York: St. Martin's, 1987.

Omari, T. Peter. *Kwame Nkrumah: An Anatomy of African Dictatorship.* Accra, 1970.

O'Meara, Dan. *Forty Lost Years: The Apartheid State and the Politics of the National Party, 1948-1994.* Athens: Ohio University Press, 1996.

Ousby, Ian. *The Cambridge Guide to Literature in English.* New York/UK: Cambridge University Press, 1993.

Pakenham, Thomas. *The Boer War.* Macdonald, 1982.

Pakenham, Thomas. *The Scramble for Africa: 1876-1912.* Jonathan Ball Publishers, 1991.

Parker, Kenneth, ed. *The South African Novel in English.* 1978.

Paton, Alan. *Towards the Mountain: An Autobiography.* David Philip, 1980.

Paton, Anne. *Some Sort of a Job: My Life with Alan Paton.* New York: Viking, 1992.

Peck, Richard. "Nadine Gordimer: A Bibliography of Primary and Secondary Sources 1938-1992." In *Research in African Literatures,* March 1, 1995.

Pedler, F.J. *West Africa.* New York: Methuen, 1951.

Perham, Margery, and J. Simmons. *African Discovery: An Anthology of Exploration.*The Travel Book Club, 1943.

Petersen, Kirsten Holst, and Anna Rutherford, eds. *Chinua Achebe: A Celebration.* North Pomfret, VT: Heinemann, 1991.

Phillips, Claude S. *The African Political Dictionary.* Santa Barbara, CA: ABC-CLIO, 1984.

Pieterse, Cosmo, and Dennis Dueren, eds. *African Writers Talking: A Collection of Radio Interviews.* New York: Africana Publishing, 1972.

Pratt, Cranford. *The Critical Phase in Tanzania, 1945-1968: Nyerere and the Emergence of a Socialist Strategy.* New York/UK: Cambridge University Press, 1976.

Putz, J. H. von Egidy, and P. Caplan. *Namibia Handbook and Who's Who.* Magus, 1989.

Rake, Alan. *Who's Who in Africa: Leaders for the 1990s.* Metuchen, NJ: Scarecrow Press, 1992.

Rattray, R. S. *Ashanti.* New York/UK: Oxford University Press, 1923.

Ray, Benjamin C. *African Religions: Symbol, Ritual, and Community.* Englewood Cliffs, NJ: Prentice Hall, 1976.

Reshetnyak, Nikolai. *Patrice Lumumba.* Novosti Press, 1990.

Ritter, E. A. *Shaka Zulu.* New York: Longman, 1955.

Roberts, Andrew. "The Lumpa Church of Alice Lenshina." In *Protest and Power in Black Africa.* Edited by Robert Rotberg and Ali Mazrui. New York/UK: Oxford University Press, 1970.

Roscoe, Adrian A. *Mother Is Gold: A Study in West African Literature.* New York/UK: Cambridge University Press, 1971.

Sampson, Anthony. *Black and Gold.* North Pomfret, VT: Hodder & Stoughton, 1987

Sampson, Anthony. *The Treason Cage: The Opposition on Trial in South Africa.* 1958.

Sarpong, Peter. *The Sacred Stools of the Akan.* Ghana Publishing Corporation, 1971.

Sarte, Jean Paul. *Lumumba Speaks.* Boston: Little, Brown, 1972.

Scientists: The Lives and Works of 150 Scientists. Detroit: U*X*L, 1996.

Senghor, Léopold Sédar. *Selected Poems.* Translated by John Reed and Clive Wake. New York: Atheneum, 1969.

Shepperson, George, and Thomas Price. *Independent African.* 1958.

Shibeika, Mekki. *The Independent Sudan,* 1959. and P. M. Holt.

Shillington, Kevin. *Ghana and the Rawlings Factor.* New York: Macmillan, 1992.

Short, Philip. *Banda.* London: Routledge & Kegan Paul, 1974.

Slater, Montague. *The Trial of Jomo Kenyatta.* North Pomfret, VT: Secker & Warburg, 1955.

Smith, David, and Colin Simpson. *Mugabe.* Salisbury: Pioneer Head, 1981

Smith, George Ivan. *Ghosts of Kampala: The Rise and Fall of Idi Amin.* New York: St. Martin's, 1980.

Smith, William Edgett. *Nyerere of Tanzania.* London: Victor Gollancz, 1973.

Soggot, David. *Namibia: The Violent Heritage.* Rex Collings, 1986.

Soyinka, Wole. *The Man Died: Prison Notes of Wole Soyinka.* New York: Harper, 1972.

Soyinka, Wole. *Myth, Literature, and the African World.* New York/UK: Cambridge University Press, 1976.

Soyinka, Wole. *Ake: The Years of Childhood.* New York: Random House, 1981.

Sparks, Allister. *The Mind of South Africa.* London: Heinemann, 1990.

Sparks, Allister. *Tomorrow Is Another Country.* Struik, 1994.

Spencer, John H. *Ethiopia at Bay: A Personal Account of the Haile Selassie Years.* Algonac, MI: Reference Publications, 1984.

Spleth, Janice. *Léopold Sédar Senghor.* New York: Twayne, 1985.

Stockwell, John. *In Search of Enemies: A CIA Story.* New York: Norton, 1978.

The Struggle for Africa. Edited by Mai Palmberg. Zed Press, 1983.

Stuart, James, and D. McK. Malcom, eds.*The Diary of Henry Francis Fynn.* Shuter & Shooter, 1986.

Sweetman, David. *Women Leaders in African History.* Portsmouth, NH: Heinemann Educational, 1984.

Taylor, Stephen. *Shaka's Children: A History of the Zulu People.* New York: HarperCollins, 1994.

Theobald, A.B. *The Mahdiya: A History of the Anglo-Egyptian Sudan, 1881-1899.* 1951.

Thompson, Leonard. *History of South Africa.* New Haven, CT: Yale University Press, 1990.

Trimingham, J. Spencer. *A History of Islam in West Africa.* New York/UK: Oxford University Press, 1974.

Tufuo, J. W., and C. E. Donkor. *Ashantis of Ghana: People with a Soul.* Anowou Educational Publications, 1989.

Tutu, Desmond. *An African Prayer Book.* North Pomfret, VT: Hodder & Stoughton, 1995.

Tutu, Desmond. *Hope and Suffering: Sermons and Speeches.* Skotaville Publishers, 1983.

Tutu, Desmond. *The Rainbow People of God: South Africa's Victory over Apartheid.* New York: Bantam Books, 1995.

Vail, John J. *Nelson and Winnie Mandela.* New York: Chelsea House, 1989.

Vaillant, Janet. *Black, French and African.* Cambridge, MA: Harvard University Press, 1990.

Verrier, Anthony. *The Road to Zimbabwe: 1890-1980.* London: Jonathan Cape, 1986.

Von Rensberg, A. P. J. *Contemporary Leaders of Africa.* Haum, 1975.

Wallace, Aubrey. *Eco-Heroes: Twelve Tales of Environmental Victory.* San Francisco: Mercury House, 1993, pp. 1-21.

Warren, Dennis M. *The Akan of Ghana.* Rev. ed. Pointer Limited, 1986.

Weh, Tuan. *The Love of Liberty: The Rule of President William V. S. Tubman in Liberia, 1944-1971.* New York: C. Hurst/Universe Books, 1976.

Wepman, Dennis. *Jomo Kenyatta.* Broomall, PA: Chelsea House, 1989.

Who's Who 1997: An Annual Biographical Dictionary. A & C Black, 1997.

Wilentz, Gay. *Binding Cultures: Black Women Writers in Africa and the Diaspora.* Bloomington: Indiana University Press, 1992.

Wills, A. J. *An Introduction to the History of Central Africa: Zambia, Malawi, and Zimbabwe.* New York/UK: Oxford University Press, 1985.

Wilson, Derek. *A History of South and Central Africa.* New York/UK: Cambridge University Press, 1975.

Wilson, Monica, and Leonard Thompson, eds. *The Oxford History of South Africa.* Volume 2. New York/UK: Oxford University Press, 1975.

Windrich, Elaine. *Britain and the Politics of Rhodesian Independence.* Africana Publishing, 1978.

Wingate, F.R. *Mahdism and the Egyptian Sudan.* Originally published in 1891. 2nd ed. London: Frank Cass and Co., 1968

Woods, Donald. *Biko.* London: Paddington Press, 1978.

Young, Kenneth. *Rhodesia and Independence.* Eyre & Spottiswoode, 1967.

Zolberg, Aristide R. *One-Party Government in the Ivory Coast.* Rev. ed. Princeton, NJ: Princeton University Press, 1969.

Periodicals

Africa Confidential. June 1, 1990; December 6, 1991.

Africa Report, May-June 1981; January/February 1988; July/August 1991; November/December 1993.

Berkeley, Bill. "Paying for Past Crimes: Uganda's Murderous Lessons." In *The Alicia Patterson Foundation Reporter.* Volume 16, number 3, 1994.

Callaloo, winter 1990, pp. 87-101.

"Can He Save the Elephants?" In *New York Times Magazine,* January 7, 1990.

Chicago Tribune, March 20, 1988.

The Economist, August 30, 1997; November 29, 1997, p. 104.

Gilbey, Emma. "The Lady: The Life and Times of Winnie." *New York Times Magazine,* May 14, 1995, pp. 24-29.

Goshko, John M. "Soft-spoken Man Who Gets Things Done." In *Mail and Guardian,* December 20-23, 1996.

"The Green Belt Movement." In *Geographical Magazine,* April 1990, p. 51.

Hultman, Tami. "Portrait of a Grass-Roots Activist." In *Utne Reader,* November-December 1992, pp. 86-87.

"An Interview with Kenya's Zookeeper." In *Audubon,* September 1990.

Los Angeles Times, July 31, 1984; December 7, 1986.

Maathai, W. "Foresters without Diplomas." In *Ms.,* March-April 1991, p. 74.

McNeil, Donald G. Jr. "Coup Charges Dropped, and Zambia's Ex-Leader is Freed," *New York Times,* June 2, 1998.

McNeil, Donald G. Jr. "Its Past on Its Sleeve, Tribe Seeks Bonn's Apology," *New York Times,* May 31, 1998.

Mehegan, David, "Nadine Gordimer's Next Chapter," *Boston Globe,* November 29, 1994, p. 69.

"The Most Dangerous Game." In *New York Times Magazine,* January 7, 1996.

Ms., July 1975; January 1987; September 1987.

The Nation (Nairobi), October 26, 1997; December 22-28, 1997.

New Republic, April 27, 1974.

Newsweek, May 8, 1972; September 4,1978.

New York Times, July 24, 1977; May 27, 1981; July 9, 1984; January 14, 1986; November 7, 1986; April 22, 1987; December 28, 1987; March 8, 1988; March 13, 1988; June 11, 1988.

Time, May 8, 1972.

Paris Review, summer 1983.

"Protectors of Forests Take Home the Prizes." In *Wall Street Journal,* May 10, 1991, p. B1.

Rolling Stone. October 20, 1994, pp. 55-56.

Saidi, Bill. "How the World Is Always Forgiving KK." *Zimbabwe Independent,* January 16, 1998.

The Standard (Nairobi). January 5, 1993.

Sunday Times (Nairobi). December 27, 1992.

Time, September 4, 1978; February 10, 1986; November 23, 1987; November 6, 1989; September 1, 1997.

Washington Post, March 3, 1992.

World Press Review, June 1986.

Other

Breaking the Silence (video documentary), 1988.

Garner, Dwight, "The Salon Interview: Nadine Gordimer," March 1998: www.salonmagazine.com/books/int/1998/03/cov_si_90int.html

Gersony, Robert. *Summary of Mozambican Refugee Accounts of Principally Conflict-Related Experience in Mozambique.* Washington, DC: U.S. State Department, 1988.

Guardian News Service report by Robin Denselow dated August 5, 1997.

King's College Newsletter, December 1984.

Maathai, W. "The Green Belt Movement: Sharing the Approach and the Experience." International Environmental Liaison Center, 1988.

Nwangwu, Chido. "USAfrica: The Newspaper." USAfrica ONLINE. www.usafricaonline.com, August 4, 1997.

"Revolutionary Worker Online." www.msc.net.rwor, #920, August 17, 1997.

UXL Biographies CD. Detroit: Gale, 1995.

WUSB 90.1 FM (Stony Brook, NY) radio broadcast featuring Lister Hewan-Lowe, June 21, 1986.

Index

Italic type indicates volume numbers.
Boldface type indicates entries and their page numbers.
(Iill.) indicates illustrations.

Wangari Maathai

A

B

C

D

E

F

G

H

I

J

K

L

M

N

O

T

U

V

W

Y

Z